By the same author

A JAMAICAN PLANTATION (*with M. J. Craton*)
THE BLACK PRESENCE

JAMES WALVIN

Black and White

The Negro and English Society
1555–1945

ALLEN LANE THE PENGUIN PRESS

Copyright © James Walvin, 1973

First published in 1973

Allen Lane The Penguin Press
74 Grosvenor Street, London W1

ISBN 0 582 12726 2

Printed in Great Britain by
Hazell Watson & Viney Ltd
Aylesbury, Bucks
Set in Linotype Pilgrim

For Gwyn

Contents

List of Illustrations		ix
Acknowledgements		xi
Preface		xiii
CHAPTER ONE	First Reactions, 1555–1700	1
CHAPTER TWO	The Impact of Africa	16
CHAPTER THREE	From Humanity to Commodity	31
CHAPTER FOUR	The Black Community, 1700–1800	46
CHAPTER FIVE	The Free Black Voice	80
CHAPTER SIX	The Legal See-saw. Slavery and the Law to 1772	105
CHAPTER SEVEN	The Somerset Case, 1772	117
CHAPTER EIGHT	From Mansfield to Emancipation. Slavery and the Law, 1772–1833	132
CHAPTER NINE	Back to Africa	144
CHAPTER TEN	Black Caricature: The Roots of Racialism	159
CHAPTER ELEVEN	The Voice of Reason: The Restoration of Black Humanity	177
CHAPTER TWELVE	Disintegration: Black Society in the Nineteenth Century	189

Contents

CHAPTER THIRTEEN	Into the Twentieth Century: 1900–1945	202
	Conclusion	217
	Bibliography	220
	Index	231

List of Illustrations

		facing page
1	Olaudah Equiano (Exeter City Museums and Art Gallery)	50
2	Ignatius Sancho by Gainsborough (the National Gallery of Canada, Ottawa)	50
3	Job ben Solomon c. 1734	50
4	Charles, 2nd Duke of Richmond and Lennox by Zoffany (National Galleries of Scotland)	51
5	The family of Sir William Young by Zoffany (Walker Art Gallery)	51
6	The Wedgwood Plaque (Wedgwood Museum)	82
7	Slaves at work on a West Indian plantation (West Indian Committee Library)	82
8	The Duchess of Portsmouth and a servant by Mignard (National Portrait Gallery)	83
9	The 2nd Duke of Perth and a servant (National Galleries of Scotland)	83
10	The Arab Princess by W. Frier (National Galleries of Scotland)	83
11	Two of the many black sailors on British ships in the 18th and 19th centuries (National Maritime Museum, Greenwich)	146
12	Two graphic comments of sexual relations between black and white (British Museum)	147
13	An anti-humanitarian caricature (British Museum)	178
14	The Ethiopian Serenaders, from Henry Mayhew, *London Labour and the London Poor*	178
15	Molineux. Heavy-weight champion boxer of England c. 1810	179
16	Black drummer, Grenadier Guards c. 1790	179
17	A still-life of an 18th-century Negro (By courtesy of the Victorian Art Gallery, Bath)	179

Acknowledgements

I am deeply indebted to a number of friends and colleagues for help and advice in the making of this book. Since 1967 Michael Craton has been my collaborator and guide, and throughout his enthusiasm, knowledge and friendship have encouraged and sustained me. Gerald Aylmer and John Parker kindly read the typescript and their comments have made this a better book than it would otherwise have been. Furthermore Professor Aylmer created opportunities for me to complete this work. To Christopher Fyfe my debts are twofold, firstly for his elegant scholarship and secondly for his friendly advice and assistance. Lt-Col. Lloyd-Baker made available the Sharp papers. John Ingamells enlightened me about eighteenth century portraits. Among many others whose help and knowledge have proved vital, I owe particular debts to the following people: Michael Banton, Rod Macdonald, Claire Cross, John Butt, Paul H. Hardacre, John Finnes, Mollie Gillen, Claude Ury, William Plomer, Peter Keating, David Neave, the Marquess of Northampton and the late Lord Learie Constantine. To a great number of colleagues at York I extend a generalized thanks for having given more freely of their time and expertise than any author has a right to expect.

I am particularly indebted to the Public Record Office and to the archivists of the following county record offices who responded so quickly to my various demands and questions: West Sussex, Devon, East Sussex, Cumberland, Essex, Nottingham, Lincoln, Shropshire, West Suffolk, Kent, Cornwall, Lancashire, Derbyshire, Caernarvon, Greater London Council, Northumberland, Stafford, Wiltshire, Northampton, Leicester, Somerset, Hampshire, the Corporation of London, Buckingham, Cambridge, Isle-of-Wight, Pembroke, Gloucester, Oxford, Warwick, Cheshire, Glasgow, Norfolk, Hertford, Monmouth, Glamorgan, Anglesey, Flintshire, East, West and North Ridings of Yorkshire, Merioneth, Worcester and Durham.

Of the libraries whose facilities have proved useful, the following gave me the greatest assistance: the Goldsmith's Library, Institute of Jamaica, British Museum, Scottish National Library, Bristol Public

Acknowledgements

Library, York Minster Library, City of London (Guildhall) Library, National Library of Wales, Cheltenham Public Library, Picton Library (Liverpool), Bath Municipal Library, Plymouth Public Library, Methodist Missionary Society Library and the SPCK Library.

I am grateful to the keepers and curators of the following galleries and museums: The National Portrait Gallery, the Tate, the Victoria and Albert, the National Army Museum, the National Maritime Museum, and of the following municipal galleries and museums: Sheffield, York, Ulster, Liverpool (Walker), Birmingham, Glasgow, Brighton, Southend, Aberdeen and Bedford.

Much of the material in this book first saw the light of day as lectures at the University of York; colleagues and students there and at the University of the West Indies (Jamaica), McMaster and Waterloo Universities (Canada), and the Universities of Edinburgh and Bristol have greatly assisted its evolution. The Institute for Advanced Studies in the Humanities in the University of Edinburgh gave me time and facilities to complete this book; for that I thank them.

J. W.
University of York

Preface

Negroes have lived in England since the mid-sixteenth century. The original purpose of this book was to tell their untold story but it soon became clear that this aim was deceptively simple. To isolate the history of the black community from the fabric of white society would be both artificial and unsatisfactory, for generations of Negroes have been profoundly affected by the attitudes of white society towards them. There was thus a need to examine the images of the Negro seen by white society; to study the white reactions to black society. What follows is the ambitious attempt to write both a history of the black community in England and the history of certain white reactions to that community. The study terminates on the eve of modern black immigration (the point at which most people imagine black history in England to start), for the reason that the period since 1945 requires a separate study by social scientists better able to handle the subtleties and complexities of modern social analysis.

Throughout, the expression black 'community' is employed in two distinct ways. Firstly, to describe all those individuals distinguished from white society by their blackness, no matter how widely separated they might be; secondly, in the more specific sense of a tightly knit social organization, restricted in location, and possessing a distinct demographic and social structure, values, relationships and *esprit* peculiar to itself. The word *Black* is used throughout to denote people of African origin or descent. Unless in quotation or paraphrase the peculiarly English use of the word 'coloured' is avoided.

As the title suggests this study is concerned primarily with the historical relationship between white English society and its various black minority groups. Occasionally a wider framework of reference is used, for example in Chapter Thirteen when black minorities in Wales are discussed, but although I sometimes write of Britain, my prime concern is with England.

CHAPTER ONE

First Reactions, 1555-1700

Early in 1555 John Lok returned from his second voyage to Guinea, carrying with him 'certaine blacke slaves, whereof some were tall and strong men, and could wel agree with our meates and drinkes'. Not surprisingly the Africans swiftly discovered that 'The colde and moyst air doth somewhat offend them'.[1] Thus began, in a small haphazard fashion, the importation by merchant adventurers of black West Africans into England, a prototype movement of population which was to be developed and perfected as trade to and from West Africa flourished over the course of the next two and half centuries.

Arriving in the troubled years of Queen Mary's reign, the imported Africans added to the growing curiosity and speculation about that wider world to the south of Europe which, since the initial daring probes of the Portuguese a century before, had gradually been drawn closer to Europe by the expansion of trade and international rivalries. As early as the 1450s Andalusian seamen had gingerly nosed their way south, hugging the north-western coastline of Africa in search of the commercial rewards of tropical Africa they knew to exist south of the Sahara. It was however the Portuguese who, by their skill and enterprise, outflanked the Sahara and laid claim to some 2000 miles of African coastline by the 1480s. In 1486 John II of Portugal proclaimed himself Lord of Guinea; in 1493 a series of Papal Bulls confirmed his claim to a monopoly of land in that region. Thus for years to come, adventures in West Africa were undertaken in the teeth of diplomatic, military and commercial threats from the pioneering Portuguese.[2]

It was natural enough that commercial curiosity and speculative optimism would prevail over diplomatic caution. English interest in the region to which the Portuguese had laid claim developed as an offshoot of Anglo-Iberian trade when 'a few bold Englishmen . . . received news of the African discoveries of the Portuguese' about

1480.³ With a few notable exceptions, however, English trade along the African coastline was of little importance until the pioneering triangular runs of William Hawkins in the 1530s and the firm establishment of an English trading presence on the Barbary Coast in the 1550s.⁴ After this it was only a matter of time and daring before the English Barbary merchants quietly slipped further south to tropical Africa and into the sensitive region of Portuguese dominance.⁵ Thus the Blacks brought back to England in the 1550s were, like the spices and tusks from the same region, evidence of the unusual opportunities of black Africa.

While the sight of Africans was a relatively new phenomenon, information about them had been common in Europe for many centuries before their importation by English traders. Black Africa and its inhabitants were perhaps unknown at the verifiable level of exploration and personal experience, but they were familiar as the objects of description and discussion in literature. Africans were clearly defined as abstract images in the minds of generations of Englishmen long before they could be seen on the streets of London. This was largely due to the popularity of a medley of manuscript and printed accounts of foreign travel which proved influential in moulding a European curiosity about the world beyond the frontiers of Europe.

Africa in particular was the subject of some amazing stories. Classical, biblical and medieval accounts formed the context for the growth of information and speculation among Europeans about the black continent and its inhabitants. Classical sources above all others were influential, for they moulded both the scriptural and the medieval awareness of it. As early as the seventh and eighth centuries B.C., Greek poets mentioned black human beings. Homer for example described a well-known herald of Odysseus as black-skinned and woolly-haired.⁶ It was clear that the Greeks' dealings with Egypt put them into contact with Negroes from further south or beyond the desert,⁷ a contact which influenced many Greek writers, in particular Herodotus. By the fourth century B.C., the Greeks had even met with Negroes from West Africa, and from this point contact between the Hellenistic (and later the Roman) world and black Africa was commonplace. Greeks and Romans visited black Africa. Even more Africans found their way to Greece, Italy, and perhaps farther north, and can be seen represented in abundance in extant

Greco-Roman pottery, sculpture, painting and coins as well as in literary material. By the time the Greek Strabo (c. 60 B.C. to A.D. 21+) wrote his influential *Geography* he was able to describe in rough but essentially accurate detail the geography of the continent. 'The shape of Africa is that of a right-angled triangle.'[8] Moreover Strabo claimed that it was a land mass which, despite its enormous size,[9] was capable of circumnavigation.[10] From such classical sources educated medieval society was able to glean fragmentary, but nonetheless distinct, information about a black continent and black humanity, beyond the fringes of the Greco-Roman world.

Scriptural sources offered ample supporting evidence. For many Europeans, their first literary entrée to the mysteries of Africa came in a variety of biblical references. When, for instance, early African explorers of the sixteenth and seventeenth centuries tried to explain the association between African blackness and the heat of Africa, they were merely repeating a theme which could be traced to Old Testament sources: 'I am black but comely.... Look not upon me because I am black, because the sun hath looked upon me.'[11] Even more specific was the association to be found in the book of Jeremiah: 'Can the Ethiopian change his skin or the leopard his spots?'[12] Egypt – where Negroes were known to live – and the Nile figured prominently in a variety of scriptural stories.[13]

The source of the Nile and the land to the south of the river were an issue of speculative debate in medieval travel stories. As early as the thirteenth century English writers had resorted to both scriptural and classical sources on Africa. Roger Bacon quoted Herodotus, Pliny, Isidore and Sallust, as well as biblical authority. Pliny in particular furnished medieval writers with an abundance of remarkable information about African life, although the degree to which his more astounding claims were believed varied from author to author. Chaucer, for instance, was the most famous of many writers who made liberal use of existing classical information about Africa and Africans. As late as the sixteenth and seventeenth centuries, English writers quoted biblical evidence when dealing with the problem of African blackness.[14]

More influential in the long term, but equally derivative, was the plethora of travel accounts which, between the middle ages and the sixteenth century conveyed to the educated European the colourful and bizarre wonders of the outside world. Foremost among these accounts was Mandeville's *Travels*, completed shortly after 1360 from 'practically every source then available'.[15] Mandeville's monumental plagiarism swept the reader along on a magical mystery tour of foreign lands, creating, rather than satisfying, a hunger for information about the world at large. Widely read in manuscript and later in printed form, Mandeville's *Travels*, unlike the work of classical geographers, stimulated and encouraged exploration and, 'for all his romancing . . . gave a clear summary of the stock of cosmographical knowledge and theory available to an educated European of the late Middle Ages'.[16] Unable to distinguish between fact and fiction, the reader of Mandeville found his attention riveted on the accounts of wonder, and no other country apparently contained more, or more remarkable, wonders than Africa.[17] The reader of the beguiling narrative was bombarded by the scarcely credible. Of all the marvels described none seemed as enthralling as the Kingdom of Prester John, a land based on a medieval rumour which, in the telling, had been inflated and had shifted its location from Asia.[18] Prester John's was a Christian kingdom beyond the encirclement of Islam, abounding in wealth, peace and miraculous freaks of nature. It was a land, said Mandeville, where rivers flowed with precious stones, where virtue and goodness reigned supreme and which, moreover, the author had seen – in the heart of Africa. 'Trow all this for sickerly I saw it with mine eyes and mickle more than I have told you.'[19]

Almost contemporary with Mandeville's work, a more scholarly treatise by Giovanni da Garrignano specifically located Prester John in Ethiopia.[20] Since Coptic monks from the ancient Ethiopian church had indeed lived for many years in Jerusalem and had even sent representatives as far afield as Italy, the concept of a Christian kingdom in Africa seemed less fantastic than Mandeville's account might suggest. Equipped with a belief in Prester John and spurred on by the need to seek Christian allies to outflank the encompassing world of Islam, the Portuguese in the mid-fifteenth century began to probe the coast of West Africa with an eye to finding a route inland to his kingdom. Eventually the Portuguese made contact with the Ethiopian court in 1487[21] and while it lacked the anticipated miracles, it had, until discovery, been a powerful stimulus to the Portuguese missions to Africa. Sometime in the decade after the first Portuguese approaches to the Ethiopian court, in the 1490s, Mandeville's *Travels*, which had introduced English readers to the Prester John legend in its earlier manuscript version, was given wider prominence in its first printed versions.[22] Thus in the last decade of the fifteenth century, fact appeared to confirm the most amazing stories.

Mandeville's *Travels*, while conditioning opinion about what to expect from the world at large, must have seemed only slightly less remarkable than the truth which began to filter back to Europe at precisely the same time. The truth about the huge round world and the revelations about the colours and conditions of mankind beyond the frontiers of Europe were stranger than legend. But because the newly discovered facts were assimilated simultaneously with the spread of fictional travel accounts, fact and fiction became inextricably fused.

African reality dawned on Europe from the mid-fifteenth century, with the return of Iberian sailors from West Africa. There were of course existing trading ties, however tenuous, which had bound Europe to black Africa at an even earlier date. The Greeks as we have seen had had trading contacts with the continent, while the Romans had developed thriving commercial relations, via Egypt with 'Nubia'.[23] By the early fifteenth century, however, much of the recent first-hand knowledge was derived from the Arabs and Berbers, whose overland routes from the southern Mediterranean to the southern fringes of the desert had for long remained the sole direct link between Europe and sub-Saharan Africa. During the fifteenth century, Arab information about tropical Africa filtered back through the contacts forged between the Arabs of North Africa on the one side, and the Jews of Aragon and Majorca, and the Italian traders on the others.[24] As trade gradually developed, black Africans found their way to Europe along the tortuous overland routes. Thus in the fifteenth century, black servants were to be found in Tuscany,[25] and they undoubtedly travelled into northern Europe.

In the fifteenth and sixteenth centuries – years of breath-taking adventure and exploration – the Portuguese proved themselves the pioneers of maritime initiative, guided in that direction, particularly after 1415, by the persistence and vision of Prince Henry. In that year a Portuguese military expedition took the Moroccan port of Ceuta, capturing along with its commercial wealth a mine of information about the trading potential and trade routes south. Attracted by the now proven world and the tempting commodities of West

Africa, Henry assembled around him a school of scientists, cartographers, shipbuilders and sailors whose prime task was to harness the latest information and discoveries to the daunting task of opening sea routes to the markets approached overland by the Arabs. Dispatching annual expeditions, each one sailing farther south than the last, Henry succeeded in winning for himself a papally-approved monopoly of trade and coast. But West Africa soon proved too tempting a commercial proposition and too great a challenge for other Europeans to resist a stealthy drift south.[26] Bit by bit, the trading adventurers seemed to be adding credibility and strength to the age-old stories which had wrapped Africa in a cocoon of rumour and speculation.

The merchant adventurers opened up a new world, where human blackness was perhaps the most immediately striking phenomenon. But Mandeville had given some indication of this already: 'The people that wone [live] in that country are called Numidians, and they are christened. But they are black of colour; and that they hold a great beauty...'[27] Some sixty years after the first printed version of Mandeville's *Travels*, Richard Eden published factual accounts of the first English voyages to Africa, those of Thomas Windham to Guinea in 1553 and of John Lok to Mina in 1554-55.[28] Incorporated in Richard Hakluyt's *Principal Navigations* in 1589, Eden's description of Africa and its people consisted of a fine interweaving of recently discovered truth and long-established rumours. Not content with mere exposition, Eden elevated speculation to the level of observed and proven experience, peering behind the steamy forests and round the bends of distant rivers, where, he claimed, lived those people 'which we now call Moores, Moorens or Negroes, a people of beastly lyvynge, without a god, law, religion, or common wealth, and so scorched and vexed with the heate of the sunne, that in many places they curse it when it riseth'.[29] Over the following 250 years this part factual, part fictional response to Africa was to characterize much of the English understanding of the black continent. Truth fed the expansion rather than the expulsion of mythology, and rumour unshakably fastened itself on reality. From the 1550s growing knowledge of black Africa, far from flushing out the residue of centuries of ingrained mythology, in fact reinforced that mythology and, by keeping Africans at the forefront of political debate, actually gave new strength to the old beliefs.

First Reactions, 1555–1700

By the late sixteenth century Englishmen no longer had to rely on printed accounts of Africa for they could see the human reality of the continent walking the streets of English seaports in the form of imported Blacks. In the course of the century, the number of Africans brought to England increased dramatically, paralleling the growth of West African trade and the upsurge of demand in the Spanish New World for cheap black labour. The 'certaine blacke slaves' brought by John Lok in 1555 were only the first of many such Africans forcibly deposited in England by merchant adventurers, particularly after the accession of Elizabeth, when traders were given full rein to challenge the Iberian monopoly in West Africa and on the high seas.[30]

In the first instance, Africans were brought to England for training to assist English trading ventures in Africa,[31] a design which was initially successful and which was to continue in a much altered form well into the nineteenth century. Italian aristocrats had for some time employed black retainers, obtained via the overland routes. After the opening of English sea routes to West Africa English noblemen were swift to follow their European peers. As early as 1569 Lord Derby employed a black servant.[32] Because of their rarity, exotic nature and curiosity value, black slave-domestics began to figure prominently in more and more noble households. After the English involvement in African slave-trading received royal approval from Elizabeth and was successfully pioneered by John Hawkins, Africans became increasingly common in England. They were the most valuable of all the cargoes shipped into the Spanish New World colonies and were useful as crew members of undermanned vessels heading west from Africa. On the return leg, surplus healthy slaves provided a bonus, or a social acquisition, for returning English sailors. As English trade between Africa and the New World increased, more and more Africans landed in England in this fashion; as the human ballast and property of the white sailors, to be sold or used at will in England.

Throughout the first two centuries of black settlement in England the servant class provided work for the largest group of black workers. By the late sixteenth century black servants were to be found employed not only by those close to the court[33] but also by others of a much humbler social station.[34] Most Africans seem to have lived in London – a reflection of the mercantile importance of the capital – but some settled in other ports which received and fed the Atlantic shipping trade.³⁵ A few, far from remaining enslaved, became relatively prosperous residents. One such group of Negroes built their own house in London in 1597, contrary to building regulations,³⁶ revealing an independence which must have alarmed contemporary Englishmen.

Indeed no less a figure than the Queen herself had already expressed herself forcibly about the growth of a black minority in the capital. In the last decade of the century the expanding population of England was troubled by famine. As hunger swept the land, England was faced with a social problem which taxed the resources of government to the limits. Immigrants added to the problems. No group was so immediately noticeable as the Blacks. In a letter to the lord mayors of the country's major cities, Elizabeth noted 'that there are of late divers blackamores brought into this realm, of which kind of people there are already here to manie consideryng howe God hath blessed this land with great increase of people of our nation as anie countrie in the world'. The Queen therefore ordered 'that those kinde of people should be sente forth of the land', in particular those Africans recently imported by Sir Thomas Baskerville.³⁷ In the July of 1596 the Queen reiterated her objection to black settlement; 'those kind of people may be well spared in this realme, being so populous'. An ideal opportunity to reverse the flow of Blacks came with an offer from Casper van Senden, a Lübeck merchant, to ship Negroes from England to Spain and Portugal, as part of a deal to recoup some of his losses on an earlier mission. Elizabeth agreed to the suggestion, ordering her subjects to turn over their black servants to van Senden and 'to be served by their owne countrymen [rather] than those kind of people'.³⁸

But the 'problem' of black settlement defied easy solution. In January 1601, Elizabeth issued a Proclamation repeating her licence to Senden to take 'such Negroes and blackamoores which . . . are carried into this realm . . . who are fostered and powered here, to the great annoyance of her own liege people'. To add religious insult to material injury, not only did the Africans consume food needed by Englishmen but 'most of them are infidels having no understanding of Christ or His gospel'.³⁹ It is difficult to see how Senden could have been more successful in 1601 than in 1596. Although he had been given what appeared to be a lucrative franchise, it remained impractical. Blacks had become too securely lodged at various social levels of English society to be displaced and repatriated. Some were totally independent of white masters, living as humble but propertied Englishmen,[40] while others, by becoming firm favourites in wealthy households, secured the protection afforded by the wealth and rank of their masters.[41] Moreover Elizabeth's generalization about the Blacks was not totally accurate. Not all for instance were 'infidels'[42]; some too had been born in England.[43] Thus owners of black slaves were able successfully to resist the royal decree, while many independent Blacks were able to avoid the threat of a round-up, and stayed in England. As an attempt to ease the nation's social problems, the plans to deport the Blacks failed. Negroes were no less in evidence in London in the years after the royal decrees than they had been before.

To a certain extent Elizabeth herself was responsible for black settlement, for she had approved and sponsored the growing English involvement in the trade in black slaves which had, in its turn, produced black immigration into England. More significantly, the Queen herself employed Africans at court – as had her father – one as a court entertainer along with 'an Italian named Monarcho . . . Thomasina the Dwarf . . . [and] Ipolyta the Tartarian',[44] and another as a page. It was clearly difficult for her to take a stand against the employment of Blacks when monarchs and their court favourites had themselves seen fit to find a niche for them at court.[45]

Not least among the changes brought about by the accession of James I was the social style of court life. Energetic and at times drunken vulgarity swept aside the respectful reserve which had marked the last years of Elizabeth.[46] Conspicuous fashionable consumption was flaunted, and Negroes, as part of that fashion, became more in evidence at court. The king employed a group of black minstrels [47] while his wife, Anne of Denmark, used black servants.[48] Even more striking was the court performance of Ben Jonson's *Masque of Blackness* in which Africans took part alongside the Queen, while ladies of the court blackened their faces for their parts.[49]

Royal patronage of black servants set a social style which was reflected at other levels of early Stuart society. This was made possible, in the first instance, by the increasing numbers of Negroes who found their way to England. Their arrival was not simply the result of growing demand for black servants, but largely of the expansion of the slave trade and the settlement of the West Indian slave colonies in the course of the seventeenth century. But in its turn, the demand created in England for imported Blacks gave such importations an added stimulus.

In the early seventeenth century, Negroes predominantly used as servants were clothed in the splendid and at times bizarre liveries which, in the eighteenth century, were to become their distinctive hallmark.[50] As the number of Blacks increased, however, more and more left the ranks of the domestic class, slipping out of the stereotyped role imposed on them by English society. In the process some of them were assimilated almost to the point of equality with white Englishmen, particularly in religious and sexual matters,[51] but much depended on the degree of freedom conceded to the Negro. Since by the early seventeenth century black slavery was common in England, those Blacks lucky enough to be free found themselves in a highly vulnerable position, unable to rely on their employers for completely fair treatment [52] or even to trust society at large for their continuing freedom. With the growth of the slave trade and the expansion of chattel slavery in the British West Indian islands, it is likely that more enslaved than free Africans were settled in England. They were, after all, brought into England in the same estate of man as their brothers in the New World – as the possessions of Englishmen. In mid-century, for example, the Guinea Company asked one of its factors in West Africa to 'buy for us 15 or 20 lusty young Negers of about 15 years of age, bring them with you for London'.[53] By this time, newspapers had begun to register the existence of chattel slavery in England. The most frequent newspaper references to Blacks dealt with runaway slaves. 'A Negro-boy, about nine years of age, in a gray Searge suit, his hair cut close to his head, was lost on Tuesday last, August 9, at night in S. Nicholas Lane, London.'[54] As a slave, the Black was entirely dependent on his English master. By escaping, the slaves took with them their master's property in the form of the clothes they stood in and were thus guilty of theft.[55]

In the years after the Restoration Negroes became everyday sights on the streets of London. The restored Charles II paid £50 for his black servant,[56] while his Queen employed her own.[57] By this time, Blacks could be found in diverse social-economic positions. Samuel Pepys employed a black cooking maid 'who dresses our meat mighty well'[58] and at his beloved Admiralty, a free Negro worked as a clerk.[59] Demand for young healthy Blacks increased, so much so

First Reactions, 1555–1700

that Africans were brought direct from the coast of Guinea for sale in England, rather than along the usual indirect route via the West Indies.[60] By 1680 Blacks were so common in London that it was alleged of the lady of fashion that 'she hath always two necessary implements about her; a Blackamoor and a little dog'.[61] Not for the first time (nor the last) the Black in England was to be placed on a level with the animal kingdom.

Moreover Negroes were not restricted to London. They could be found scattered across the country, obliged to live wherever their owners resided – as far north as Whitehaven in Cumberland,[62] as well as in London and in the environs of the capital.[63] Nor were they restricted to the seaports. George Adkins 'a blakimore' lived in Woburn, Bedfordshire, in 1682.[64] Robert 'the blackamore servant to Sir George Blundell' lived with his master in Cardington in the same county.[65] Twelve black slaves and their families lived in Nottinghamshire in 1680. In Lincolnshire at about the same time the Jenkinson family of Claxby-by-Normanby owned a black slave who was later killed by his master in a fit of drunken rage.[66] Charles Mason, M.P. for Bishop's Castle, Salop., for the last few years of the seventeenth century employed, and had baptised, a West Indian slave.[67] Another, Richard Zeno, lived with his master in Friston, East Sussex.[68] Thus the dispersal of Blacks throughout the country was pronounced long before the peak of black slave immigration in the mid-eighteenth century. Although an overall majority lived in ports, and perhaps a majority of those in London, many individual Blacks lived up and down the country, dependent on the will of their white masters, and following them into the peacefulness and quiet of retired life in rural England.

Handsome, and sporting a showy livery, the black attendant caught the public eye and his owner basked in the reflected social glory. By using the Black as a purchasable commodity and converting him into a mere adjunct of their social whims, Englishmen gave a new shape to chattel slavery. It is true that slaves in England, even at the height of slave imports in the mid-eighteenth century, were not brutalized to the same degree as plantation slaves but in becoming a colourful appendage to the fashionable lady or gentleman, the Black in England was nonetheless similarly consigned to the level of non-human property.

The engine behind slave importations into England was not the demand of the domestic labour market but political and economic changes in the Caribbean. The settlement of the West Indies and their conversion to a sugar monoculture was made possible by the availability of cheap labour from West Africa. Until the mid-seventeenth century the slave trade – the umbilical chord of West Indian development – had been haphazard and disorganized. After 1660 this rapidly changed. Under Charles II the taste for black servants at home was as nothing compared to the voracious appetite of the West Indian islands for black labour. The escalation of English slave trading between West Africa and the West Indies between 1600 and 1700 was staggering. To understand the numerical and qualitative growth of the black community in England from the mid-seventeenth century, it is vital to understand the wider context from which it sprang. To appreciate the life style of those muted beings who formed the backbone of the English black community, we need to understand the context of imperial and maritime growth which enabled the British empire to straddle the Atlantic. The growth, the nature and even the hidden sensibilities of England's Blacks can only be fully appreciated by realizing that the Africans were a single element in a booming empire. At the beginning of the eighteenth century the Atlantic empire was located primarily in the New World, embracing the lucrative sugar islands, the vast landmass of North America, and dominance of the high seas. But much of its strength was derived from the sweat and muscle power of West African slaves. Without the Blacks of Africa, whole areas of England's New World empire would have been mere territory, for it was they who were the sinews of much New World development. When staring at liveried Blacks in England it must have been difficult to envisage the invaluable role they played within the imperial framework.

Notes

CHAPTER ONE: *First Reactions, 1555–1700*

1. 'The Second Voyage of John Lok, 1554–5', in Richard Hakluyt, *The Principal Navigations, Voiages, Traffiques and Discoveries of the English Nation*, Glasgow, 1904, 12 vols, vi, 176.
2. J. W. Blake, *Europeans in West Africa, 1450–1560*, London, 1942, 2 vols, i, 18–19, 185–99.
3. ibid., ii, 263.
4. ibid., ii, 269, 271–6.
5. This occurred sometime between 1553–55; ibid., ii, 282–9.
6. Frank Snowden, *Blacks in Antiquity*, Harvard University Press, 1970, 101; not all scholars agree that this denotes a Negro. I owe this point to John Parker.
7. ibid., 103.
8. *The Geography of Strabo*, London, 1887, 3 vols, iii, 275.
9. ibid., iii, 274.
10. ibid., i, 148–50.
11. *The Song of Solomon*, 1 : 5–6.
12. *Jeremiah*, 13 : 23.
13. *St Matthew*, 2 : 13–14.
14. Eldred Jones, *Othello's Countrymen, The African in English Renaissance Drama*, London, Oxford University Press, 1965, 2–5.
15. Malcolm Letts, *Mandeville's Travels*, Cambridge University Press for Hakluyt Society, 1953, 2 vols, vol. i, p. xxvii.
16. J. H. Parry, *The European Reconnaissance*, London, Macmillan, 1968, 25.
17. A. P. Newton, ed., *Travel and Travellers of the Middle Ages*, London, Kegan Paul, 1934, 166.
18. C. R. Beazley, *The Dawn of Modern Geography*, New York, P. Smith, 1949, 3 vols, iii, 88; M. Letts, 'Prester John', *Transactions of the Royal Historical Society*, 4th series, xxix, 1947.
19. *Mandeville's Travels*, i, 193.
20. C. F. Beckingham and G. W. B. Huntingford, eds, *The Prester John of the Indies*, Cambridge, Hakluyt Society, 1961, 2 vols, i, 1.
21. ibid., 1–2.
22. Malcolm Letts, *Sir John Mandeville: the man and his book*, London, Batchworth, 1949, 121.

23. M. Rostovtzeff, *The Social and Economic History of the Roman Empire*, 2nd edn, Oxford University Press, 1957, 2 vols, ii, 68n.
24. A. P. Newton, *Travel and Travellers of the Middle Ages*, 168–73.
25. I. Origo, 'The domestic enemy; The eastern slaves in Tuscany in the 14th and 15th centuries', *Speculum*, July 1955, xxx, no. 3, 321–66.
26. B. Penrose, *Travel and Discovery in the Renaissance*, Harvard University Press, 1960, 33–47, 125–8.
27. Jones, 6; *Mandeville's Travels*, i, 33.
28. Jones, 8–9; Blake ii, 251–60.
29. 'The Second Voyage of John Lok, 1554', Hakluyt, vi, 167.
30. A. L. Rowse, *The Expansion of Elizabethan England*, London, Macmillan, 1955, 173–4.
31. 'The first voyage of William Towerson', *Hakluyt*, vi, 217.
32. C. S. L. Davies, 'Slavery and the Protector Somerset; the Vagrancy Act of 1547', *Economic History Review*, xix, 1966, 548n.
33. *Calendar of State Papers, Domestic* [hereafter *Cal. S. P. Dom.*], 1595–97, 7 April 1597, 381.
34. ibid., 28 May 1599, 199.
35. See mention of Negro in will of Nicholas Wichehalse of Barnstaple, 28 August 1570, *Report and Transactions of the Devonshire Association*, xxxviii, 1906, 240; also Negro baptisms, Nov. 1594, 'Parish Register of St Andrew's, Plymouth', ed., M. C. S. Cruwys, *Devon and Cornwall Record Society*, 1954, 57; for London, see *Returns of Aliens in the City and Suburbs of London*, Aberdeen, 3 vols, 1900–7, iii, 407; 1598–1629, 28; 54; 55. See also *Notes and Queries*, April 1961, 138.
36. E. M. Leonard, *The Early History of English Poor Relief*, Cambridge, 1906, 297n.
37. *Acts of the Privy Council*, xxvi, 1596–97, 16.
38. ibid., 20–1.
39. 'Licensing Casper van Senden to deport Negroes' (1601), *Tudor Royal Proclamations, 1588–1603*, ed, J. L. Hughes and J. F. Larkin, Yale University Press, 1969, 221.
40. *Notes and Queries*, April 1961, 138.
41. See n. 32, 35 above.
42. *Return of Aliens in the City and Suburbs of London*, iii, 407.
43. See n. 35 above.
44. Quoted in E. Welsford, *The Fool*, London, Faber, 1935, 170.
45. *Cal. S. P. Dom., 1595–97*, 7 April 1597, 381.
46. For a colourful impressionistic picture of the Court see Christopher Hibbert, *Charles I*, London, 1968. Also David Mathew, *The Jacobean Age*, London, Longmans, 1938.
47. J. A. Rogers, *Nature Knows No Color-Line*, New York, 1952, 161.

First Reactions, 1555–1700

This and the same author's *Sex and Race*, quoted throughout, are unusual and at times unreliable sources. But both contain some invaluable material. I never quote from Rogers without having cross-checked his point, or his evidence.

48. Portrait of Anne of Denmark, 1617, by Paul van Somer, in the National Portrait Gallery, London.
49. Rogers, *Nature Knows No Color-Line*, 161.
50. *Cal. S. P. Dom.*, 1627–1628, 521; *Notes and Queries*, 1917, 146.
51. *The Records of a Church of Christ, 1640–87*, ed. E. B. Underhill, for the Hanserd Knollys Society, London, 1847, 33–6; *Parish Register of St Andrews, Plymouth*, 587.
52. March, 1620, 'Petition of John Anthony a negro', *Cal. S. P. Dom.*, 1619–1622, 131
53. The Guinea Company to James Pope, 17 September 1651, in Elizabeth Donnan, *Documents Illustrative of the Slave Trade to America*, 4 vols, Washington, 1930–35, I, 128.
54. *Mercurius Politicus*, 11 August 1659, quoted in *Quarterly Review*, 1855, 187.
55. *London Gazette*, 15 January 1689, quoted in *Notes and Queries*, 1917, 146.
56. Rogers, *Nature Knows No Color-Line*, 161.
57. K. L. Little, *Negroes in Britain*, London, Kegan Paul, 1948, 166.
58. Quoted in ibid., 166.
59. Rogers, *Nature Knows No Color-Line*, 165.
60. *Cal. S. P. Dom.*, 1667–68, 95.
61. Quoted in Rogers, *Nature Knows No Color-Line*, 157.
62. St Bee's Register, 7 January 1700/1. Archives of Cumberland and Westmorland, Carlisle.
63. J. Kennedy, *A History of the Parish of Leyton*, London, 1894, 116–17.
64. *Bedfordshire Parish Records*, iii. Information from County Archivist, Bedford.
65. ibid., viii.
66. Information communicated by the County Archivist, Nottingham Record Office.
67. *Transactions of the Shropshire Archaeological Society*, 2nd series, x, 53.
68. Information communicated by the Archivist, East Sussex Record Office.

CHAPTER TWO

The Impact of Africa

The major European maritime powers from the sixteenth century onwards began to make a deep impression on a number of West African societies. Europeans in search of gold, spices, tusks and, later, black labour, redefined and restructured the economies and ultimately the societies of the region. In the initial explorations of the African coastline curiosity and daring were manifestly important inducements, but these were auxiliary factors compared to the main reason for African adventures – commercial enterprise. Africa seemed to offer untold profit. The first wave of white expansion into Africa, like the second in the late nineteenth century, was conceived in the commercial dreams of European speculators and born of shrewd investment.

Europe's impact on Africa, while economically inspired, was not simply commercial. The social and cultural ramifications of the European trading presence were complex and deep. Conversely, the impact made by Africa upon Europe was not confined to the economic sphere. African goods brought profit, colour, pleasure and social distinction to the upper reaches of European society, although it was to be some time before sugar, the most important if indirect product of black labour, was to change the tastes of the common people. Europeans responded to the newly discovered world with a piercing curiosity which has left its mark on white reactions towards Africa and the Africans to this day.

English knowledge of Africa was not restricted to the West Country and London merchants and sailors whose early contacts with the Iberians so stimulated the African adventures of the 1550s and 1560s. There existed, as we have seen, a widespread residual curiosity about the world at large, inherited by educated Englishmen from diverse sources. Stories told by returning sailors seemed to give the seal of confirmation to the older beliefs. Their accounts were too remarkable, and too consonant with popular taste, to be

The Impact of Africa

limited to the maritime mercantile community. Accounts of the latest overseas ventures were swiftly purveyed to a wider reading public by editors and publishers who appreciated the commercial opportunities afforded by foreign travel. In a modern society, when international horizons are limitless and international contacts commonplace, it is difficult to appreciate the excitement created by the hazardous explorations which drew Europeans closer to the unknown world around them. As early as 1511 Richard Eden had published an English account drawn from Portuguese sources,[1] dealing with black Africans. But the most important book dealing with Africa was published in 1589 by Richard Hakluyt, who gathered a variety of travel accounts, including some seminal accounts from Africa, incorporating them into his classic *Principal Navigations, Voiages and Discoveries of the English Nation*.

Hakluyt expanded and revised this collection continually until his death in 1616. Unfortunately some of the individual narrations which he passed on to an eager reading public contained serious flaws and distortions. For his material on the early English voyages to Guinea – Windham's to Benin in 1553 and John Lok's to Mina in 1554–55 – Hakluyt was obliged to rely on the earlier manuscript produced by Richard Eden. Eden had embellished these narratives with fantasy.[2]

Nothing, however, could have appeared more remarkable than the truths about Africa. Inevitably, considering the nature of the missions there, much of the narrative was concerned with commercial possibilities. Africa was, after all, 'the golden land'.[3] Gold and ivory abounded. 'They brought from thence at the last voiage foure hundred pound weight and odde of gold, of two and twntie carrats ... and about two hundred and fifty Elephants teeth of all quantities. Of these I saw and measured some of nine spans in length, as they were crooked. Some of them were as bigge as a man's thigh above the knee, and weyed about fourescore and ten pound weight a peace.'[4] These were some of the more obvious riches which drew the Europeans in the first place. But already the Spaniards and Portuguese had realized that 'black ivory' was even more valuable.

The excitement of Africa for these early travellers, narrators and readers was not limited to the profitable commerce of the region. The continent abounded with natural wonders which gave the

17

narrator of each exploration the opportunity to hold the Elizabethan Englishman spellbound. African weather, vegetation, animal life and humanity presented a kaleidoscopic spectrum of the scarcely credible. The most striking physical feature of the coast was the heat. Africa seemed to be a veritable furnace where the graded seasons of Europe fused into one long sweltering hell: 'In the stead of Winter they have a cloudy and tempestuous season . . . smothering hote, with hote showers of raine, and somewhere such scorching windes, that what by one means and other, they seeme at certaine times to live as it were in fornaces, and in maner already half way in Purgotorie or hell.'[5] Wind, rain, heat (even the heat from the moon) were described in frightening terms. While the land roasted, the sea around threw up equally amazing freaks; water spouts 'as bigge as the great pillars of Churches'.[6] Inland waters were no less terrifying; rivers and creeks were battered by 'whirlpools and fluxions'.[7] The cumulative impact of news from Africa on a credulous audience is difficult to overestimate. In an age when the forces of nature belonged to the realms of the inexplicable, the supernatural and the divine, African nature seemed as awesome, and as terrifying and as disturbing as the wildest fantasies of mythology and fairytale. The immortal world of dragons and natural miracles was not, after all, pure invention. It had been found at last by the African adventurers.

The readers' powers of comprehension were stretched to the limit by a seductive combination of detail about Africa's natural wonders and about the inhabitants, human and animal. Evidence of all these aspects of African life was not new, but from the mid-sixteenth century it was given freshness and immediacy for English readers by being contemporary, and described for and by Englishmen. Unusual freaks and creatures of nature, which had seemed more imaginary than real, had finally been seen by English travellers. The elephant for example 'which some call an Oliphant' rapidly became something of a preoccupation with travellers. Its amazing physical shape and size, coupled with its docility and teachability, marked it out as one of Africa's greatest animal curiosities. An early voyage brought back an elephant's head 'of such hugh bignesse' to prove to people at home that what they said was true. Other less lovable animals helped to complete Africa's image as a bizarre, perverse savage continent. There were dragons who could even dispatch an elephant; white elephants, 'tygers', 'and beasts called Rhinocerotes'; and the inland waters 'bring forth the like beasts as the Crocodile'.[8] But nothing in the animal kingdom drew the quizzical attention of travellers and readers more than the human inhabitants of the region.

The Blacks, unlike their northern neighbours the Arabs and Berbers, fell within the scope of curiosity but beyond the pale of comprehension of Elizabethan Englishmen. They were at once human yet 'uncivilized'. Few contemporaries (unlike the plantocratic commentators of the eighteenth century) doubted that the African was indeed human. He did after all display all the features of *homo sapiens*, but almost every aspect of his physical, social, sexual and religious life placed him beyond understanding. When describing the animal kingdom, or the geophysical conditions of Africa, contemporaries generally allowed the 'facts' to be self-explanatory. But the African was more difficult to deal with. His physical being, family and tribal life, his patterns of trade, religion and agriculture all needed explanation as well as description. In the telling, however, an image of the African was conveyed to the English reader which often owed as much to the values and biases of the writer as it did to African reality.

A good illustration of this was contained in Richard Eden's account of John Lok's second voyage. Eden wrote of 'people which now inhabit the regions of Nubia ... with divers other great and large regions about the same [who] were in the old time called Aethiopes and Negitae, which we now call Moores, Moorens or Negroes ... so scorched ... by the heat of the soone, that in many places they curse it when it ryseth'.[9]

In particular two aspects of African life made a deep impression on English visitors; the blackness and nakedness of the people. Both characteristics placed them at the opposite physical and social pole to Elizabethan Englishmen and it is easy to see how the African came to be seen as a dramatic inversion of their most deeply cherished social and cultural values.

From the first, heat was associated with blackness; 'throughout all Africke, under the Aequinoctial line, and neere about the same on both sides, the regions are extrme hote, and the people very blacke'.[10] The crucial question was whether the heat of the sun actually caused the blackness. In the first two centuries following the opening of West Africa, the question became the subject of a far-reaching intellectual debate centred on important biological and cultural issues, not simply about Africans, but involving the English themselves. It was logical that people should assume a connection to exist between darkness of skin and the heat of Africa, but the questions could not be discussed purely in logical terms. When in 1578 George Best, a much travelled Elizabethan sailor, published his *Discourse*, his purpose was to explain the habitability of all parts of the world. In the process he set out to analyse and demolish the influential opinion which claimed African blackness to be caused 'only by the parching heat of the Sunne, which how it should be possible I cannot see'. There were, as Best pointed out, other equally hot regions of the world where the indigenous people were not black. Furthermore, there were examples of Africans brought to England whose histories upset the theory. 'I myselfe have seen an Ethiopian as blacke as a cole brought into England, who taking an English wife, begat a sonne in all respects as blacke as the father was, although England were his native countrey, and an English woman his mother; whereby it seemeth that blackness proceedeth rather of some natural infection of that man, which was so strong, that neither the nature of the Clime, neither the good complexion of the mother concurring, could any thing alter, and therefore, we cannot impute it to the nature of the Clime.'[11]

It was evident that Blacks did not turn white in colder climes and that whites did not turn black, or produce black children, by living in Africa. Best was perceptive enough to locate the source of human blackness in biological factors, but he was unable to move one step further. To suggest that black and white had different genetic origins was to query fundamental scriptural beliefs about genesis which, in a society severely circumscribed by religion, was to expose oneself to serious personal danger. Best therefore fell back on the traditional view that blackness was divinely inspired, stemming from the curse of Noah upon his son Ham for the son's disobedience; 'as an example for contempt of Almightie God, and disobedience of parents, God would a sonne should be borne whose name was Chus not only it selfe, but all its posteritie after him should be so blacke and lothsome, that it might remaine a spectacle of disobedience to all the worlde. And of this blacke and cursed Chus came all these blacke Moores which are in Africa.'[12]

This same topic continued to tax the imagination of Englishmen

The Impact of Africa

in the mid-seventeenth century. In 1646 the distinguished physician and writer Sir Thomas Browne published his *Enquiries into Vulgar and Common Errors*, in which he brought to the old topic of human blackness the freshness of a critical mind, cutting through older traditional explanations and elevating the subject to the level of scientific investigation. But even Browne was unable to take his analysis to its logical conclusion and to scutinize accepted views about the origins of mankind. Browne remorselessly undermined the argument that human blackness could be explained by the heat of the sun but although he too pointed to biological and environmental factors as the true explanation, he was unable or unwilling to follow the logic of his argument.[13] Even in the late eighteenth century, when Englishmen came near to a satisfactory explanation of human blackness they preferred to fall back on traditional views which had changed little. In 1772 Granville Sharp, the sophisticated and enlightened friend of the Blacks in London, was able to write: 'I had always supposed that Black Men in general were descended from Cush.'[14] Biblical references to the African's blackness – or rather a belief that blackness was scripturally explained – placed severe limitations on the conceptual framework within which generations of Englishmen were forced to tackle this difficult and delicate problem.

But there was an added complication facing Best, Browne and, to a lesser extent, Englishmen of Granville Sharp's generation, when trying to answer this question. There existed virtually no intellectual distinction between discussion of the African in particular and of mankind in general. Debate about the African raised a series of questions which obliged the English to look at themselves and their own values. In the sixteenth and seventeenth centuries in particular Englishmen's intellectual attention was turned inwards, directed at themselves, as a result of probing the taxing issues raised by black Africa. Thus in an inverted way Africa, along with other recently discovered areas, made a profound impact on their intellectual world. If, as all the contemporary evidence seemed to suggest, the biblical account of the origins of man was unacceptable in the light of his biological diversity, the attempt to deal with African blackness was only one aspect of the changing philosophical framework. The existence of the African placed a strain on a series of fundamental English beliefs: the genesis of mankind, the nature of beauty and, most perplexing of all, the reliability of biblical explanation.

Whatever the complications about the origins of African colour, it was reasonable to assume that African nakedness was in some way related to the heat. On the coast of Guinea, reported William Towerson in 1555, 'are mighty bigge men who go al naked except something before their privie parts'. Even more offensive was the fact that 'the men and women go so alike, that one cannot know a man from a woman but by their breasts, which in the most part be very foule and long, hanging downe low like the udder of a goate'. Female nakedness apparently offended what few sensitivities the English seamen possessed. 'Divers of the women have such exceedingly long breasts, that some of them will lay the same upon the ground and lie downe by them.'[15] African men were similarly endowed with unusual sexual attributes – or so it was claimed. Even before the European encroachment on West Africa, there was a widespread belief that the African possessed an unusually large penis.[16] In time this belief was to grow into an international myth of major proportions and came to form the basis for much sexual excitement, resentment and, ultimately, racial antagonism between black and white.[17] In those first encounters in the sixteenth century the myth of black sexuality was given strength and meaning by the nakedness of the Africans. Englishmen were able to look at parts of the male and female anatomy which they rarely, if ever, saw publicly revealed at home. Not unnaturally their attention, and their comments, were directed at this unusual aspect of African life.

To compound English bewilderment when faced by Africans for the first time, the Blacks, in search of a beauty which the English could scarcely comprehend, disfigured their bodies; '... most part of them have their skin of their bodies raced with divers workes, in maner of a leather Jerkin'.[18] Black, naked, tatooed, 'with curlde and short wool on their heads',[19] the Africans stood in sharp physical and social contrast to the explorers themselves. The Blacks presented a living reversal of prevailing English values of beauty and goodness, a fact which increasing numbers of Englishmen came to appreciate after Hakluyt published his famous accounts in 1589.

Elizabeth's reign witnessed a growing concern with printed accounts of foreign travel. In particular, the 1570s witnessed an outpouring of literature on Africa,[20] and a consequent increase in

The Impact of Africa

factual information about the continent. In the wider context of foreign travel Hakluyt's contribution was monumental. His 'exhilarating accounts of voyages to all quarters of the globe ... constituted a national hymn, a sermon, an adventure story, and a scientific treatise'. Hakluyt brought an expanding and excited readership within reach of the newly discovered wonders of Africa.[21] As an immediate result, intellectual curiosity about the world was greater than ever before.[22] But simply to read Hakluyt posed a severe challenge to the Englishman's most deeply ingrained cultural and social values. His narratives revealed diverse peoples of the world, whose lives and behaviour were totally inexplicable within the value system of the English readers. Of all the phenomena described in Hakluyt's volumes, none was more startling or difficult for the Englishman to comprehend than the black African.

At precisely this time, as we have seen, ever more Africans were introduced into England as servants. Thus any doubts or curiosities about the printed accounts could be tested against the human evidence to be found in particular in London. This fact is particularly relevant when we think of Shakespeare's treatment of Negro characteristics. Whatever the 'facts' of Africa, there could be no disputing the manifest contrast between the black and white human. This contrast, which rapidly became apparent in the middle years of Elizabeth's reign, was all the more acute in England because there, more so than elsewhere in Europe, 'the concept of blackness was loaded with intense meaning'. So too was its related but opposite meaning. 'White and black connoted purity and filthiness, virginity and sin, virtue and baseness, beauty and ugliness, beneficence and evil, God and the devil.'[23]

Whiteness and purity had become even more important since the accession of the Queen for they were the symbols of the Queen's beauty, and a manifestation of the purity of virginal, queenly government. Elizabeth's white skin, pale looks and rouged cheeks were the objects of her admiring subjects' curiosity. They constituted an image of beauty which Elizabeth herself deliberately fostered. When entering the capital on one occasion, 'her litter was uncovered that she might shew herself to the people, clothed all in white, her face sickly pale'.[24] In the middle of her struggle with Mary Queen of Scots, Elizabeth felt it sufficiently important to ask one of Mary's courtiers who was the fairer of the two. It was as if Elizabeth,

23

throughout her reign, asked the mirror on the wall who was the fairest of them all. It is revealing in this context to remember that the word 'fair' was the contemporary synonym for beauty. Until 1603 it was also equated with the Queen herself.

> Her cheeke, her chinne, her neck, her nose,
> This was a lilly, that was a rose;
> Her hand so white as whales bone,
> Her finger tipt with Cassidone;
> Her bosome, sleeke as Paris plaster,
> Held up two bowles of Alabaster.[25]

Into this world of fairness and purity, of whiteness and virginity, the black African entered, in person and in print, his very colour and being an overt inversion of prevailing values of beauty and goodness.

Similarly, blackness expressed distinct English cultural values. 'Deeply stained with dirt; soiled, dirty, foul. Having dark or deadly purposes, malignant; pertaining to or involving death, deadly; baneful, disastrous, sinister ... iniquitous, atrocious, horribly wicked.' Such were some of its connotations in a society which began for the first time to absorb a black minority.[26] It was the startling contrast between the cultural values symbolized in black and white terminology, and given human form by black settlement in England, which made the impact of Africa on England so immediate and deep. The interplay and clash between black and white was swiftly seized on by creative Englishmen as an intellectual challenge which offered great literary and dramatic potential.

In late sixteenth and early seventeenth century drama and literature, the use of blackness – and indeed of black Africans – was a commonplace. Many of these references would have been largely meaningless to a contemporary audience had not the writer been able to rely upon a general understanding of the significance of his ideas and terminology. When evoking African or black imagery, writers were in effect appealing to the conscious and subconscious responses of white people recently made aware of the enormous differences between black and white.

Shakespeare more than any other contemporary was able to achieve considerable dramatic effect by conjuring up the image of blackness and Africa, and of making a subtle interplay between black and white. At times he reflected the reactions of his fellow Englishmen to Africans; at others he put aside prevailing attitudes and offered instead a dissenting reaction to blackness which responded more closely to his own feelings. He was for instance undoubtedly reflecting popular taste by suggesting that the African – or Ethiope – was an image of ugliness. 'I'll hold my mind were she an Ethiope', says Claudio in *Much Ado*.[27] In the same vein, the word was used as an insult. 'Away, you Ethiope!' Lysander shouts at Hermia in *Midsummer Night's Dream*.[28] Similarly, the word Ethiope was used to denote base behaviour as well as nasty people.

> Such Ethiope words, blacker in their effect
> Than in their countenance.[29]

The distinction made by contemporaries between themselves and Africans can be gauged by the comments of Pandarus about Cressida:

> I care not an she were a blackamoor,
> 'Tis all one to me.[30]

His view however was rare among Shakespeare's Englishmen. They were more likely to agree that 'Black is the badge of hell'.[31]

While Shakespeare played on his contemporaries' jaundiced reactions to black humanity, there is proof, scattered throughout his works, that personally he did not approve of, or believe in, the common mythology about Africans. Nor was he alone in this. In the society around him there was already evidence that some people responded to Africans favourably. 'Black men are pearls in beauteous ladies' eyes.'[32] Shakespeare's personal views about Blacks found their clearest expression in the sonnets, and pervade the whole of *Othello*.

> In the old age black was not counted fair
> Or if it were, it bore not beauty's name;
> But now is black beauty's successive heir,
> And beauty slander'd with a bastard shame.[33]

Of his 'mistress', Shakespeare wrote,

> If snow be white, why then her breasts are dun;
> If hairs be wires, black wires grow on her head.[34]

It is almost certain that Shakespeare had read – and indeed used – Richard Hakluyt's *Voiages* in his researches, but he had no need of second-hand sources for accounts of African physical features. They could be seen in the courtly circles with which he was familiar.³⁵

Until the great wave of abolitionist and pro-slavery literature in the late eighteenth century, no work in English captured the varied English responses to black humanity better than *Othello*, written sometime between 1604 and 1611. By that time Shakespeare had to hand one of the best accounts to date of Africa – Leo Africanus's *History and Description of Africa*, translated and published by John Pory in 1600.³⁶ *Othello* is notable, however, not for the factual content derived from such sources, but for the language of blackness and sex which was immediately recognized and understood by Shakespeare's audiences.³⁷ When Iago told Brabantio, 'your daughter and the Moor are now making the beast with two backs', that 'an old black ram/Is tupping your white ewe', and that 'your daughter [is] cover'd with a Barbary horse', he was being much more than 'dirty'. He was using 'the integrated imagery of blackness and whiteness, of Africa, of the sexuality of beasts and the bestiality of sex'.³⁸ The play would have been utterly confusing to the audience had they felt no understanding of Shakespeare's interplay of black and white.

Published accounts dealing with black sexuality had of course been given prominence long before *Othello* was performed, and Shakespeare simply inherited popular views on the topic, but he was able to use them with great success. Had not Hakluyt already informed the public that Africans – naked Africans – 'contract no matrimonie, neither have respect to chastitie'?³⁹ Leo Africanus, translated only a few years before the appearance of *Othello*, had told how Africans 'have great swarmes of Harlots among them: whereupon a man may easily conjecture their manner of living'.⁴⁰ In the mid-sixteenth century, Walter Waterman had informed his readers that Africans 'fall upon their women even as they come to hande without any choyse'.⁴¹ There was a clearly defined association in the popular mind between black humanity and unusually powerful sexuality and attraction. It was on this theme that Shakespeare played unmercifully in the course of *Othello*. Crammed into the play are all the tensions and subconscious fears which could be found in society at large in relation to the Blacks. One of the central elements in *Othello* and in Shakespeare's England was that a man's colour *did* matter – at least if he were black – for it was the key to most of his social relationships. Negroes *were* different, were treated and behaved differently, simply because of their blackness and the reaction of white society towards that blackness.

By the early seventeenth century perhaps the most crucial element defining relations between black and white was the growth of black slavery. White attitudes were swift to develop along the lines of economic fact. This was another element of black experience which found a pointed reflection in Shakespeare's work.

> You have among you many a purchas'd slave,
> Which, like your asses, and your dogs, and mules,
> You use them in abject and slavish parts,
> Because you bought them.[42]

Frequently, however, the black slave was decked in the finest clothing and jewellery. The more lavish the dress and finery, the more obvious was the master's wealth, and the Black in England constituted an advertisement of his owner's position. A hint of this lies in: 'It seems she hangs upon the cheek of night like a rich jewel in an Ethiope's ear.'[43]

Thus Shakespeare's portrayal of black humanity reflects, at one level, the varied character and the subtle social nuances of black experience which he could only have acquired from first-hand knowledge. To this extent he gives some indication of the nature and role of the Blacks living in England in the early seventeenth century. More important are the fundamental white social responses to black humanity which were central to Shakespeare's analysis of relations between black and white. Without an understanding among his audience of the significance of his black and white symbolism, much of what he wrote on the subject would have fallen on barren ground. That he was able to play upon the overt and subconscious reactions of Englishmen to the wider social implications of black humanity, tells us a great deal about English society. Englishmen appreciated Shakespeare's use of colour symbolism because, in the first place, it belonged to a centuries-old tradition. Furthermore they had lived in a reign when cultural values and norms of beauty had come to be expressed precisely in terms of colour. The impact of Africa on their society can be gauged from the degree to which language about the African entered into the vernacular. As 'Ethiope' or 'blackamoor' the African became part of the everyday language of Englishmen.

Black and White

The literary tradition of providing English readers with new information from Africa did not end with Hakluyt's death.[44] More accounts were compiled from his manuscripts by Samuel Purchas in the years up to 1626.[45] In its turn, Purchas's monumental collection became a source of information for creative writers of the seventeenth century. The compilation of Purchas, like that of Hakluyt before him, helped to foster a belief in the importance of the blackness of the African. When, almost a century later, the brothers Awnsham and John Churchill published their *Collection of Voyages and Travels*, they were joining a distinguished tradition of English editors whose life work was to bring the distant world into the more remote and peaceful crannies of English society. Churchill's *Collection*, like Hakluyt's and Purchas's before, was ultimately cannibalized by an army of writers (including the present author) dealing with the African. Setting aside derivative works, Hakluyt, Purchas – and to a lesser extent Churchill – kept the image of Africa before the reading public for a century and a half. As the seventeenth century advanced, and as black labour became vital to England's overseas empire, interest in Africa increased proportionately. But the basic foundation of knowledge about Africa had been laid by Hakluyt and Purchas in the years of formative contact with Africa.

In the middle and late eighteenth century, as the slave lobby and abolitionists sought to justify their politics, they turned to the corpus of information enshrined in the great collections of travel stories. But, like many before them, they were mistaken in assuming the total accuracy of Hakluyt and his successors. The errors and fantasies written into these works were responsible for the perpetuation of inaccuracy among later writers who turned to Hakluyt and Purchas for a truthful guide to Africa. Thus, by a complicated but nonetheless unbroken descent, the myths of the early years were absorbed and embellished by later generations of Englishmen. The African as a part of mythology, rather than the African as reality, entered into the unconscious and the daily considerations of the English. In the last resort, the myths of Africa were to prove more resilient and influential than its truths.

Notes

CHAPTER TWO: *The Impact of Africa*

1. Richard Eden 'Of the newe landes of ye people ...' Antwerp, 1511, in Edward Arber, *The First English Three Books on America*, London, 1895.
2. Blake, *Europeans in West Africa*, ii, 251–9.
3. 'The First Voyage to Guinea, 1553', *Hakluyt*, vi, 147.
4. 'The Second Voyage of John Lok, 1554', *Hakluyt*, vi, 163.
5. ibid., 170.
6. ibid., 171.
7. ibid., 172.
8. ibid., 164, 165, 169, 167.
9. ibid., 167.
10. ibid., 176.
11. George Best, 'Discourse, 1578', *Hakluyt*, vii.
12. ibid.
13. Sir Thomas Browne, 'Enquiries into vulgar and common errors', *The Works of Sir Thomas Browne*, ed. G. Keynes, 2nd edn, London, Faber 1964.
14. Granville Sharp to Jacob Bryant, 19 October 1772, Granville Sharp, *Letter Book, 1768–1773*, 158. For details of the myth about Ham's curse, see Winthrop Jordan, *White over Black*, Penguin edn, Baltimore, 1969, 17–20.
15. 'William Towerson's first voyage 1555', *Hakluyt*, vi, 184, 187.
16. Jordan, 158–9.
17. See in particular Chapter Four below.
18. 'William Towerson's first voyage', 1555, *Hakluyt*, vi, 184.
19. 'The Second Voyage of John Lok, 1554', ibid., 176.
20. R. R. Cawley *The Voyagers in Elizabethan Drama*, Boston, Modern Languages Association, 1938, 10.
21. Jordan, 3; see also E. G. R. Taylor, *The Original Writings and Correspondence of the two Richards Hakluyt*, Hakluyt Society, London, 1935.
22. Cawley, 1.
23. Jordan, 7.
24. J. E. Neale, *Queen Elizabeth I* (Cape, 1934), Penguin Books, 1961, 42.
25. Quoted in Jordan, 8.

26. These definitions are taken from the Oxford English Dictionary. Some indication of the continuing use of black symbolism can be be seen in present-day expressions: black looks/list/ball/guard/leg/mail/mark, etc.
27. *Much Ado About Nothing*, V, iv.
28. *Midsummer Night's Dream*, III, ii.
29. *As You Like It*, IV, iii.
30. *Troilus and Cressida*, I, i.
31. *Love's Labour Lost*, IV, iii.
32. *Two Gentlemen of Verona*, V, ii.
33. *Sonnet*, cxxvii.
34. *Sonnet*, cxxx.
35. Chapter One above.
36. Leo Africanus, *The History and Description of Africa*, ed. Robert Brown, Hakluyt Society, London, 1896.
37. By far the best historical analysis of *Othello* is in Jordon, 37–9.
38. ibid., 37–8.
39. 'The Second Voyage of John Lok, 1554', *Hakluyt*, vi, 168.
40. Leo Africanus, 187.
41. Quoted in Jones, 8.
42. *Merchant of Venice*, IV, ii.
43. *Romeo and Juliet*, I, iv.
44. Jones, 16.
45. Samuel Purchas (1575?–1626).

CHAPTER THREE

From Humanity to Commodity

John Hawkins, a scion of the great West Country naval family took to the sea as naturally as most men take to land. His father, William, had been an influential pioneer in the 1530s, making the exciting first English runs to West Africa and Brazil. But despite the daring of the father it was John who was to be pre-eminent in the family's fame. In the reign of Elizabeth John Hawkins carved out a special place in naval annals by a series of voyages in which he steered a delicate line between legal and piratical ventures into the Spanish New World. He pioneered the first major English slave voyages between West Africa and the West Indies, offering an indication, to future generations of speculative sailors, of where the profits lay.[1]

Hawkins had made a number of voyages to the Canary Islands before 1562. During his visits he had been informed that 'Negros were very good merchandise in Hispaniola, and that store of Negros might easily bee had upon the coast of Guinea'.[2] With the financial and political help of well-placed friends in London, he was able in 1562–63 to embark on the first English slave run along the triangular route which was later to be the most pernicious but most lucrative of England's trading highways. Paying a brief visit to Teneriffe, Hawkins headed south to Sierra Leone 'where he stayed some good time, and got into his possession partly by the sworde and partly by other meanes to the number of 300 Negros'. Turning his three vessels westward towards the New World, he took his human cargo to Hispaniola 'and made vent of the whole number of his Negros: for which he received in those 3 places by way of exchange such quantities of merchandise that hee did not onely laid his owne 3 shippes with hides, ginger, sugars, and some quantities of pearles, but he fraighted also two other hulkes with hides and the like commodities'.[3] The trip had been an enormous success, beyond Hawkins's expectations, amply justifying the faith placed in him by his

Black and White

backers. It was a prototype for much of the future development of the English slave trade.

Hawkins was not the first to embark on a slave mission to West Africa. As early as 1444 black Africans had been brought as slaves into Europe. Shortly afterwards the traffic had become a profitable and much sought after area of European commerce. It was the opening up of the New World, with its vast emptiness, luxuriant islands and untapped economic energy which made the readily available black labour of West Africa uniquely valuable.[4] As the Portuguese opened up West African settlement and trade, the Spaniards cast their imperial mantle across huge stretches of the Americas and across the Caribbean islands. The native peoples of the region soon proved inadequate to the tasks the Spaniards demanded of them. Inevitably, the Spaniards turned their attention to the part of the world which yielded such quantities of pliant labour – West Africa.

Exactly when black slaves were landed in the Spanish colonies for the first time is not clear. Traditionally it is claimed that Columbus carried some on his first voyage across the Atlantic and there is clear evidence that some had been settled in Hispaniola by 1502.[5] Eight years later more slaves had been imported, largely Christianized Africans bought in Lisbon. The market demand in Hispaniola rapidly outstripped the meagre supply of Christian Africans from Portugal, consequently more and more slaves were simply 'bozal' Negroes, that is those bought and shipped west direct from Africa. Through the sixteenth century, licences for slave trading bought and operated by Spaniards, Italians and Flemings, formed a lucrative source of income for the Portuguese who were able to enforce their monopoly claims to West Africa. In demographic terms the trade rapidly began to alter the face of the Spanish West Indies. By the mid-sixteenth century the annual importation of black slaves has been widely calculated as high as 10,000 but the real figure is likely to be in the hundreds rather than the thousands.[6] Hawkins in 1562–63 was thus merely cashing in on a long established and lucrative trade. Long before the English began to dabble in the black slave trade, the African had already become a purchasable commodity in his homeland, in the New World and in the ledgers of European trading houses.

When Hawkins set out in 1562 there were no firm precedents for

From Humanity to Commodity

the English treating Africans as 'merchandise'. The concept that a human being, albeit the distant and unknown African, could be treated as commodity was alien to the English, not for philosophical or humanitarian reasons, but simply because the English had had no economic need to regard or treat the African as such. Furthermore it flew in the face of English legal practice, for the institution of slavery in England had been moribund for many years. The Iberians however were swiftly reinstating bondage as a major social institution. When Hawkins took his opportunity, Blacks formed the backbone of the new plantation system along the Brazilian coastal region,[7] and throughout the Spanish islands of the West Indies. It was for instance claimed of Hispaniola that 'there are so many Negroes in this Island as a result of the sugar factories that the land seems an effigy or an image of Ethiopia itself'.[8] Paradoxically, after the initial ravaging contact with the Amerindians, the Spaniards sought to preserve the local peoples from the afflictions of forced labour, and were forced to abandon their predilection for Christian Africans. Instead they were obliged to use any kind of healthy African available. Even then there were never sufficient numbers for their needs. Letters from Spanish officials in Hispaniola consistently sought increased supplies of slaves. 'Here the chief urgency is Negroes', wrote one in 1542.[9] This pattern was repeated throughout the islands – Hispaniola, Cuba, Puerto Rico, Trinidad and Jamaica; 'Negroes are essential in the Indies since the Spaniards do not work here.'[10] Prices of slaves rocketed, to the consternation of the colonists and officials, and to the scarcely concealed glee of the slave traders.[11] It was in this situation that Hawkins, inheriting the commercially adventurous eye of his father, realized the rich potential afforded by the growing Spanish West Indian addiction to slaves. He, and other Englishmen, simply stepped forward to profit from the economic vulnerability of the Spaniards. Even at this early date, the Spanish empire had badly outstripped its supply lines. Without fresh infusions of labour from other parts of the world, labour which the Spaniards were unable themselves to recruit, the economic development of the colonies would be dramatically altered. The rapid expansion of the Spanish empire thus contained within itself the seeds of its own downfall.

Las Casas, the protector of the Amerindians, favoured the importation of black slaves so as to shield the local people from the rigours of this work. But he was to recant his views before his death, blaming himself for the evils perpetrated against the Africans. Even despite his repentance, 'he was not certain that his ignorance and goodwill would excuse him in God's eyes'.[12] But he worried in vain, for while his pleas to Spain for further supplies of slaves may have proved influential, the crucial factor in bringing Africans to the Spanish islands was the crude economic needs of the mines and, later, the plantations. Without labour the islands were useless luxuries, and Africa was known to contain an easily accessible and easily recruited source of cheap labour, apparently suited to the climatic conditions of the Indies. Once the colonial economy had been connected to the source of black labour, there seemed to be no viable alternative if the islands were to function properly. And all this had taken place long before Hawkins embarked on his first voyage, indeed it had made his voyage possible.

The Atlantic empire was technically divided between Portugal and Spain, Portugal monopolizing West African trade and Spain controlling most of the Americas. In practice however the Portuguese claims had been exploded by successful English trading missions. In 1563 Hawkins similarly burst the bubble of Spanish New World monopoly.[13] In all this Elizabeth I had a keen diplomatic and financial interest. The Queen had diplomatic reason enough to hate the Spaniards, but Hawkins's piratical invasion of their monopoly afforded her much more than diplomatic joy. Elizabeth, no less than Hawkins's backers, was ever anxious to capitalize on the daring of her sailors. When therefore Hawkins planned later voyages along the triangular run Elizabeth gave him support and invested in the undertaking. But she had to abide by diplomatic niceties and appear to remain independent of her sailors' open piracy. The Queen played an unconvincing double game, encouraging Hawkins to trade in slaves inside the Spanish monopoly, but consistently denying any such plans to the Spanish ambassador. The Spaniard was not so easily deceived even (or rather especially) by the Queen herself, for by this time, 1567, Hawkins's name had become a dangerous byword among the Spaniards for violation of their rights. There was of course an enormous discrepancy between Spanish imperial policies and the needs of the Spanish settlers, who were prepared, if no one was looking, to flaunt the imperial regulations no less than Hawkins. It was on this contradiction inside the Spanish empire that Hawkins could rely when he nosed his way into the Caribbean. That Hawkins was able to sell his slaves, despite the strictures of Spanish officials, speaks for the desperate position of the Spanish colonies. Whenever he began preparations for a further voyage – and such preparations were naturally open and obvious – no one believed that his intentions were other than to embark on further slave trading missions. From the first the Spanish ambassador knew that Hawkins planned, in his third mission, to flaunt Spanish rights, and was equally aware that the Queen was behind him. 'The principal merchandise is to barter for negroes', he informed the King.[14] Hawkins could find only one real outlet for these Negroes, and that was in the Spanish islands.

Elizabeth's active cooperation in what proved to be a disastrous expedition is well documented. As the Spanish ambassador had assumed, Hawkins had spelled out to the Queen the details of his plans; 'to lade negroes ... and to sell them in the West Indyes, in trade of golde, perles and esmeraldes'.[15] Unfortunately for the Queen, this third mission, so unlike the first two, proved to be a disaster, costly in men and money. The losses of that voyage effectively halted English slave trading until more congenial circumstances revived English interest in the next reign.

The slave missions of the sixteenth century had been *ad hoc* and haphazard enterprises and government assistance had been recruited only when the lure of profits proved irresistible to a hard-pressed monarchy. Thus by the turn of the century, though the English had indeed become enmeshed in selling Africans as a commodity, in the absence of New World colonies of their own they lagged well behind the Iberians in organizing an imperial economy on the bent backs of black humanity.

The importance of black labour to European maritime countries in the first half of the seventeenth century increased beyond all recognition. European diplomatic struggles, played out in the West Indies and in West Africa, largely arose from the need to stake a claim to the fruitful Indies and the vital trade in black Africans. But the initiating Iberians rapidly lost ground to the new arrivals. Spain's crumbling empire lost effective claim to an exclusive control of the West Indies, and the English, French, Dutch and Danes easily infiltrated the ragged Spanish defences and settled the available islands. Like a tide in full flood, the English rapidly swept from one West

Indian island to another. They began to settle Bermuda in 1609, St Kitts (with the French) in 1623, Barbados in 1625 and thence rapidly Nevis, Antigua and Montserrat.[16] By the time Jamaica was wrested from the enfeebled Spanish grip in 1655, the earlier English settlements to the south-east had already followed the lead set by the Spaniards and having adopted plantation settlement now began to convert the islands to monoculture in sugar or tobacco.

Letters to England from West Indian colonists, merchants and traders echoed the sentiments of the Spanish colonies a century before. Negroes – and yet more Negroes – was the plea of the new settlers; 'and the more they buie, the better able they are to buye, for in a year and a halfe they will earne (with God's blessing) as much as they cost'.[17] Unfortunately for the English, the Dutch had effectively displaced the Portuguese as the most powerful trading presence in West Africa, backing up their gains with even more effective claims to monopoly of the West African trade, helped in that direction by a powerful joint stock company. In contrast, the English were sluggish in organizing West African trading ventures. Patents were given to traders on the Guinea coast by James I in 1618 and Charles I in 1631 but no carefully organized economic framework developed which was able adequately to compete with the Dutch, or to satisfy the voracious demand for slaves in the West Indies. Furthermore, the Civil War, by dividing the loyalties of the English traders, greatly hindered the development of English interests in Africa.[18]

Rapid progress was however made after the Restoration in 1660. Political attention was once again redirected to the potential of Africa, more particularly since the Dutch stood in the way of satisfying the crying need of the West Indies for black labour. When the Company of Royal Adventurers to Africa was reorganized in 1663 it was backed by ex-Cavaliers, headed by the King and the Duke of York. This group was eventually replaced in 1672 by the Royal African Company, which held effective sway for the rest of the century.[19] From the first the new Company, buttressed by royal investment and support, traded in Africans as slaves. A century after Elizabeth had tentatively given royal approval to the slave trade, the English monarchy firmly committed itself – and some of the Crown's private fortune – to the trade. When the Royal Charter of 1663 was issued, it gave to the Company 'the whole, entire and only trade for the buying and selling bartering and exchanging of for or with any negroes, slaves, goods, wares, merchandises whatsoever'.[20] The King thus gave personal public support to a system of slave-trading which was dramatically to alter the structure of the English economy, scar the face of West Africa and populate the West Indies with an alien people. When in 1621, an English merchant trading on the Gambia, had been offered slaves, he declined saying 'that this sort of trade was not used by the English'.[21] Forty years later, such a sentiment would have sounded absurd.

Before the opening up of Jamaica in the later seventeenth century, the development of Barbados was the greatest single stimulant to the growth of the English slave trade – as Hispaniola had been to the Spanish a hundred years before. To feed the burgeoning sugar industry, African slaves were deposited in the island by the thousands. In economic terms the imported Black was a mere commodity, albeit a highly valuable one. Barbados set the pattern which was to be followed throughout the English islands. Local whites 'sell them [Negroes] from one to the other as we do sheep'.[22] Nor was this view of the Black as commodity restricted to West Indian whites. It was a concept shared by a large and growing body of English merchants and financiers. On the London market, the African became a fundamental item in an increasingly complex international trading nexus; he was purchased by English goods, exchanged for West Indian produce and used as a beast to work the fruitful land of the colonies. In such an involved web of trade it is clearly difficult to elevate any one of a series of equally crucial factors to a position of prime importance. But within the framework of the triangular trade, the African rapidly became central to the massive growth of maritime trade, and its offshoots of banking and insurance.

After 1655, but more particularly after the Restoration, Jamaica added a new economic dimension to the West Indian empire. Jamaica was the largest of the English islands, largely untamed, luxuriant and inviting. It was accepted as 'the Garden of the Indies' with land 'as good as any is in the West Indies, and very fruitful if it be planted'.[23] But like Barbados fifty years before, Jamaica needed labour. To populate the island, Africans were carried across the Atlantic in ever greater numbers. The black population increased dramatically and by 1670 it was apparent that the imported population explosion could soon have serious repercussions for local whites. The Jamaicans had swiftly foreseen 'that the proportion of Blacks might in a short tyme be such, that a Rebellion of them would bee easy'.[24] Planters were hoist with their own petard. Unable to work their lands profitably without massive infusions of black labour, they built up a society of brute Blacks whose very numbers were to send chills down the spine of succeeding generations of planters. The moral was clear – as George Cruickshank pointed out many years later.

> The planter's dream doth plainly seem
> To point a moral deep:
> If you choose to whack a nigger's back,
> You should never go to sleep.[25]

Jamaica and Barbados were only exceptional cases of a pattern common to all the West Indian islands. Once the islands had been conquered, economic growth was made possible by the creation of a plantation system. To work them, black labour was recruited, following the Spanish pattern of the previous century. In the process the triangular trade developed, drawing into its web government, private finance and virtually the whole fabric of West Indian society.

The terminology used to describe the African in the period of seventeenth-century West Indian expansion gives some indication of English attitudes towards him. Hawkins referred to the black 'merchandise' but such an open equation of the African with commodity was rare even by the early seventeenth century, despite the fact that in practice he was treated as such. It was much more common to speak of the African in human, as opposed to chattel terms. As late as the 1660s the Royal African Adventurers spoke of the Africans transported to the New World as 'Negro-Servants'.[26] A public declaration of the same Company spoke of the 'supply of Servants ... from Africa'.[27] This legal fiction was adopted by the Committee of the Privy Council for Plantations, who reported in 1664 that 'the servants are classed under two heads, black and whites. The blacks bought by way of trade ... [are] the most useful appartenances of a plantation and the perpetual servants.' [28]

In 1672 when the new Royal African Company was granted its charter, official terminology began at last to reflect the reality of the African's chattel status. Henceforth, decreed the Charter, only the African Company was permitted to 'import any redwood, elephants' teeth, negroes, slaves, hides, wax, guinea grains, *or other commodities.'* [29] Two years later, a Royal Proclamation continued to use the expression 'Negro Servants' but the context had changed, for the 'Negro Servants' were grouped with 'Gold, Elephants' teeth, *or any other Goods or Merchandise or the product or Manufacture of the said Places'*.[30]

Descriptions of the African involved more than an issue of vocabulary, for they mirrored the deeper social substance of economic fact and attitudes. To contemporaries the status of the African was of immediate economic importance. While in practice he had been consigned to the level of a chattel, this was purely a function of the growth of plantation society. Initially there was no legislation from Parliament which imposed this status on the Black. But this situation changed dramatically in the later seventeenth century as the African rapidly became the most valuable commodity imported into the West Indies. Since the ideal of seventeenth-century economics was monopolistic mercantilism, all goods travelling inside the empire had to be transported by English ships. It was, from this viewpoint, vital that a clear legal definition of the status of the imported Negro should be arrived at, in order to make the slave trade conform to the terms of the various Navigation Acts regulating the nature and growth of maritime trade. In 1677 the Solicitor-General's opinion was sought 'whether negroes ought to be esteemed goods or commodities intended by the Acts of Trade, which provide that no commodities intended by the Acts of Trade be imported or exported out of His Majesty's plantations, but in ships that belong to the people of England'.[31] The opinion of the Solicitor-General was clear and unequivocal; 'that negroes ought to be esteemed goods and commodities within the Acts of Trade and Navigation'.[32] Thus the process of dehumanization of the African was given the stamp of government approval. In the same year, to compound the African's tribulations, an English court gave common law backing to this view: 'Negroes being usually bought and sold among Merchants, so Merchandise.' [33]

Economic usage had prevailed over the earlier tendency to regard the Black as human. In the reign of Charles II not only was the English slave trade organized to dovetail more neatly with the requirements of the West Indies, but the government in London committed itself wholeheartedly to this process. English legislation, English common law and the Crown, had assisted and agreed to the ultimate dehumanization of the African. But the English were soon to learn, via black slave settlement in England, that this view of the African flew in the face of the growth of freedom in England. In the century when the English were preoccupied with battles for their own freedoms, they were active in denying even more fundamental freedoms to their black captives.

By 1700 the African's status was clearly defined. Despite the uncertain attempts of the Privy Council to blunt the sharper edges of plantocratic brutality towards the Africans,[34] English government and law had conceded and bolstered the colonial assemblies' view of the Blacks as chattels.

Much of the legislation dealing with the Negro in the eighteenth century was firmly based on the chattel status of the Black which had been defined in the previous century. Diplomacy too was tainted with the same view. In 1713 for instance the Treaty of Utrecht granted the right to supply slaves to the Spanish West Indies.[35] 'Black Ivory' had become a valuable chess piece fought over in the diplomatic council chambers of Europe. In 1726 the South Sea Company Act expressed the hope that 'the transportation of Negroes from this island [Madagascar] might become a very beneficial branch of trade to the kingdom'.[36] Parliament was similarly instrumental in buttressing the planters' view that Negroes were merely an economic adjunct to a plantation. An Act of 1732 spoke of 'the Houses, Lands, Negroes and other Hereditaments and Real Estates'.[37] New legislation in 1776 classified imported Africans alongside 'all Manner of Goods and Merchandises whatsoever'.[38] As late as 1790 an Act to encourage immigration into British North America, the Bahamas and Bermuda, spoke of 'Negroes, household furniture, utensils of husbandry or cloathing'.[39]

English legislative support for the Negro's commodity status was paralleled by common-law judgments. In 1749, for example, Lord Chancellor Hardwicke affirmed that the Negro 'is as much property as any other thing'.[40] While it could be argued that Parliament and the English courts were only approving what had already become established fact in the empire, it is nonetheless true that there was a two-sided process at work. Legislation and court judgments, in confirming economic reality, simultaneously made easier, and paved the way for, the development of West Indian and, ultimately, English chattel slavery. When, late in the eighteenth century, the planters found themselves under serious attack from the humanitarians, they were able to take comfort from and make political capital out of the fact that the English Parliament had been responsible for the dehumanization of the African.[41] Friends of the African were quite mistaken in believing that 'the right of the planter to his Negro is only founded on the acts of his provincial assembly'.[42] The English had been only too keen to assist the development of a form of bondage which brought such rich returns to the mother country. Law, as well as economic usage, had helped to convert the African from humanity to commodity. By the law, claimed a planter, the Negro 'is made matter of trade; he is said to be property; he is goods, chattels, and effects, vestable and vested in his owner'.[43]

During the first four decades of the eighteenth century, the African trade was an issue of bitter political controversy between supporters of the Royal African Company and those interested in free trade in West Africa. The two sides clashed on how best to promote the expansion of African trade, but they agreed that the African trade was vital to Britain and the West Indies: 'The African Trade is a Trade of the most Advantage to this Kingdom of any we drive, and as it were all Profit, the first Cost being little more than small Matters of our own Manufactures, for which we have in Return, Gold, Teeth, Wax and Negroes, the last whereof are much better than the first being indeed the best Traffic the Kingdom hath, as it doth give occasionally so vast an Employment to our People both by sea and Land.'[44]

On the one central issue there was complete agreement between the two sides.

The most approved Judges of the commercial Interests of these Kingdoms have ever been of Opinion that our West Indian and African Trades are the most naturally beneficial of any we carry on. It is also allowed on all Hands, that the Trade to Africa is the Branch which renders our American Colonies and Plantations so advantageous to Great Britain; that Traffic only affording our Plantations a constant Supply of Negroe-Servants for the culture of their Lands in the Produce of Sugars, Tobacco, Rice, Rum, Cotton, Fustick, Pimento, and all other our Plantation-Produce: So that the extensive Employment of our Shipping in, to, and from America, the great Brood of Seamen consequent thereupon, and the daily Bread of the most considerable Part of our British Manufacturers, are owing primarily to the Labour of Negroes; who, as they were the first happy Instruments of raising our Plantations; so their Labour only can support and preserve them, and render them still more and more profitable to their Mother-Country. The Negroe-Trade therefore, and the natural Consequences resulting from it, may be justly esteemed an inexhaustible Fund of Wealth and Naval Power to this Nation.[45]

Furthermore it seemed, to yet another commentator, to offer benefits that stretched into the unforeseeable future, 'when gold ceases to be valuable in the world; when Men cease to wear Cloathes, and when Mankind leave off cultivating the Earth, and when the Ground ceases to bring forth its Pruductions, then, and not till then, can the Trade to Africa be lost'.[46] What this author failed to mention here was the unique importance of the African. The 'trade to Africa' was made possible and viable by the pool of African slaves waiting for the ships. All those dealing in slaves, and writing to justify their involvement, took it for granted that the African was a commodity, to be traded like all other African goods.

Somewhere between 1600 and 1700 the English view of the African had changed. By 1700 an Englishman was able to write in his will of a Negro, 'I take [him] to be in the nature and quality of my goods and chattels'.[47] This position was not reversed until the early successes of the humanitarians in the late eighteenth century. But in the late seventeenth and early eighteenth centuries it was sufficient to affirm the overall economic importance of the slave trade and the indispensability of the Black, to convince contemporaries of the justice of black chattel slavery. Economic facts were felt to be sufficient to speak for themselves without preface or apology for the treatment meted out to the African.

In the paper war which raged around the issue of the Royal African Company's monopoly, the most frequent comparison drawn was between the Negro and the animal kingdom, in particular the horse.[48] To the extent that the African carried out the brute labour in the fields, the comparison was accurate, but until the nineteenth century the African was often *literally* viewed in this light. In 1783, when the Lord Chief Justice, Lord Mansfield, summed up in the horrific case of the ship *Zong*, he reluctantly informed the jury that the deliberate drowning of slaves 'was the same as if horses had been thrown overboard'.[49] Lord Hardwicke in 1749 had given legal approval to this interpretation of the Negro as mere animal stock. They 'wear out with labour, as cattle or other things ... they are like stock on a farm'.[50] As late as 1849 Thomas Carlyle openly equated the African with the horse.[51]

'A West Indian estate,' wrote a planter in 1788, 'consists of two parts; lands with their adjuncts, buildings, etc., and the living stock, viz. cattle and negroes, all of which are as much the property of the planter as it is possible for the most authentic statutes of the British Senate and Colonial Assemblies to make them.'[52] The transmutation of the African from human to chattel was thus complete and Parliament no less than economic practice had, to use the words of a West India planter, 'set the mark and stamp of property upon Negroes'.[53] To concede humanity to the African would be to destroy the economic role created for him in the plantations. If we grasp what happened in English attitudes towards the Negro in the period of imperial expansion, how the English slowly came to view him as a non-human, much of the treatment meted out to him in the West Indies, and in England, becomes comprehensible if no more forgivable.

Notes

CHAPTER THREE: *From Humanity to Commodity*

1. 'First Voyage of John Hawkins, 1562-3', Hakluyt, x, 7-8; J. A. Williamson, *Hawkins of Plymouth*, London, A. & C. Black, 1949; J. W. Blake, *European Beginnings in West Africa*, Longmans, 1937.
2. 'First Voyage of Hawkins', Hakluyt, x, 7-8.
3. ibid.
4. J. H. Parry and P. M. Sherlock, *A Short History of the West Indies*, 3rd edn, London, Macmillan, 1968; Donnan, *Documents Illustrative of the Slave Trade*, i, 1.
5. Donnan, i, 14.
6. ibid., 17; Philip Curtin, *The Slave Trade; a census*, University of

Wisconsin Press, 1969, 25, the definitive study, computes an annual figure between 500 and 810.
7. C. R. Boxer, *The Portuguese Seaborne Empire, 1415–1825*, London, Hutchinson, 1969, 96.
8. 'Gonzalo Fernandez de Oviedo y Valdes, 1535–1557', in Eric Williams, *Documents of West Indian History*, Port-of-Spain, 1963, i, 142.
9. 'Attorney of Hispaniola to Charles V, 1542', ibid., 143.
10. 'Judge Hutardo of Hispaniola, 1550', ibid., 144.
11. 'Royal officials of Hispaniola to Charles V', 30 March 1550, ibid., 151.
12. 'Las Casas, 1559', ibid., 157.
13. Donnan, i, 10.
14. 'Guzman de Silva to Phillip II, 1567', ibid., 66, n. 2.
15. *Cal. S.P. Dom.*, 1547–1580, 299.
16. Parry and Sherlock ch. 4.
17. 'George Downing to John Winthrop, 26 August 1645', Donnan i, 125.
18. ibid., i, 74–80, 83.
19. ibid., i, 85–6. For a list of members of the Royal Adventurers, 1667, see ibid., 169. Details of the Royal African Society in K. G. Davies, *The Royal African Company*, London, Longmans, 1957.
20. Donnan, i. 88.
21. Quoted in Edward Long, *Candid Reflections*, London, 1772, 22.
22. 'Henry Whistler 1645–55', Eric Williams, *Documents*, 290.
23. ibid., 286.
24. 'Reflections on the Jamaica Slave Trade, 1670', Donnan, i, 174.
25. George Cruickshank, *The Comic Almanack, 1834–1843*, London, n.d., 185.
26. Company of Royal Adventurers, 1662/3, Donnan, i, 156.
27. Declaration of the Royal Adventurers, 1662/3, ibid., 158, see also petition of 1684, ibid., 166.
28. *Calendar of State Papers, Colonial America and West Indies* [hereafter C.S.P. Col. Am. W.I.], *1661–1668*, 229
29. *C.S.P. Col. Am. W.I., 1669–1674*, 412. The italics are mine.
30. Royal Proclamation, 1674, Donman i, 195–6. The italics are mine.
31. *C.S.P. Col. Am. W.I., 1677–1680*, 118.
32. ibid., 120.
33. 'Butts v. Penny, 1677', H. T. Catterall, *Judicial Cases Concerning American Slavery and the Negro*, 5 vols, Washington, 1926–36, i, 9.
34. *C.S.P. Col. Am. W.I., 1681–1685*, 386; Elsa Goveia, *West India Slave Laws of the 18th Century*, Caribbean Universities Press, London, Ginn, 1970.
35. Parry and Sherlock, 100–1.
36. Quoted in Long, *Candid Reflections*, 26.
37. 'An Act for the more easy recovery of debts in His Majesty's planta-

tions and colonies in America', VII Geo. II, cl. iv., *Statutes at Large*, 1730–1746, vi, 74.
38. 'An Act for opening and establishing certain ports in the Islands of Jamaica and Dominica' 3 Geo. III, 49, cl. v, *Statutes at Large*, 1751–1770, 263.
39. Quoted in Robin Winks, *The Blacks in Canada*, Yale University Press, 1971, 26.
40. 'Pearne v. Lisle, 1748', Catterall, i, 12.
41. Long, *Candid Reflections*, 33.
42. William Knox, *Three Tracts* . . ., 1768, 15.
43. *Considerations on the Negro Cause*, by a West Indian, London, 1772, 35.
44. *A Discourse of the Advantage of the African Trade to the Nation*, n.d., 5.
45. *The National and Private Advantage of the African Trade*, London, London, 1746, 1–2.
46. *The African Company's Property to the Forts and Settlements in Guinea Considered* . . ., 1709, 2.
47. Will of Thomas Papillon, 1700/1. Kent Archives, v 1015. T. 44.
48. *Observations on Some of the African Company's late Printed Papers*, 1709; *A Letter from a Merchant in Bristol* . . ., 1709, 2.
49. P. Hoare, *Memoirs of Granville Sharp*, London, 1820, 241.
50. 'Pearne v. Lisle, 1749', Catterall, i, 13.
51. Thomas Carlyle, *Discourse on the Nigger Question*, 1849.
52. *Considerations on the Emancipation of Negroes*, London, 1788, 3.
53. *Considerations on the Negro Cause*, by a West Indian, London, 1772, 11.

CHAPTER FOUR

The Black Community, 1700-1800

The black population of England by the mid-eighteenth century had begun seriously to worry contemporaries. It was large, growing, virtually unknown to white society and desperately poor. Even more alarming was the fact that most Blacks seemed to live in the capital. Calculations of the size of the black population were vague and sometimes contradictory. In 1764 the *Gentleman's Magazine* hazarded a guess of 20,000, noting that it was expanding all the time.[1] A year later the *Morning Chronicle* raised the figure to 30,000. But we have to set both these startling figures against the calculations used in the period of the Somerset case in 1772. In the course of that long drawn-out and totally misunderstood legal hearing, Edward Long, the vituperative Jamaican planter, was busy writing his tract *Candid Reflections* as a contribution to the plantocratic case. He was deliberately trying to alarm his readers about the consequences of black freedom and black immigration into Britain. But the first figure he used for the black population was a mere 3,000. While the tract was in proof form a figure of 14,000 to 15,000 Blacks in England was mentioned in the Somerset hearing. Long consequently rushed through a postscript to the tract, raising his guess to 15,000, adding 'My reader, I hope, will excuse my having stated their number so low as three thousand...'[2]

The Court of King's Bench and no less a figure than the Lord Chief Justice himself had accepted the figure of 15,000 as a reliable indication of the black population.[3] After 1772 therefore, 15,000 was the lowest possible calculation anyone could use, despite the fact that it was based on pure speculation, as had been the wild guesses of the popular press ten years before. Since both the slavery lobby and the philanthropists had political reasons for inflating the size of the black population, 15,000 became the standard minimum. On the strength of this oft-repeated guess generations of historians have taken the figure to be an accurate reflection of reality.[4] If anything lends justification to using this high figure it is the fact that Granville Sharp, the philanthropist who knew, and was known by, the Blacks better than any other white man, privately accepted a figure of 20,000 for the country as a whole.[5]

More alarming still for those disturbed by black settlement in England was the increasing speed and scope of immigration. Contemporaries seemed gripped with a fear that the country was beset by a tidal wave of black immigrants. Between 1772 and 1789, wrote one panic-stricken observer, 'the numbers of slaves who have attended their masters and their families from North America and the islands to Great Britain and Ireland, cannot have been much less than 40,000'.[6] Even those planters who depended on black servants on the long laborious voyage 'home' felt that some measures would have to be taken to arrest the influx of Negroes. Long himself urged that 'some restraint should be laid on the unnatural increase of blacks imported'.[7] In the absence of restrictive immigration laws however it was impossible to prevent the continuing, though wildly exaggerated, influx of Blacks into England.

By the mid-eighteenth century, Negroes were arriving from all points of the compass; from Africa, the West Indies, from North and South America. They landed in all sorts of conditions; as slaves, servants, freemen and even as prosperous and fêted individuals. Overwhelmingly, however, they landed as black slaves, the human property of a homecoming Englishman. Some found their way to England as the slaves of British officials who had served in the far-flung corners of the Atlantic empire. The Commander in Chief of British forces in North America, the British Consul in Madeira, Lord Rodney, the naval commander in the West Indies, all returned home with black slaves who served them faithfully until their master's death.[8] Planters, returning home (though many had never seen England) to enjoy the fruits of absentee leisure, landed in London and Bristol surrounded by the black retinues which had so characterized their opulence in the West Indies. 'The conduct of these people,' wrote one witness, 'approaches nearer to show and extravagance than the northern inhabitants.'[9] Ships, home from the triangular or Atlantic trades, docked in London, Bristol and later in Liverpool, with the riches and the cargoes of the New World. Stacked away like any other commodity, was the occasional black slave, brought to England as the human flotsam and jetsam of overseas trade. In Bristol it was accepted custom that 'commanders of slaving vessels were allowed to transport a few slaves in each cargo for their personal profit'.[10] Indeed by the late eighteenth century imported slaves had become a regular bonus for sailors of all ranks, a custom which led to a series of legal cases in English courts.[11] Some Blacks landed in England as refugees, escaping the horrors of plantation life, although sometimes, as stowaways, they were discovered and forced to serve a new master. Others came to England as free sailors, spending only brief visits in port before heading back to sea once more. Contemporaries however were concerned, not with the transient Blacks, but with those who stayed.

Visitors to England were forcibly struck by the number of Blacks to be seen in town and countryside alike. Writing of London in 1710, a visitor remarked: 'There are, in fact, such a quantity of Moors of both sexes in England that I have not seen before.'[12] Nor were they restricted to London, 'nay in almost every village are to be seen a little race of mulattoes, mischievous as monkeys, and infinitely more dangerous'.[13] The capital however was well known for its sizeable black population. In 1769, when the Tsarina of Russia wanted a 'number of the finest best made black boys, in order to be sent to Petersburgh as attendants on her Russian Majesty', her agent came to London to buy them.[14] Towards the end of the century they were to be found right across the city, though they lived predominantly in the black ghettoes of Mile End, Paddington and along the riverside. By this time others too had moved out, following their retiring masters into widely scattered areas of rural England.[15]

After 1783 hostility to the black population crystallized in a spate of publications directed against further immigration. What had stimulated this response had been the conclusion of the American war, and the depositing in England of some of the black slaves who had been unlucky enough to fight for the British in North America. They arrived in London to join the already considerable number of black beggars. According to one hostile witness 'the city of London, and the country about it [was] lately infested with American negroes'.[16] The most immediate result of this fresh wave of black immigrants was the scheme, supported by private philanthropists and the government of William Pitt alike, to encourage black emigration to Sierra Leone.[17] But the anxiety which white society nervously displayed towards the black population stemmed, not

The Black Community, 1700–1800

from the demographic reality of black immigrants, but from a confused intermeshing of largely imaginary factors. From the mid-eighteenth century, English society reacted partly to the real or imagined size of the black population it knew so badly, and partly to the fear that expanding immigration was threatening to swell the black ranks even further. All these factors were to be repeated in the controversy over immigration in the mid-twentieth century.

Immigration, perhaps more than the size of the resident black population itself, was the spark which unleashed a chain reaction of startled responses. As late as 1830 the spectre of further black immigration was conjured up by the slave lobby as an argument against emancipation of the slaves. Were the slaves freed, argued one slaver, 'I think it not unlikely that one in twenty ... of the black population would find their way to England in the first ten year'.[18] It is certainly true that London's black population was sufficiently large and sufficiently well-known to attract and protect criminal black refugees from abroad,[19] but the scale of black immigration threatened by the slave lobby bore no relation to reality. But it was successful in frightening the English and turning them against those Blacks already in the country.

There existed among the Blacks a certain degree of unity, deriving from their colour and the hostility of white society towards them, but below this unity there was a distinct social and political fragmentation. Many, perhaps even a majority of imported Blacks, had come to England as slaves. After 1772 the most famous of these was James Somerset, cause and occasion of the celebrated Mansfield judgement of that year. In overall terms, slaves may have constituted a majority, but at any one time their total numbers were constantly eroded for the simple reason that slaves, one after the other, fled from bondage, heading for the poor alleyways and warrens of London. These runaways formed the kernel of a very distinct group of Blacks who were free and largely self-sufficient. In the course of the eighteenth century around this group there developed a free black community. Free Blacks moreover needed all the collective strength they could gather, for they were always liable (certainly until the abolition of the slave trade itself in 1807) to recapture and re-enslavement by profiteering captains. Nor need they be shipped back to slavery in the West Indies, for slavery flourished in England throughout most of the eighteenth century. Slaves, said Lord Mansfield in 1772, were 'sold on the exchange and other places of public resort by parties themselves resident in London, and with as little reserve as they would have been in any of our West India possessions'.[20]

Until the moral and legal climate of opinion towards slavery changed dramatically in the last twenty years of the century black slaves in England were treated and used as commodities; they were bought, sold and inherited like other items of property. In 1701, Thomas Papillon of London bequeathed to his son a Negro 'whom I take to be in the nature and quality of my goods and chattels'.[21] When Blacks were sold, receipts were exchanged to prove the legal possession of the human property.[22] As late as 1822, Thomas Armstrong of Dalston in Cumberland, bequeathed a slave in his will.[23] Black chattel slavery, commissioned by usage and sanctioned by various legal processes, was a commonly accepted institution in eighteenth-century England. What undermined it was the resistance of the slaves themselves and their determination to seize their freedom.

Not all Blacks were imported as slaves and not all slaves ran away. There was a third distinct group who, for reasons known only to themselves, remained loyal to their masters, either as slaves or freemen. These were generally rewarded on their master's death. Sabina, the black maid to William Rudd in Bedford, received a cottage, £5 a year and half her master's household effects in return for years of loyalty.[24] The plantocratic lobby, however, always anxious to denigrate the Negro as an individual, was successful in persuading the reading public that inconsiderate selfishness was common to all Blacks. This argument so angered friends of the Negro that part of the philanthropist case was to present the truth about black service. 'Lives there a man in Britain who can say that he has never seen an instance of an African negro acting his part in life with propriety and decorum? Has he never seen a negro respected and trusted by the family he served? Has he never seen a free negro industrious in business, attentive to his own family or kindly attached to those with whom he has formed domestic connections?'[25] Another philanthropist, writing in 1824 claimed to know 'a family in the vicinity of London who have retained a free negro in their service nearly twenty years, who is remarkable for his intelligence, good morals, diligence, attachment and fidelity'.[26] Sometimes a slave was manu-

Olaudah Equiano c. 1789

Ignatius Sancho by Gainsborough

Job ben Solomon c. 1734

Charles, 2nd Duke of Richmond and Lennox by Zoffany. Distinctive red and black livery for the Duke's black servant

The Family of Sir William Young. Another of Zoffany's fine portrayals of black domestics in 18th-century England

mitted by a grateful master, but again, it was a favour normally granted when the master died.²⁷ Many Blacks in eighteenth-century England felt themselves unable to wait for their master's death, in the dim and distant hope of legalised manumission. Instead they freed themselves in perhaps the only way possible – by escape and sanctuary among their fellows.

Smaller, and less significant for the local black population, was the tiny group of Blacks sent or brought to England in the eighteenth century for education. These pioneers from West Africa and the West Indies were intended to fill posts of responsibility and trust, particularly in Africa. More often than not, however, their education, far from helping them to assimilate easily to the English economic process, was employed to counter English interests on return to Africa. The numbers involved were generally small. In 1789 for instance there were an estimated fifty boys and twenty-eight girls in Liverpool, London, Bristol and Lancaster, all from the Sierra Leone region.²⁸

Yet another distinct, but ever changing group, of Blacks that affected English society in the eighteenth century was the maritime fraternity. They were, as we have seen, generally transient, but like the students they formed a black group which has remained a constant element in English society from the eighteenth to the twentieth century. Given the nature and destination of a substantial part of England's maritime trade it was inevitable that Africans, both as freemen and as slaves, would find employment on English ships and would spend time in English ports. Both Bristol and London became famous in the course of the eighteenth century as the homes of transient sea-faring Blacks. In London, Stepney became the traditional home of black sailors. A local clergyman, Dr Mayo, spent his life among them, and it was alleged of him that 'no clergyman in England ever baptised so many black men and mulattoes'.²⁹ Englishmen became so accustomed to the idea of Blacks as sailors that they were felt to be ideally suited to the life; they 'take easily to a sea-life and become ... very excellent seamen'.³⁰ Many of course had little choice in their career, having been pitched into a sailor's life, as many others had become plantation slaves. So successful were the Blacks as sailors – or so desperate was the shortage of white men – that by the late century it was claimed that up to a quarter of all seamen in the navy were black (though this figure ought to be treated with the same scepticism as the immigration and population figures).[31]

Black serving-maids were common in England from the early seventeenth century, but the overwhelming majority of Negroes in England, from the seventeenth to the late eighteenth century, were male; a reflection primarily of the slave recruiting patterns in West Africa, but also of the greater demand for black footmen and male servants. By 1785 it was claimed of the black population that only a 'very small proportion of this number were female'.[32] The consequences of this sexual imbalance were profound and far reaching, both for the Blacks themselves and, in a wider context, for their relations with white society. A majority of black males would find it impossible to form permanent relations with women of their own colour and inevitably many settled down with local white women of the class the blacks were closest to – the poor whites. Sexual relations between black and white flourished, a fact which alarmed and angered white commentators. 'The lower order of women,' fumed Edward Long, 'are remarkably fond of the blacks, for reasons too brutal to mention',[33] (though this did not prevent Long from mentioning them). Thirteen years later, in 1785, another English writer noted the same phenomenon; 'the strange partiality shown for them by the lower order of women'.[34] Few saw these relations for what they really were: a natural consequence of the dearth of black women, similar to the reliance of West Indian planters on black women in the absence of white. Nor did observers mention that this 'partiality' was not restricted to poor white women.

Respectability was bestowed on a racially mixed union if the couple married, but most of the free Blacks who escaped from their masters lived beyond the pale of formal society and beyond the reach of the church. Like the poor whites, it is doubtful whether marriage was an institution to which they even aspired. There were however various examples of mixed marriages, the most notable being between Equiano, the most famous African in late eighteenth-century England, and a Cambridgeshire lady.[35] Another free Negro, Charles Morett, raised a mixed family in the small village of North Ashton;[36] the landlady of a York tavern was married to a Black.[37] More unusual, but not uncommon, were marriages between Englishmen and black women.[38] Such happy unions were held up by white humanitarians as the ideal for racial harmony. When in 1816 William Wilberforce organized a dinner to celebrate the international outlawing of the slave trade, he invited Negroes from the streets of London (insisting however that they dined in a separate room). The highlight of the evening was the presentation, to the reassembled crowd, of a Negro and his English wife, accompanied, to the applause of the gathering, by their 'partly coloured-child, the fruit of their mutual loves'.[39]

Few were willing to see the results of mixed relations in such a light, for the simple reason that racial mixing was not simply a demographic matter. For centuries past, sexual relations with Negroes had been overlaid by the myth of black sexual prowess. This belief, shared by both white men and women, became something of an institution in the course of the eighteenth century and was used to explain, or deride, mixed unions. The strength of, and widespread support for, this myth was perhaps one of the most powerful factors in moulding the racial attitudes between the two sides. At one level the idea that Negroes were exceptionally sexually endowed offered an obvious exception to the generally held belief in the overall superiority of white men; in the delicate, sensitive area of sexuality, even the most superior white men conceded that the Negro took pride of place. Dr Johnson's servant Francis Barber, for instance, was pursued from Lincolnshire to London by a local girl. With her, and with many others, sighed Dr Johnson, 'Frank . . . carried the empire of Cupid further than most men'.[40] This magnetic appeal moreover was not reserved for the lower classes. At about the same time, the Duchess of Queensberry's infatuation for a black servant caused great scandal in society. Her protégé, the former black slave Soubise, was educated by the Duchess to be an English gentleman, versed in the arts of riding, music and polite conversation. But his main talent lay elsewhere and he soon became as famous in the boudoirs of stately homes as he was in London's whore-houses. He was 'as general a lover as Don Juan'. Ultimately his financial extravagances and personal wildness forced the Duchess to send him to India. There he established a successful riding school, only to die in a fall from a horse.[41]

Sexual relations between black and white were, then as now, often the cause of great emotional crises. The birth of a black child to an English woman caused her husband – who was white – to abandon her and the child, in the small Berkshire village of Midgham.⁴² The upper classes were equally involved in sexual entanglements with Negroes. The Earl of Craven threw out his mistress when, to use the Earl's own euphemism, he caught her 'on the knee of my black footman, Mingo'.⁴³ For a gentleman to be caught in bed with a black woman, or for the black servant to gain the affections of his white mistress, was the height of social folly. Yet both frequently occurred, to the private amusement and public shock of society. Cartoonists and caricaturists, those graphic barometers of English society in the late eighteenth century, took great delight in bringing to their curious audience the saucy truth or mischievous innuendo of sexual relations between black and white. There were of course instances of happy, stable relations between black and white which managed to survive the pressures of society. But these were generally ignored as society of all levels fixed its sordid gaze on the more titillating aspects of sexual relations.

Explorers in West Africa from a very early date had displayed a curiosity bordering on the obsessional about the sexual habits of the Africans. West Indian whites too were interested in the sexual behaviour of their black slaves and both groups had extensively reported their observations and analyses to the reading public in England. The enormous differences which separated tribal and slave morality from conventional English society were usually put down to basic and incurable black 'immorality'. In the course of the eighteenth century however this black 'characteristic' began to reveal itself, not in Africa or the slave colonies, but in England itself. Planters, who had relied on black women to while away the lonely plantocratic evenings, became puffed up with spleen and social concern when they saw the degree of interracial sex in England. What disturbed them, and many other Englishmen, was not the 'immorality' itself, but rather its social consequences. Foremost was the 'problem' of miscegenation. The sight of 'tawny children playing in the Squares'⁴⁴ and of a numerous mulatto class, drove white masters into tirades of abuse; 'the English blood will become so contaminated with this mixture and from the chances, the ups and downs of life, this alloy may spread so extensively as even to reach the middle, and then the upper orders of the people, till the whole nation resembles the Portuguese and Moriscos in complexion of skin and baseness of mind'.⁴⁵ When, after 1787, the scheme to recruit London's poor Blacks for settlement in Sierra Leone was first launched, it was given enthusiastic support as a move to 'prevent the unnatural connections between black persons and white'.⁴⁶

Some alleged consequences of miscegenation became the source of mythology. Mulattoes for example were claimed to be the human equivalent of mules, despite the very strong evidence to the contrary.⁴⁷ Public curiosity was always aroused by the more unusual results of miscegenation. A gaping public was invited to inspect George Alexander Grattox, the 'Spotted Negro Boy' a 'fanciful child of nature formed in her most playful mood ... the greatest curiosity ever beheld'.⁴⁸ Alarm, rather than curiosity however was the most common response to miscegenation. The terminology used to describe it gives some idea of the writers' fears. One spoke of 'the rapid increase of a dark and contaminated breed';⁴⁹ Edward Long, always reliable as a spokesman for racial extremism, described miscegenation as a 'venomous and dangerous ulcer that threatens to disperce its malignancy far and wide, until every family catches infection from it'.⁵⁰ While this bitter reaction was common in printed matter from the 1770s, it is also true that foreign visitors commented on the kindly tolerance shown by the English towards racially mixed unions.⁵¹ There can be no doubt, however, that by a substantial and influential section of English society, miscegenation was regarded as a threat to the structure of that society. Consequently racial mixing became a central issue in the opposition to the development of a black community in England.

Servants constituted one of the largest occupational groups in eighteenth-century England⁵² and as the century advanced an increasing proportion of them were black, many of them enslaved domestics. As in the seventeenth century, royalty set the social pace by using black servants. William III, George I, George II, the sons of George III and later William IV, employed Negroes in a variety of menial capacities.⁵³ The nobility was swift to follow the example set by their royal masters, though in numbers and pomp neither royalty nor aristocracy could compete with the planters. Black servants became so common among the aristocracy that the Duke of Dorset, whose family had employed them for the best part of 200 years, abandoned the practice in favour of Chinese servants.⁵⁴ Some masters were able to secure black workers through their contacts with the colonies. But it was also possible to buy them direct from returning sailors, and even on the open market in London.

Black and White

There were at least two taverns in Wapping which served as specialist sale rooms for young black servants.[55] But for those who wished to keep black servants on a slave basis there was the very serious problem of escapes.

Blacks imported as slaves on arrival often 'cease to consider themselves as slaves in this free country nor will they put up with an inequality of treatment'.[56] The reasons for this were complex. In the slave colonies there had always been a close correlation between colour and occupational role. Once in England, the black slave was swift to realize that menial work was not the unique preserve of the Black. This realization was apparently an important element in the dislocation and loosening of ties between the Black and his master. It was only a matter of time before the black servants 'put themselves on a footing with other servants, become intoxicated with liberty [and] grow refractory'.[57] It was into the free black community in London that freshly arrived, freshly dissatisfied slaves escaped. The free Blacks offered both a bait and a haven for new arrivals, and made it their business 'to corrupt and dissatisfy the minds of every black servant that comes to England'.[58] Once this was accomplished the slave was effectively lost inside the black community and was transmuted, by his own actions, into a free man.

The taste of freedom, even when soured by poverty, proved irresistibly attractive. To make matters worse for the former owners a runaway slave was virtually worthless. He could never again recapture the trust needed in a domestic servant, while his experience of freedom rendered him too risky to be returned to the slave colonies. No other Englishman could employ him in the light of his former master's technical ownership. Most of the runaways had been trained and had worked as domestics and had no skills in other fields. Few had the artisan skills which would help them gain entry to a profession, but even the skilled runaways had to face the obstacles laid down by guilds and unions.[59] John Hanson, a successful black joiner in Liverpool, was exceptional.[60] Even fewer were trained for English agricultural labour and often lacked the incentive to leave the security of the capital for the risks of country work. 'They were neither husbandmen, manufacturers nor artificers.'[61] Young, malleable Blacks could of course be trained, as for instance the young slave offered for sale in Bristol in 1728, 'fit to be Instructed in any

Handycraft Trade'.⁶² Such investment, however, could well prove costly and wasteful if the Black opted for the more rigorous life of a free man. Whatever the exceptions to the overall rule, most Negroes, 'being acquainted with no other place but London'.⁶³ found themselves free but unemployed and unemployable at the heart of an urban area already plagued by social unrest. Freedom for the runaway slave was to be endured rather than enjoyed.

In this they were in no way exceptional. They shared a cultural environment of poverty common to thousands of whites. Relations between the poor whites and the poor Blacks form a curious contrast to relations between the white master class and the Blacks, which were generally based on fear, distrust or a mutually acceptable paternalism. With the poor whites, the Blacks shared the dirt and the hunger of London's poor districts. There were few signs of the tensions and resentments between the two sides that one associates with similar situations in a more modern context. The reasons for this may be complex, but a simple answer lies in the appalling conditions shared by everyone. Life was so hard and enjoyments so few that it could scarcely be claimed that immigrant Blacks were taking anything from the whites; there was nothing to take in the first place. Poor whites and Negroes looked on each other with friendly cooperation. The best example of this was the traditional shelter given by poor whites to runaway slaves, preventing the masters from claiming their human property.⁶⁴ Like the poor whites, the free Blacks were forced to scratch for a living on the grimy fringes of legality, sharing the same problems and coming up with the same solutions. They became another, albeit a distinct, element in the subculture of the urban poor.

The results were swift, and predictable. Soon 'they fall into the company of vicious white servants and abandoned prostitutes of the town; and thus are quickly debauched in their morals, instructed in the science of domestic knavery, fleeced of their money, and driven to commit some theft or misdemeanour'.⁶⁵ William Beckford, scion of the great Jamaican plantocratic family, wrote of London's 'poor neglected negroes ... who become pick-pockets, thieves or murderers in consequence of emancipation'.⁶⁶ Those Negroes who were freed 'in general plunged into vice and debauchery' and large numbers of them 'died miserably within a short time'.⁶⁷ Negroes not employed as servants, sniffed another irate Englishman, 'are either thieves or mendicants'.[68] This stream of invective directed against the free Blacks by worried Englishmen failed to conceal what was, after all, a genuine social problem. But it was a problem not peculiar to Negroes, namely the inability of a substantial part of the urban population to survive within the framework of legality. There was nothing new in this, but by the late eighteenth century it was all the more noticeable because the sufferers were black.

In the eighteenth century resorting to crime frequently reflected, not so much on the individual, or in this case on the black population, but on the nature of the legal system and society's general paralysis when faced with the testing issue of urban poverty. Edward Long's 'dissolute, idle, profligate crew'[69] of Blacks turned to crime for much the same reason as London's Irish – as a means of survival in a hostile environment. Inevitably some Blacks paid for their crimes with prison sentences and even with their lives.[70] Black criminals could be found outside the capital among those dispersed into the country or tramping through it on the way to London; in some respects life in rural England was no less difficult and pitiless than life in the city. Black criminals found their way into the jails of Bedford and Shrewsbury; others were transported from Cheshire and Cumberland.[71] The case of Thomas Jennings, sentenced to death for burglary at Faversham in Kent, offers an insight into the dilemma of the black poor. Born in New York, he had served in the Royal Navy, eventually being discharged in England 'a stranger in this country without any visible means of support and of a very mean capacity'.[72] His crimes were clearly not of his own making.

Public attention was drawn to the situation of the black poor, and to black criminal behaviour, after 1783 and the importation of Loyalist American slaves.[73] By 'begging about the streets' the Blacks suffered 'all those evils and inconveniences consequent on idleness and poverty, famine, disease and inclemency of weather'.[74] The black beggar who amassed a fortune on the streets of London was exceptional, if not apocryphal.[75] Most were crushed by circumstances, finding themselves 'unfeelingly driven from place to place by parish officers'.[76] It was alleged in fact that London parishes were unwilling to receive them,[77] an attitude which finally forced the national government to intervene on their behalf.[78] But as late as 1815, the black poor were regarded as a separate social problem. 'The only way we can dispose of them', said one parish officer, 'is to

The Black Community, 1700–1800

fix them on the parish where they fall as casualty.'[79] Similarly in rural communities, the burden of caring for the black poor fell upon the parish.[80] From the eighteenth century to the twentieth the special burden of the black poor and unemployed was to trouble Englishmen who were unable, or unwilling, to see the social reality of the situation. In the eighteenth as in the twentieth century people were only too eager to blame the victims.

In the eighteenth century white hostility towards the Negroes stemmed from easily recognized causes: miscegenation, the burden on the poor rates, the threat to private property posed by runaway slaves and the incidence of crime. Perhaps the most frequently heard complaint was the alleged threat to white employment. As early as 1731 the corporation of London forbade the recruitment of Blacks into companies in the City.[81] It was as servants that Blacks were chiefly employed. Many Englishmen found it perplexing that masters should opt for black menials when there was never any shortage of white domestics.[82] It was felt that the black worker 'excludes an equal number of poor white natives from that bread to which they are entitled to a prior claim'.[83] The black labour threat even extended to the high seas, according to one West Indian Governor: 'I cannot conclude this letter without informing your Lordship that the Number of Negroe slaves employed in navigating the Trading Vessels in these seas (particularly from Bermuda) seem to me to increase so much as to require the attention of the British legislature, as it throws English seamen out of employment.'[84] We know that this simply was not the case. On the contrary, masters frequently had great difficulty recruiting a full complement. Moreover, had black employment been so great a threat as was claimed – at sea and at home – there would surely have been some murmur of dissent from those most likely to be affected – the poor whites. In fact the complaints came from men whose livelihoods could never be threatened by Blacks. White sailors and white domestics, far from resenting their black co-workers, were generally content to work and live on friendly terms with them.

Despite the friendship and help of some Englishmen, the black population was in a very vulnerable situation. Prone to recapture and re-enslavement, the Black was in constant danger of brutalization. It was even disputed whether murder of a Negro would constitute homicide in an English court of law.[85] Outrageous and sadistic punishment of Blacks was common, and often went unpunished, the best known example being the shocking injuries received by Jonathan Strong in 1765. Rescued by the generous Granville Sharp in the winter of 1765, Strong had been beaten by his master 'upon his Head with a pistol till the Barrel and Lock were separated from the Stock. ... The poor Fellow was more than six months under a Surgeon's care.' Perhaps the most common outrage against the Negro was to oblige him to wear a padlocked collar. Sharp, vigilant as ever in the black cause, was shocked to find another Black 'having a Brass collar round his neck with a Direction on it'.[86] Nor was this practice secret or furtive. English artisans made a thriving living from it. 'Matthew Dyer intimates to the public that he makes silver padlocks for Blacks or Dogs; collars etc.' [87] As late as 1814 there were known cases of Blacks in London kept in chains.[88] Ironmongers in the capital in the 1760s offered for sale an implement known as 'the Iron Gag Muzzle' designed for use on Negroes.[89] The view of the Negro as a mere chattel was not simply a matter of legal definition for in the daily treatment meted out to large numbers of Blacks, the English reduced their black property to the level of an ignorant beast.

Even had there been no cases of specific brutality, slavery would have remained a brutalized existence, stripping the Negro of his humanity and feelings. Freedom furthermore often failed to redeem the situation. The poor Negro had constantly to be on his guard against rapacious whites who would profit by his capture, even after 1772 when the Lord Chief Justice had ruled against the forcible repatriation of slaves from England. As late as 1790 Hannah More told Horace Walpole of a harrowing incident in Bristol. A 'poor negro girl was dragged out from a hole in the top of the house where she had hid herself, and forced on board ship'.[90] This particular risk was not removed until abolition in 1807. But of all the punishments inflicted on the black community, perhaps the most difficult to bear was that which is most difficult to trace – widespread racial hatred. As one would expect, literature from the slave lobby seethes with such hatred, but there are signs of racial tension on a wider social level. When in 1815 a mulatto applied for a teaching post in Bisley, his friendly referee was forced to comment, 'Unfortunately he is a Mulatto, a native of the West Indies, which circumstance, added to a family of nine children, has kept him down in the world – Where so dark a complexion is not objected to, he would make a very valuable Schoolmaster.'[91] Even Ignatius Sancho, one of the most obsequious of eighteenth-century Blacks, was constantly rebuffed by 'the national antipathy and prejudice ... towards their woolly headed brethren'.[92]

Faced by constant animosity and dangers, the black population turned to the only reliable support – their own numbers and sense of community. Immersed in an alien white world, Blacks from a variety of backgrounds shed tribal and cultural differences in an effort to fend for themselves. A spirit of black cooperation evolved which manifested itself in many ways. 'London', wrote a visitor, 'abounds with an incredible number of these black men who have clubs to support those out of place.'[93] If a Black were pursued by law officers, he could always rely on the protection of his fellows.[94] For newly arrived slaves, the free Blacks held out the inducement of freedom. Thus the community offered people of African descent a haven from the rigours of the outside world and a protection against the more obvious risks facing them.

Equally important was the distinct social world which the black community created for itself from the residue of African culture and the institutions they found in England. The initial impetus behind the unification of Blacks into a community was the one African characteristic they could never lose, their colour. It was the sight of other Africans which drew them together into a bond of social sympathy[95] and which cut across the primary divisions of tribalism, and African or Creole lines.[96] Together they met, lived, and entertained themselves in little black enclaves within the city of London. The houses of well-placed Negroes often became a focal point where others met and sheltered or simply passed their spare time.[97] Social occasions were frequently exclusively black. In 1764 'no less than 57 of them, men and women, supped, drank, and entertained themselves with dancing and music, consisting of violins, French horns and other instruments, at a public-house in Fleet Street, till four in the morning. No whites were allowed to be present for all the performers were Black.'[98] While the social habits of the English were adopted by the immigrants, they created from the tavern-life, the music and drinking, a social world of their own, imposing on existing patterns a distinctively black style.

In some respects slavery in England had common characteristics with that in the plantation societies, but the differences were more pronounced. The function of the domestic slave in Jamaica or Virginia was different, and his status quite distinct, from those of the black domestic in England. The prime distinction between the two lay in the separate legal systems governing slavery on the two sides of the Atlantic.[99] There were also less important differences. The domestic slave in England was immediately recognisable by his livery. As we have seen, from an early date masters took great care to see that their Blacks 'should be handsomely clothed',[100] sometimes in the finest foppery available, from ruffled shirts, silver buttons and buckles to powdered wigs (both black and white).[101] A Bristol slave ran away wearing 'a brown coat, turn'd up with red, Plad waiscoat and leather breeches'.[102] Time and again newspaper advertisements for runaway slaves leave the most vivid impression in the descriptions of their clothes. Glimpses of their finery can also be seen in numerous eighteenth-century portraits of English aristocrats, in which their black servants are tucked away in the corner of the canvas, providing a contrast to their masters' features and a reminder of their lost reality. But the splendid liveries worn by the Blacks ought not to deceive us. Unlike their white fellow-workers, who frequently wore similar clothing, the Blacks were often obliged to wear the metal collar of the slave. Nor were all of them dressed in elegant style. The clothes of those with less wealthy masters reflected their owners' lower social class. One such escaped slave was described as 'very ill-made, being remarkably pot-bellied – he had when he went away a coarse dark brown Linen Frock and Thickset Waistcoat, very dirty Leather Breeches and on his Head an Old Velvet Jockey Cap'.[103]

Perhaps the most distinguishing feature of slaves and free Blacks in England was their language and level of literacy. In the West Indies a distinctly new tongue emerged from the remnants of African languages and bastardized English (or French and Spanish). Furthermore West Indian whites bitterly resisted the advance of black literacy, assuming (as propertied opinion often has), that there was a causal connection between literacy and social and political dissent. Slave-owners in Britain however seemed less affected by this view and gave their black workers the rudiments of literacy and education. Sancho and Equiano, who are discussed in Chapter Seven, were extreme examples of the fruits of black literacy, but many other slaves were educated by their masters, without making the same impact on white society. Blacks working alongside white domestics, and working directly under an English master, would obviously need a more perfect command of English than the West Indian domestic or field slave. English Blacks evidently retained strong elements of African intonation,[104] but they did not develop the *patois* of the West Indian slaves, though this may have been common among Blacks when they were speaking among themselves.

Language reflects the social requirements of the society it springs from, but in its turn it can be an influential stimulant to the growth of that same society. In the case of the eighteenth-century Blacks, spoken English was a significant element in their assimilation into English society. In the West Indies on the other hand, the absence of the need for English was important in the growth of a distinct Creole society. Newspapers give an indication of the way the white master class in England was largely responsible for spoken English among the Blacks. Advertisements of sales and runaways frequently comment on this vital occupational asset for the black domestic. Cato, a Bristol runaway, 'speaks English very imperfect',[105] claimed his master. Others were more fluent. One black girl was described in a newspaper of 1769 as working 'at her needle tolerably, and speaks English perfectly well'.[106] A Bristol runaway in 1746 spoke 'very good English',[107] but another was notable for his 'English stammering speech'.[108]

Literacy among Negroes was rarer than spoken English. In the face of the overall resistance to the spread of lower class literacy,[109] which was manifested in particular in the 1790s, it seems odd at first sight that the few literate Blacks frequently owed their ability to their masters. Equiano, for instance, was sent to school by his mistress;[110] Sancho was educated by his white patrons.[111] Nor was education given solely to free black domestics; enslaved Blacks were sometimes educated by their owners.[112] Negroes fluent in two languages were sometimes used as interpreters and intermediaries[113] in the African trade but they had scarcely any influence with the English Negroes. Black literacy was often instrumental in helping an individual rise up the social ladder. Again, Sancho and Equiano are good cases in point, but others followed them in a less exalted and publicized way. In 1765 a Black in London was ordained into the Church of England,[114] while others put their education to the task of working hard and saving for their uncertain futures.[115] Only with skills or education could the free Black command regular paid work and few could have been as lucky or thrifty as James Martin, who lived in Bristol. Bought as a slave in the West Indies, he died as a free Englishman, leaving a legacy to the African Association for their missionary work in Africa.[116] Free Blacks did prosper and travel around England like any other free members of the community, lodging undisturbed in taverns,[117] owning businesses and generally prospering. But that such men were able to emerge from the world of the black poor hardly alters the overall picture of poverty and limited freedom which was the hallmark of the eighteenth-century black community.

Certain sections of the black population turned to the religion of their masters with a zeal unknown in the slave colonies until the nineteenth century.[118] In part this was due to the greater incidence of freedom in England, but the most important factor behind black Christianity was the widespread belief, shared by black and white alike, that conversion and baptism automatically bestowed full freedom on the Negro. Black members of a church were rare, but not unknown, in the seventeenth century. A 'blackamoor maid, named Frances, a servant to one that lived upon the back of Bristol', joined the Baptist Church of Christ in Broadmead in the 1640s 'which thing is somewhat rare in our days and nation, to have an Ethiopian, or blackamoor, to be truly convinced of sin, and of their lost state without the Redeemer, and to be truly converted to the Lord Jesus Christ, as she was'. Moreover the girl set the other members of the church an example of devoted piety, 'for this poor Ethiopian's soul sorrowed much for God, and she walked very humble and blameless in her conversation to her end'.[119] A century later such black devotion to Christianity – of various brands – had become commonplace, and most converts seem to have been attracted to the Church of England.

It was widely believed that baptism or marriage made the Negro free,[120] even after the famous ruling of the Attorney and Solicitor Generals in 1729 to the effect that 'baptism doth not bestow freedom on him nor make any alteration in his temporal condition in these kingdoms'.[121] English owners were divided about baptism for their slaves. Some resisted as bitterly as the planters in the West Indies, whereas others were only too eager to have their black 'pagans' converted into Christians. The special attraction of religion, for

Negroes of varied tribal backgrounds, is brilliantly illustrated in a description of a London black christening at St Giles's parish church in 1726.

1st came the reputed Father, a Guiney Black, a very clever well-dresst Fellow, and another Black who was to be the Godfather. 2dly, The Midwife or rather her Deputy, a White Woman, carrying the sooty little Pagan, who was to be metamorphos'd into a Christian. 3dly, the Mother, who was also a Black but not of the Guiney Breed, a well-shap'd, well dress'd Woman. 4thly, the two intended Godmothers, attended by 6 or 8 more, all Guiney Blacks, as pretty, genteel Girls as could be girt with a girdle, and setting aside the Complexion, enough to tempt an old frozen Anchorite to have crack'd a Commandment with any of them.[122]

Doubtless it was the Christian virtues of docility and industry that were supposed to follow this 'metamorphosis' which may have persuaded so many white masters to have their slaves converted to the faith, though the cases we know of suggest that baptized Blacks also happened to be firm favourites with the family.[123]

There was little or no pattern about the incidence of black baptism. Negroes were accepted into the Church at all ages and not primarily, as with the white community, among the very young and infants. The timing of a baptism would depend on the position and rank of the parent or parents, on the time spent in England (in the case of adults), and on the relationship with the white master.[124] In 1760 'three adult Negroes [were] converted to Christianity and baptized' in Warfield, Berkshire.[125] In a neighbouring parish, William Diego was baptized at the relatively early age of four and a half.[126] Equiano, baptized in St Margaret's, Westminster, was fourteen; Jack London, converted in Norham in 1763, was eight years old.[127] Others, like the case described above, were brought into the church at birth, but this would clearly depend on their parents already being members of the Church. Maria Sambo, who had married an Englishman, Warren Hull, in Earls Colne near Colchester in 1731, brought up all her children in the local parish church.[128] Ministers in Yorkshire were unhappy about baptizing local Blacks without the prior consent of the Archbishop.[129] One such Yorkshire slave, Beswick, 'a Youth of no Learning, and but of slender capacity', remained the only regular member of his parish church not to have been baptized, although both the local ministers 'have instructed him in order to be baptized, if your Grace shall so

Black and White

order it'.[130] Across the Pennines in Lancaster, the local parish records show that all the local black converts were adults.[131] All over the country, Negroes of all ages turned to their masters' religion.

Individual masters or mistresses clearly exerted great influence on the particular persuasion adopted by the slave or black servant. John Wesley was able personally to convert some Negroes simply by knowing their master. On a visit to a house in Wandsworth Wesley noted that 'two Negro servants ... and a mulatto appear to be much awakened'. Within the year, he returned and 'baptized two negroes belonging to Mr Gilbert ... one of these is deeply convinced of sin; the other rejoiced in God her Saviour and is the first African Christian I have known'.[132] Long before this date however the SPCK had been actively converting Africans. In 1754 three 'fine negro boys' were brought to London and placed with a 'very diligent schoolmaster'. Within seven weeks 'one of them could say the Lord's Prayer and the Apostle's Creed and the others answered well'.[133]

Conversion and baptism involved much more than the mere adoption of an alien religion. It generally led to the giving or confirmation of new names. Once again it can be seen how the adoption of English cultural patterns was a factor in the assimilation of the black population. Frequently an African name was dropped because it was unmanageable, and an anglicized name given, even before baptism. Thus Olaudah Equiano became Gustavus Vassa.[134] Rarely did Africans keep their African names. When they did, their English masters added an English Christian name to make matters simpler. But this was usually the case when the African was in England only temporarily for education or training, before returning to West Africa. Thus Quaque, Cudjoe and Coboro were given the extra names Philip, William and Thomas.[135] Negroes frequently took their masters' names,[136] or took the name of the locality as their own. John Lancaster lived in Lancaster;[137] two Blacks in Carlisle took that name for themselves.[138] Another Black, in Bedford, adopted the town's name as his own.[139]

Names were given to Negroes, naturally enough, even when they remained enslaved and unbaptized. As in the slave colonies, many of these names tended to be classical, or even absurd; Pompey, Cato, Scipio, Starling, Tallow, Little Ephraim, Robin John, Othello and even Pan Ran Ratto Skinner.[140] Such names were often kept, rather than replaced, after baptism. However, combinations of Christian names and surnames (whether African or traditional slave surnames) were much more common, certainly among Christian Blacks, than was ever the case in the slave colonies. But even in England the degradation of the Negro was frequently in evidence in the naming process. The ultimate denial of the Black's humanity was to give him no name at all, but to treat him merely as an appendix to his master: 'Mr Moses Goodyear of Chelsea, his Negro'.[141] All the evidence shown here unfortunately but inevitably is from white sources and it seems feasible that, when living as a black community, Negroes used different names and may even have kept their African names. But in their formal relations with white English society, they often went through a varied process of name-changing which ultimately assisted their acculturation.

Converted Blacks usually followed the religious denomination of their master, generally the Church of England. In a way this was understandable. Those people most given to owning slaves – planters, noblemen and the upper reaches of English society – were more likely, by social rank and ideological persuasion, to belong to the Church of England than to non-conformity. Since however baptism was often a reward of faithful service, or to a family favourite, it could only affect those black servants who remained within the confines of their masters' house. Perhaps a majority of Blacks by the late eighteenth century no longer lived like this, but instead had fled to the freedom and poverty of the free black community. It could well be the case that those who turned to religion formed only a small proportion of the total black population. If most Negroes lived in that free black society lying beyond the reach of white society, it is likely that, like the poor whites, they remained untouched by Christianity.

Where Christianity did make inroads into the black population, there are no signs that it brought with it the disruptive seeds of egalitarianism, as was feared by the planters. Barbadians had complained in 1680 'that the conversion of their slaves to Christianity would not only destroy their property but endanger the island, insomuch as converted negroes grew more perverse and intractable than others, and hence of less value for labour or sale'.[142] There is no evidence that this took place among the Blacks in England in the eighteenth century. Indeed those who became spokesmen for the black population, display a religious attachment which was other-worldly and far from perverse. To put it crudely, black religion did not become the cutting edge of black radicalism in England.

The printed works of the three African spokesmen in England are full of religious imagery, allusions and biblical quotations. All three seem to have staggered through life groaning beneath a burden of sin, searching for personal salvation. Sancho put down his success in life to 'God's blessing'.[143] Cugoano argued that, were men to 'observe the laws of God, and to keep His commandments, and walk in the way of righteousness, then might the temperate climes of Great Britain be seen to vie with the rich land of Canaan of old'.[144] Equiano's use of biblical material and religious themes was, if anything, even more pronounced. Told by other servants that he could not go to heaven unless baptized, Equiano persuaded his mistress to allow this.[145] With the passage of time his religious feelings became more acute. 'I was continually oppressed and much concerned about the salvation of my soul and was determined (in my own strength) to be a first-rate Christian.' To this end he plodded from church to church 'two or three times a day', seeking a satisfactory religious experience.[146] But one looks in vain, in all these black utterances on religion, for that awareness of social inequality which became so pronounced among Christianized Blacks in the slave colonies some forty years later. The Christianization of the English Blacks was not accompanied, as it was in the West Indies, by serious social unrest. Instead, it became yet another factor in their relatively smooth assimilation into English society. Christianity for that minority who turned to it, redirected black aspirations towards the hereafter. For this reason, if for no other, white masters may well have been keen on promoting the baptism of their black workers.

The role of religion in England's involvement with slavery and the slave trade is tortuous and defies simple analysis. While abolitionists from the 1780s tried, with ultimate success, to monopolize Christian sentiment in the interests of the slaves, supporters of slavery had long before, by a perverse twist, used their religion to justify the trade. It was argued that the slave trade had served a useful Christian purpose by bringing heathens within the reach of the Church,[147] despite the fact that precious few planters supported the conversion of their slaves. By an even more bizarre twist, evangelicals adopted this line of argument from the slavery lobby, and even persuaded the Blacks that they had the slave trade to thank for making their conversion possible. 'O Lord, I thank thee for sending big ship into my country, and wicked men to steal me and bring me here that I might know and love thee.'[148] At this level, Christianity was used not to condemn the trade but to praise it as a vehicle on which the Blacks could safely ride to the promised land.

The attitudes of Sancho, Cugoano and Equiano become comprehensible when we look at the religious material produced specifically for the conversion of the Blacks. Much of the ideological content of evangelical religion was little more than a crude psychological pacification programme. Black attention was to be fixed, not on the here and now, but on the hereafter. 'The better you grow yourself, and the more Negroes you teach their daily duty to God the more happy you will be when you die.'[149] The words to be used by a minister to his black flock neatly summarise the inspiration behind much of the Christian attack on black 'heathenism': 'May God keep you in this good disposition, and give you a teachable temper.' At times the message became a caricature of religious zeal: 'This is not the world for which you were chiefly made; – nor must you look for any true and lasting happiness here.' A morning prayer produced specially for Negroes contained a cogently stated programme for work and life discipline: 'O, merciful God, grant that I may perform my duty this day faithfully and cheerfully; and that I may never murmur, be uneasy, or impatient under any of the troubles of this life.' The hymn with which the Blacks were expected to greet the day, in this book of religious instruction for Negroes, echoed similar sentiments:

> Awake my soul and with the sun
> Thy daily stage of duty run
> Shake off dull sloth, and early rise
> To pay thy morning sacrifice.[150]

Black slaves permitted by their masters to turn to Christianity were confronted by an other-worldly ideology which diverted their gaze from worldly problems. Encouragement was given by masters who realized the social benefits of diversionary religion, and by those evangelicals who produced the prayers and hymns which formed the basis for black Christianity. From the mid-eighteenth century, a new, distinct brand of Christianity emerged, designed for the Blacks and 'better adapted to their capacities and conditions'.[151]

But it also served the interests of the masters and helped to maintain the status quo. The degree to which it succeeded can be seen in the burden of sin weighing on the shoulders of Cugoano and Equiano.

On the fringes of English society in the eighteenth century there existed Negroes who defy any neat analysis along social or occupation lines. These men moved in the world of popular entertainment, using their blackness or unusual colour and talents, their strengths and their oddities, to live out a stereotyped role which has stuck with Blacks to this day. A popular myth, finding its origins in a misunderstanding of the role of music in West Indian and West African society, was, to use the words of John Wesley, that Negroes have an 'ear for music'. Wesley was keen to spot the advantages of this alleged natural talent. 'Negroes above all the human species I ever knew, have the nicest ear for music. They have a kind of ecstatic delight in psalmody.'[152] Englishmen were swift to seize on this black 'characteristic' and to harness it to their own entertainment. The black runaway Starling, who 'blows the French Horn very well'[153] was not unusual in his talent for the simple reason that large numbers of Negroes were trained to play musical instruments. The black community, in its turn, used the talents given to it by its white masters, for its own amusement and social relief.[154] In army regiments black musicians came to the fore in mid-century, although there is evidence that black trumpeters had been used in the Scottish Life Guards in the previous century.[155] At the installation of the Knights Companion of the Order of the Bath in London in 1730, a fanfare was blown by twelve black trumpeters.[156] Negro musicians became common and apparently indispensable; 'If there were no niggers, who would make sugar for us, and beat the big drum?'[157] The use of Negro musicians in military bands was given a boost in 1783 when the Duke of York, son of George III, imported a group from Germany.[158] Ten years later, four companies of Middlesex Militia were attached to a band in which 'the clash pans' were played 'by a real live blackamoor, who walked between two mulattos, which had a grand appearance indeed'.[159] Dressed in flamboyant style – often Oriental dress – Negro bandsmen were to be found in a variety of late eighteenth-century regimental bands, playing drums, cymbals and trumpets.[160] Some became celebrated, including 'the leaping Negro bandsman of the Connaught Rangers with his Jingling Johnnie'.[161] At the other end of the black musical scale was the famous Billy Waters, the black fiddler who frequented the taverns and entertained the crowds of professional beggars in the rookeries of St Giles.[162] As late as the mid-nineteenth century, Taine noted the grating music coming from a black fiddler in the spirit cellars of Shadwell.[163] The practice of employing black military bandsmen died out in 1835, to be revived in the twentieth century, with the death of Francis, the last black drummer in the Grenadier Guards. Interestingly enough, even he wore a silver collar.[164]

The stage, in the eighteenth century a truly popular entertainment in every sense of the word, also attracted Negroes. Sancho himself took to the stage in the 1760s in the melodrama *Oroonoko*, the story of an African prince. Unfortunately, his career was cut short by a speech impediment. When Englishmen tried to imitate Negroes in a short-lived comic opera *The Blackamoor Wash'd White* in 1776, the theatrical mob broke up the theatre. The key to the play was the sentiment expressed by the leading character, 'O that I should ever live to see the day when white Englishmen must give way to foreign blacks'.[165] But it was not the racialist sentiment, so much as the poor quality of the play, which led to the mob's unrest. It took the great Garrick, who was a friend of Sancho, to restore peace and order. Negroes appeared on the stage outside London, in Lancashire and even in Dublin.[166] They also appeared or rather starred, in touring fairs, where their peculiar characteristics drew in bemused crowds. George Alexander Grattox, 'the Spotted Negro Boy', was imported to be displayed in public. 'His skin and hair were spotted and mottled all over brown and white.' He was understandably 'allowed by every lady and Gentleman that hath seen him the greatest curiosity ever beheld'.[167] A similar 'curiosity' was offered to the public in the person of Harlequin 'the white Negro woman', whose albinism proved too tempting a commercial proposition for her owner to keep her as an enslaved domestic.[168]

Popular entertainment in the eighteenth century was often tinged with violence and squalid brutality (it is often forgotten that public executions and punishments offered the poor their cheapest and most eagerly awaited entertainment). Amusement was often extracted from the coarse daily realities of life. Negroes were common among the poor, but their unusualness still proved a great attraction. Special physical attributes or talents made the Negro a special object of public attention. Soubise, 'an uncommonly smart and intelligent little Mingo', entertained polite society with his violin, fencing and singing. Other Blacks appealed to the more brutal tastes of society. Bill Richmond, the heavyweight champion of England, was black, born a slave in New York and brought to England in 1783. Taught to box by Lord Byron, Richmond later taught George, Prince of Wales, to box. Thomas Molineaux, another black champion, who lost his crown to Tom Cribb in 1810, had also been a slave, born and raised in Virginia.[169] There were other Blacks whose lives were even more bizarre. Macomo, the most famous lion-tamer in eighteenth century England, was African. His mulatto son continued the tradition, running a circus well into the nineteenth century.[170] At a different level, but scarcely less famous, was Harriet, the black African from Guinea, a highly successful London prostitute, famous for her fortune and sexual abilities alike.[171]

By 1800 it was still impossible to calculate the actual size of England's black population. But it had permeated most ranks of society, through the length and breadth of the country and in all walks of life. The dispersion was uneven but certainly in London Blacks were an everyday sight. They could be found grouped together in the wretched slums of the capital; they could be found in stately homes in remote rural communities, living the respected but rugged life of the servant class. Some behaved like black English gentlemen, and had been educated to that end. Others stalked the major ports of the country or settled in the smallest of rural villages where they had found themselves in the train of a retiring planter or official.

In London, and in rural settings, relations between the black and white populations were complex and constantly shifting under the pressures of economic change and fluctuating political events. Blacks were, at one and the same time, exploited (in a way inapplicable to white people), befriended, patronized, rejected and despised. Even their white friends were unhappy to see the growth of a black population inside England. The English were distrustful when the Blacks kept to themselves and led a distinct community life, and yet were equally alarmed, for different reasons, when they saw them absorbed into white society. The Lord Chief Justice had called them 'an enemy at the heart of the state'; their friends tried to send them 'back' to Africa; their enemies sold them and treated them like animals.

The Black Community, 1700–1800

The irony of the black situation was that while they had little or no control over their arrival in England, having been deposited here directly and indirectly as a result of English economic dependence on black labour, they were unable to find a home for themselves. In England the Blacks pressed too hard on a number of society's sensitive nerves. In self-defence, they evolved a community which may have served their immediate purposes, but which compounded the Englishman's fears about the black presence. Racial hatred was manifested in a variety of subtle and open ways, from open distrust of the black poor in London, to belief in the slave lobby's propaganda about the nature of the Negro as a species. It was the experience of this first major black community, with all its ancillary worries and doubts, which crystallized racial feeling. Fears and myths about the Blacks could be traced back to the travel stories of the sixteenth century. In the eighteenth century mythology seemed to be given the shape of living, breathing reality in the form of a large black subculture in England. English racialism (though this word is too crude to describe the complex social phenomenon it has come to denote) emerged in a pronounced form from mid-century; the basic tenets of that racialism were inherited by later generations of Englishmen in an uneven, but nonetheless unbroken line. My prime purpose here has been to show, not the rise of racialism itself, but the one major social change which was so intimately involved in its development: namely the emergence of an important black minority. When staring into the face of black humanity on the streets of eighteenth-century England, white Englishmen underwent a series of emotions and reactions they scarcely understood. In the last resort, the history of the first black community in England tells us as much about white society, and the roots of racialism, as it does about the thousands of Blacks whose gaunt faces and bony outstretched hands remain the proper subject of this book.

Notes

CHAPTER FOUR: *The Black Community, 1700–1800*

1. *Gentleman's Magazine*, 1764, 493.
2. Long, *Candid Reflections*, 53; 75–6.
3. *Howell's State Trials*, 1820, xx, 71; 77.
4. Most historians give this figure: M. D. George, Christopher Fyfe, Richard West, F. J. Klingberg.
5. Granville Sharp, *Letter Book, 1763–1773*, 19 (York Minster).
6. G. Francklyn, *Observations on the Slave Trade*, London, 1789, 81.
7. Long, *Candid Reflections*, 46.
8. Weybridge Parish Registers, *Surrey Archeological Collection*, 1902, xvii, 65; Gravestone of Fisher Murray 'A Faithful Black Servant' Elvington Church Yard, York; J. J. Hecht, *Continental and Colonial Servants in Eighteenth Century England*, Northampton, Mass., Smith College, 1954, 34.
9. J. Abraham, *Lettsum*, London, 1933, 53.
10. J. Latimer, *The Annals of Bristol in the Eighteenth Century*, Frome, 1893, 146.
11. Catterall, ii, 23; 26.
12. Z. C. von Uffenbach, *London in 1710*, (ed. and trans. W. H. Quarrel, 1934), 88.
13. Philip Thicknesse, quoted in C. Dover, *Hell in the Sunshine*, London, Secker & Warburg, 1943.
14. *Notes and Queries*, ii, October 1852, 411.
15. See locations mentioned in n. 124–131 below.
16. *A Letter to Philo-Africanus*, London, 1787, 17.
17. See Chapter Nine below.
18. 'A West India Planter', *Letter to the Most Hon. the Marquis of Chandos*, London, 1830, 22.
19. V. S. Naipaul, *The Loss of El Dorado*, London, Deutsch, 1969, 282.
20. Quoted in Catterall, i, 3, n. 14.
21. Kent Archives, v, 1015.T.44.
22. *Historical Manuscripts Commission*, Earl of Ancaster, London, 1907, 493.
23. Will of Thomas Armstrong, 1822, Record Office, Carlisle.
24. Will of William Rudd, 1741; (ABP/W.1745/22) Bedford County Record Office.

The Black Community, 1700–1800

25. James Anderson, *Observations on Slavery*, Manchester, 1789, 35–6.
26. *An Important Appeal to the Reason, Justice and Patriotism of the People of Illinois*, 1824, 39.
27. *Fifth Report of the African Institution*, London, 1811, 88.
28. Christopher Fyfe, *A History of Sierra Leone*, Oxford University Press, 1962, 11.
29. M. P. Banton, *The Coloured Quarter*, London, Cape, 1955, 23.
30. *A Letter from Capt. J. S. Smith* ..., London, 1786, 35.
31. N. Leys, *Kenya*, London, 1924, 367; but see Christopher Lloyd, *The British Seaman*, London, Paladin Books, 1970.
32. *Cursory Remarks upon the Rev. Ramsay's Essays* ..., London, 1785, 117.
33. Long, *Candid Reflections*, 48.
34. *Cursory Remarks*, 1785, 118n.
35. *Equiano's Travels*, ed. Paul Edwards, London, Dawsons Pall Mall, 1967, xv.
36. *Notes and Queries*, December 1878, 453.
37. *York Gazette*, 16 June 1832.
38. Bedfordshire Parish Registers, vol. xxxiv, 1758, 'Burial of Sabina'.
39. Joseph Marryat, *More Thoughts* ..., London, 1815, 105.
40. G. B. Hill, *Johnsonian Miscellany*, Oxford, 1897, i, 291.
41. *Reminiscences of Henry Angelo*, London, 1828, i, 446–52.
42. Midgham Parish Register, 1769, Berkshire Record Office.
43. *Confessions of Julia Johnson*, 1828, 28, quoted in Rogers, *Nature Knows No Color-Line*, 174.
44. Hester Piozzi, *Intimate Letters*, 1914, 243, quoted in ibid., 169.
45. Long, *Candid Reflections*, 48–9.
46. John Pugh, *Remarkable Occurrences* ... 1788, 169.
47. See for instance comments in *Gentleman's Magazine*, 1766, 403.
48. *Notes and Queries*, 9th series, vi, 1900, 56.
49. *Cursory Remarks*, 118n.
50. Long, *Candid Reflections*, 49.
51. B. Silliman, *A Journal of Travels, 1810*, New Haven, 1820, 271–72.
52. Hecht, iii.
53. Rogers, *Sex and Race*, i, 201.
54. Rogers, *Nature Knows No Color-Line*, 157.
55. Banton, *The Coloured Quarter*, 23.
56. *Gentleman's Magazine*, 1764, 493.
57. Sir John Fielding, *Penal Laws*, 1768, 144–5.
58. ibid.
59. 14 September 1731, *Proclamation by the Lord Mayor of London*, Guildhall Record Office.

60. *Tenth Report of the African Institution*, 1816, 38.
61. Long, *Candid Reflections*, 51.
62. *Farley's Bristol Newspaper*, 31 August 1728.
63. *A Letter from Capt J. S. Smith*, 35.
64. Fielding, *Penal Laws*, 144.
65. Long, *Candid Reflections*, 47.
66. William Beckford, *Remarks upon the Situation of Negroes in Jamaica*, London, 1788, 96.
67. Francklyn, *Observations*, XII–XIII.
68. *Cursory Remarks*, 117.
69. Long, *Candid Reflections*, 48.
70. *Cursory Remarks*, 119; Bedford Quarter Sessions, 1820 (QSR, 1820/235, 237; QGV 10/1) Bedford County Record Office.
71. Information communicated by County Archivists of Bedford, Salop., Cheshire and Cumberland.
72. Kent Archives Office, *Petition*, Fa/JQZ 15/2.
73. J. Tobin, *A Short Rejoinder*, 1787, 100; G. L. Craig *The History of British Commerce*, London, 1844, vol. iii, p. iii.
74. Francklyn, *Observations*, xii; *Cursory Remarks*, 117.
75. *Quarterly Review*, 1815, 131.
76. Beckford, *Remarks*, 96.
77. Francklyn, *Observations*, xii.
78. Richard West, *Back to Africa, History of Sierra Leone and Liberia*, London Cape, 1970, Chapter 1.
79. 'Report from the Committee on the State of Mendacity in the Metropolis', PP 1814–15, iii, 15.
80. Ampthill Overseers's Account, 1815, P. 30/12/1 (Bedford R.O.); Q. Sessions 1870, (Salop. C.R.); Easthampstead Parish Reg. 1793, D/P.49. 1/3 (Berkshire R.O.).
81. *Proclamation*, 14 September 1731, Guildhall Record Office.
82. *Gentleman's Magazine*, 1764, 493.
83. Long, *Candid Reflections*, 52.
84. Quoted in R. A. Fisher, 'Manuscript material bearing on the Negroes in British archives', *Journal of Negro History*, 1942, 27, 88.
85. Granville Sharp, *Letter Book*, 46.
86. ibid., 93.
87. Quoted in Little, *Negroes in Britain*, 168.
88. *Ninth Report of the African Institution*, London, 1815, 70; See also Banton *The Coloured Quarter*, 25.
89. Granville Sharp, *Letter Book*, 34.
90. Quoted in Latimer, *Annals of Bristol*, 492.
91. Letter of Richard Raikes, 5 July 1815, Gloucestershire C.R.O.

92. 5 January 1776, *Letters of the Late Ignatius Sancho*, ed. J. Jeckyll, London, 1782, 252.
93. Philip Thicknesse, quoted, in Dover, 159.
94. Banton, *The Coloured Quarter*, 93, n.18.
95. Olaudah Equiano, *The Interesting Narrative of the Life of Olaudah Equiano or Gustavus Vassa the African by Himself*, London, 1789, 2 vols. [hereafter cited as Equiano], i, 152–3.
96. *St James Evening Post*, 19–27 March, 1726; Hecht, 49.
97. Hecht, 49.
98. ibid.
99. Chapters 6–8 below.
100. 18 January 1628, Sir James Bragg to Nicholas, *Cal. S. P. Dom.*, 1627–8, 521.
101. The list of clothing for two African boys brought to England for education in 1754 contained the following '12 ruffled Shirts, 1 blue Coat and Breeches for each laced with White, laced with Silver, and Silver Buttons, 1 Scarlet Cloth Waistcoat for each trimmed with Silver, 2 Frocks and Breeches, 2 Scarlet worsted Waistcoats, 2 Silver laced Hats, 2 Berry Wiggs, 8 pairs of white stockings, 4 pairs of worsted ditto, 8 pairs of Pumps, 2 pairs of strong shoes, 2 pairs of Silver Buckles'. *Notes and Queries*, 1928, 173–4.
102. *Felix Farley's Bristol Journal*, 5 March 1757.
103. Sharp, *Letter Book*, 3.
104. See words put into mouth of Negroes by cartoonists.
105. *Felix Farley's Bristol Journal*, 5 March 1757.
106. *Public Advertiser*, 28 November 1769.
107. *Felix Farley's Bristol Journal*, 15 November 1746.
108. *Daily Courant*, 29 March 1712.
109. R. K. Webb, *The British Working-Class Reader*, Allen & Unwin, London, 1955.
110. Equiano, I, 133.
111. Jeckyll, *Letters*, iii.
112. *Felix Farley's Bristol Journal*, 16 February, 1765.
113. Francklyn, *Observations*, 209.
114. *Gentleman's Magazine*, 1765, 145.
115. *The Bristol Gazette and Public Advertiser*, 30 August 1787.
116. *Eighth Report of the Directors of the African Institution*, London, 1814, 22–4.
117. *Felix Farley's Bristol Journal*, 17 May 1746.
118. O. Patterson, *The Sociology of Slavery*, MacGibbon & Kee, London, 1967.

119. E B. Underhill, ed *The Records of a Church of Christ, 1640–1687*. Hanserd Knollys Society, London, 1847.
120. Sir John Fielding, *Penal Laws*, 144–5.
121. 'Yorke–Talbot Opinion, 1729,' Catterall, i, 3.
122. *St James Evening Post*, 19–27 March 1726, quoted in Hecht, 49.
123. Equiano, I, 134; Weybridge Parish Registers, *Surrey Archeological Collection*, xvii, 1902, 65, 69; Hecht, 42.
124. Hecht, 42; *Notes and Queries*, 1878, 338.
125. Warfield Parish Register, January 1760, Berkshire R.O.
126. Sunninghill Parish Register, 1755, Berkshire R. O.
127. *Notes and Queries*, 1878, 338.
128. Parish Registers of Earls Colne, 1731–73; information from A. D. Merson.
129. Bishopthorpe Papers (R.Bp), 30 October 1762. R.Bp 20/B/98; 20 July 1768, R.Bp 20/F/10, Borthwick Institute, York.
130. *Yorkshire Record Series* (1743), lxxi, 105.
131. *Notes and Queries*, 1931, 80.
132. 17 January; December 1758, *The Works of John Wesley*, Grand Rapids, Michegan, n.d., ii, 433, 464.
133. C. F. Pascoe, *Two Hundred Years of the SPG*, London, 1901, 256.
134. Equiano, i, 96.
135. Pascoe, 256.
136. Sir Henry Charles' slave became Charles Henry; see also Catterall, i, 20.
137. *Notes and Queries*, 1931, 80.
138. St Mary's Parish Register, Cumberland Westmoreland R.O.
139. Streatly Parish 1773, Bedford R.O.
140. Others include John Wilkes and Robinson Cruiso.
141. J. Ashley, *Social Life in the Reign of Queen Anne*, 2 vols, London, i, 81.
142. *Cal. St. Pap. Col, Am. W.I*, 1677–80, 611.
143. Sancho, *Letters*, 95.
144. Ottobah Cugoano, *Thoughts and Sentiments*, London, 1787, 138.
145. Equiano, i, 133–4.
146. Equiano, ii, 116–18.
147. R. Harris, *Scriptural Researches on the Licitness of the Slave Trade*, London, 1824.
148. *Missionary Stories*, London, 1842, 'The Prayer of the Little Negro'.
149. *Christian Directions and Instructions for Negroes*, London, 1807, iii.
150. ibid., 12, 84, 124, 137.
151. William Knox, *Three Tracts*, London, 1768, 33.
152. *The Works of John Wesley*, ii, 338.
153. *Felix Farley's Bristol Journal*, 12 March 1757.

154. Hecht, 99.
155. *Notes and Queries*, 1889, 448; 517.
156. ibid., 1889, 237.
157. Quoted, ibid., 1916, 303–4.
158. Rogers, *Nature Knows no Color-Line*, 163.
159. *Notes and Queries*, 1916, 303–4.
160. H. G. Farmer, *Military Music*, New York, Chanticleer, 1950, 35.
161. ibid., 52.
162. M. D. George, *Hogarth to Cruikshank*, London, Allen Lane, The Penguin Press, 1967, 169–70.
163. H. Taine, *Notes on England*, London, 1872, 33.
164. *Notes and Queries*, 1916, 378.
165. G. W. Slone Jnr, *The London Stage 1600–1800*, Part 4, Illinois, 1962, 1949–1999; H. W. Pedicord, *The Theatrical Public in the Time of Garrick*, New York, 1954, 56.
166. *Notes and Queries*, 1889, 164–5.
167. ibid., v, 1900, 506; vi, 1910, 56.
168. Papers on Harlequin, Q/SBb, 372/60–62. Essex R.O.
169. J. A. Rogers, *Nature Knows no Color-Line*, 163; 169–70.
170. ibid., 165.
171. ibid., 173.

CHAPTER FIVE

The Free Black Voice

At the height of the slave trade thousands of Negroes lived in England, the majority in bondage, all of them oppressed or exploited. They and the poor whites were 'marginal people' whose voices went largely unheeded and unrecorded. But the lives of a small number of Africans were described in detail, by themselves or their white friends. Four men in particular, Job ben Solomon, Ignatius Sancho, Olaudah Equiano and Ottobah Cugoano rose from the submerged mass. All but one were adopted by polite white society, in itself a feat requiring a fortuitous combination of luck and personal qualities. Few Blacks could expect similar fortune. Men able to overcome the institutional obstacles surrounding the Negro in eighteenth-century England were, by definition, exceptional. In other respects they typified the black community. They too had passed through the agonies of slavery; they too continued to suffer the rebuffs of white society. Their free voice told of common experiences; of the fears and slender hopes of their mute fellow Blacks.

The published works of or about these Africans are few but of crucial significance. Their value lies not simply in the stark and at times horrifying descriptions of the Africans' lives, but in the unique insight they offer into black society. In the eighteenth-century, as in the twentieth, black experience was moulded from three distinct elements: immediate or long past memories of Africa, the West Indies and dealings with white society. In the moments of enslavement, on board the slave ship, toiling beneath the blistering sun on the plantations or even when dressed in the absurd livery of wealthy English society, the Blacks found their lives moulded in direct and at times abrasive contact with their white masters. Black experience, then as now, tells us as much about white society faced with the Blacks, as it does about the internal history of the Blacks themselves. For this reason, the writings of black authors, even when tinged with clear evidence of 'ghosting', capture the range of crude and subtle white responses to the Blacks. Individually and collectively Job ben Solomon, Sancho, Equiano and Cugoano spoke with a free black voice, telling of a way of life which was wider and more general than their own particular experiences.

Of the four Job ben Solomon [1] alone left no personal testimony of his remarkable life. He was born a Fulani in the region of the Gambia in 1702, the son of a Muslim holy man. In 1731 when trying to sell slaves of his own, he was seized and sold into captivity by Mandingoes.[2] Shipped to America, he was bought by a Maryland planter for £45 and, faced with commitment to plantation labour, desperately sought an escape. Educated and from princely stock, Job sought to use his exalted origins to secure his release. Writing in Arabic to his father, Job hoped the letter would be delivered to the Gambia by way of London. In the process however the document fell into the hands of the philanthropist and founder of Georgia, General James Oglethorpe. Oglethorpe had the letter translated at Oxford, and was so moved by its contents that he sent for Job. After a long delay Job landed in London in April 1733 to find himself lionized and fêted by polite society, treated as an equal by some of the country's greatest scholars and heeded by the nation's élite. They had found a sophisticated African whose education they respected and whose knowledge was swiftly harnessed to the development of Arabic studies. A handsome, congenial man, Job was besieged by invitations from all quarters, notably from the Court. City merchants, scholars, philanthropists, aristocrats and those who were merely curious, vied with each other to sample the unusual spectacle of a scholarly African in their midst.

As a slave in Maryland, like most slaves throughout the English colonies, Job had had little need to master spoken English. On the voyage to England however friends taught him the rudiments of the alphabet and pronunciation. On arrival he 'was able to understand much of what was said to him and to express himself tolerably to those used to his accent'.[3] Over the course of the next year, his English improved markedly as he endeavoured to communicate with white society. But his main problems were of a more fundamental nature. Oglethorpe had in the meantime sailed for America and had missed Job. Even had Oglethorpe been on hand, Job's position would have still remained unusual, for, like so many of his fellow Africans, he landed in England a slave. The Englishmen into whose care he fell put him into lodgings in Limehouse. His position here was precarious in the extreme, for dockside areas were unsafe for the unwary Negro, who was constantly liable to recapture and re-enslavement for the colonies.

In this insecure position, in a totally bewildering environment, Job was taken in tow by Thomas Bluett who had travelled with him on the ship from America. Bluett realized the unusual quality and the talents of the African and introduced him into the company of educated friends and polite society, starting in Cheshunt where Job 'had the Honour to be sent for by most of the Gentry of that Place, who were mightily pleased with his Company and concerned with his Misfortunes'.[4] This proved an entrée to influential circles. Initially his poor English made comprehension difficult for both sides, but time and effort produced a great improvement. The kind curiosity shown towards Job made his task easier. Moving easily through refined salons he described for his audiences, in ever clearer English, the exotic realities of African life – husbandry, animal life, sexual morality and religion. Englishmen responded to Job's firsthand account of his home region with that bemused curiosity which had characterized sixteenth-century responses to traveller's tales. He provided an important new source of information for the enlightened members of his audience. He offered a wealth of anthropological detail about his homeland, details which until that time had been disseminated largely in distorted form by those Europeans whose interest lay in conveying to their readers a horrifying picture of the continent. Job's picture of Africa, while obviously remarkable to his new English friends, was an invaluable corrective to the prevailing 'evidence'; a significant first step in the long and painful process of correcting and modifying the popular image of Africa skilfully fashioned by the slave lobby.

Two of the major charges popularly levelled against Africans, their illiteracy and heathenism, were clearly inapplicable to Job. His devotion to his native Islam impressed his English friends who, like most good eighteenth-century Englishmen, took religion as an index of a man's civilization (or his lack of it). Job had read the New Testament, recently translated into Arabic by the Society for the Propagation of Christian Knowledge,[5] but he resisted the temptation of conversion for which the translation had been specifically designed. His improving bilingualism was recruited to the cause of

'Am I not a man and a brother?' Wedgwood's effective plea for black equality

The cause of it all. Slaves at work on a West Indian plantation

The Duchess of Portsmouth by Mignard. An example of the lavish clothing and jewellery in which black menials were dressed by 17th-century nobles

2nd Duke of Perth. Note the padlocked collar worn by the Negro

The Arab Princess by W. Frier. A contrast in class and qualities of beauty

scholarship, more particularly by Sir Hans Sloane, one of the greatest collectors of his age, whose Arabic manuscripts he translated and who introduced him to a wider circle. The ultimate compliment was his election to the exclusive 'Gentlemen's Society of Spalding' a distinguished group of scholars.[6]

Throughout these remarkable activities Job ben Solomon remained a slave, owned first by Oglethorpe, later by a Captain Hunt and finally by the Royal African Company, but he was eventually emancipated in December 1733, thanks to a subscription among his wealthy friends. The certificate of manumission given to him made it absolutely clear that from 27 December 1733 'the said Simon, otherwise called Job is a free Man and is at Liberty to take Passage to Africa in any of our Ships'.[7] Armed with this certificate and equipped with a watch from the Queen, a Bible from the persistent SPCK, garden tools from the Duke of Montagu and £500 worth of luggage, late in June 1734 Job sailed from London for Africa. He returned to his home village some four years after his departure, in the style of an English gentleman, dressed in 'a silk Damask Gown . . . a black velvet cap and Mindingo breeches'. Understandably overjoyed at what was, after all, little short of a miraculous delivery, Job 'galloped his horse wildly up and down firing off guns and pistols. . . . He rode so furiously that his horse "drop'd down under him, being not able to stand no longer".'[8] From bondage in the white man's wilderness, Job had returned a free man. In this he was rare and lucky; a statistical freak who had avoided the alternate hammer blows of debasement and physical collapse.

Job's stories of English society, the splendours of the Court, the crowded street scenes of London and the refinements of his English friends, doubtless went the rounds of his native people, just as his stories of Africa had held his English listeners. Briefly, Job brought together groups of people from two totally different worlds. But in England he remained an ephemeral curiosity. Untypical of his fellow Africans by virtue of his education and rank, he was accorded exceptional treatment. But he presented those who met him, and the even greater numbers who simply read about him after his departure, with a sophisticated picture of a continent which Englishmen tended to view simply as the birthplace of savages. Job ben Solomon helped to restore to the African elements of humanity which years of debasement had eliminated in English considerations.

Black and White

About the time as Job was enslaved in West Africa, an African child of two years old was brought into England. In later life he was to become the most celebrated Negro in the country. Ignatius Sancho[9] had been born on board a slaver in mid-Atlantic, spending the first two years of his life as a slave in Grenada. Sancho's life was effectively spent entirely in England and he therefore grew up as a black Englishman, partly assimilated into the lower reaches of English middle-class society. But he was never able to escape the consequences of his colour and though his blackness gave his liberal English friends and patrons a reason for befriending and patronizing him, it marked him off from the society into which he was pitched. The mature Sancho lived a poor but respectable life on the fringes of Johnsonian London, moving in circles where literary and artistic accomplishments were considered as the hallmark of a cultured man. Inevitably Sancho the African, brought up as an Englishman, made every effort to acquire those skills most admired by his patrons. Friendly with Garrick and Sterne, painted by Gainsborough and fêted by nobility, Sancho tried to harness his own limited abilities to master the arts and attainments of his friends. He wrote some poetry, two plays and a work on the theory of music.[10] But his best known work was posthumous; a collection of his letters edited after his death by Dr Joseph Jeckyll. More notable because of Sancho's unique social position than by reason of any literary merits, the letters would have been lost to posterity had they not come from the pen of an African. The *Gentleman's Magazine* harshly dismissed them as 'little more than common-place effusions, such as many other Negroes, we suppose, could, with the same advantages have written'.[11]

Initially Sancho, like most of his fellows in England, had few of the 'advantages' mentioned by the *Gentleman's Magazine*. He had started work as a servant 'in a family who judged that Ignorance was the best Security for Obedience'.[12] Not thwarted, the ambitious Sancho made great efforts at self-improvement; 'a little Reading and writing I got by unwearied application'.[13] Fortunately, he was spotted by the Duke of Montagu, who had already patronized Job ben Solomon and the black Jamaican poet Francis Williams.[14] Montagu 'accidentally saw the little Negro, and admired in him a native frankness of manner as yet unbroken by servitude, and unrefined by education. He brought him frequently to the Duchess, indulged his turn for reading with presents of books, and strongly recommended to his mistresses the duty of cultivating a genius of such apparent fertility.' Sancho's mistress was unmoved by the Duke's advice 'and even threatened on angry occasions to return Ignatius Sancho to his African slavery'.[15] Shortly after the Duke's death in 1749 Sancho, in whom the 'love of freedom had increased with years', fled to seek the Duchess's protection. After an initial rebuff, she relented and employed him as a butler. On her death she left him £70 in cash with an annuity of £30.[16] Her generosity was wasted, however, for Sancho's 'attachment to women' and love of gambling led to the swift dissipation of his money. Once more he turned to the Montagu family for help and employment.[17] But his days as a servant were numbered, 'gout and corpulence rendering him, in 1773, incapable of being further useful as a domestic'.[18] At an earlier date, Sancho had wanted to take up an acting career but had been thwarted by another physical problem, 'a defective and incorrigible articulation'.[19]

After his youthful philandering, Sancho settled down, marrying a black West Indian woman[20] and raising a large and apparently happy family of 'Sanchonettas', in his last venture, a small grocer's shop in Charles Street, Westminster.[21] But his commercial independence was threatened by poverty. His increasing family kept him on the razor thin line between sufficiency and destitution. Late in 1777 he described himself as 'a poor starving black Negro, with six children'.[22] Two years later, twelve months before his death, he moaned that he was 'never poorer since created – But 'tis a general case – Blessed times for a poor Blacky grocer to hang or drown in!'[23] His complaints about his poverty run like a dismal descant through his letters to all and sundry. He was at one point forced to refuse to pay for a letter from a fellow Black, for 'five pence is the twelfth part of five shillings – the forty eighth part of a pound – it would keep my girls in potatoes two days'.[24] Despite the generosity of his friends, Sancho's poverty remained a lifelong companion. 'Thou well knowst my poverty', he wrote to a friend in 1778 – 'but 'tis an honest poverty – and I need not blush or conceal it.'[25]

Throughout his letters, Sancho displayed strong attachment to the values of the English middle-class society to which he desperately but fruitlessly aspired. But his assimilation was far from complete. For all his Englishness[26] his innermost reservations and doubts about the position of the Black in England frequently flash through the pomposity of his prose. In the last year of his life, after almost fifty years in England, in which time he had been luckier than most other Negroes in the country, he knew that England could never be a home in any real sense. 'I am,' he wrote, 'only a lodger – and hardly that.'[27] Frequently his remarks reveal the tensions and contradictions inherent to black experience in a white society. These tensions were all the more acute for Sancho who realized that his own position was unusual because of his favoured position and proximity to respectability. He was a relatively privileged Black living in a society which had perfected, and depended on, its great slave empires; indeed Sancho's life in England was an immediate result of the English involvement with slavery. 'Dear sir,' he beseeched Sterne, 'think in me you behold the uplifted hands of thousands of my brother Moors.' Despite his influential contacts, he was aware that he must for ever remain isolated; 'one of those people whom the vulgar and illiberal call "Negurs".'[28] He was aware that his friends were exceptional in conceding his own equality. Those possessing 'charity enough to admit dark faces into the fellowship of Christians'[29] were, as he knew, few and far between. Much more common was the curious and sometimes abusive response of white society towards the Black. Returning with his family from Vauxhall one evening, Sancho recorded: 'We went by water – had a coach home – were gazed at etc. etc. – but not much abused.'[30] He was less fortunate later, when 'they stopped us in the town, and most generously insulted us'.[31] He was aware from bitter personal experience that the Blacks were despised by certain sections of white English society, 'from Othello to Sancho the big – we are either foolish – or mulish – all-all without a single exception'.[32] But he was luckier than most and was able periodically to forget – or ignore 'the national antipathy and prejudice . . . towards their woolly headed brethren'.[33]

Sancho's sense of ethnic isolation was compounded by the sight of the daily inhumanities perpetrated around him by those in power. 'I say nothing of politics – I hate such subjects – the public papers will inform you of mistakes – blood – taxes – misery – murder – the obstinacy of the few – and the madness and villany of a many.'[34] He died in the middle of what he called 'a detestable Brothers' War',[35] the American Revolution, some years before the tide of humanitarianism gave the Blacks the distant prospect of freedom, if not

The Free Black Voice

equality, and he frequently captures the despair of his black brothers trapped in a society which appeared to offer them little hope or comfort. He lived in times when universal humanity and kindness seemed as remote as his native land. In these circumstances it is scarcely surprising that his sense of ethnic identity revealed itself time and again in his letters. What hurt him more than anything else was the inability of the English to see the evils of their own society while simultaneously being all too willing to believe the very worst stories about Africa. As if to prove his point, the Gordon Riots of 1780 threw London into a turmoil, marked by what Sancho described as 'the worse than Negro barbarity of the populace'.[36]

Swift to spot a friend to his people – 'I thank you for your kindness to my poor black brethren' – Sancho persistently pleaded for the well-being of his fellow Blacks. Sometimes this took an odd form. 'I have observed a dog will love those who use him kindly – and surely, if so, negroes in their state of ignorance and bondage, will not act less generously, if I may judge them by myself.'[37] Here, as elsewhere, Sancho used his blackness to bring home to his English friends and correspondents the iniquities of English treatment of the Blacks. Overt political pleading was never foremost in his letters, but by constantly nagging his correspondents about the condition of the Blacks, he kept the issue alive in their thoughts.

Inevitably Sancho mixed with other Blacks in London. After the great variety of women he had been involved with as a young man he did choose to marry a fellow Black.[38] Throughout his life he was clearly affected by a strong sympathy for the universality of black problems. He was for instance fond of talking about 'my brother Negroes'[39] and frequently made great play of his own colour.[40] He enjoyed describing himself in a playful sense, as 'a coal-black, jolly African';[41] on another occasion he called himself 'a poor thick-lipped son of Africa!'[42] Where possible he personally helped his black brethren, but denied that this had anything to do with the man's colour. 'I like the rogue's looks, or the similarity of colour should not have induced me to recommend him.'[43] Sancho described this particular friend as 'a merry chirping – white tooth'd – clean – and light little fellow; with a woolly pate – and face as dark as your humble; Guinea-born, and French bred – with the sulky gloom of Africa dispelled by Gallic vivacity'.[44]

87

Less enthusiastic were Sancho's efforts for Soubise, the black protégé of the Duchess of Queensberry who has been already mentioned. Educated as a gentleman, Soubise in his prime was the most sought after Black in England; lionised and bedded by dozens of English ladies.[45] Unfortunately his extravagance, coupled with the scandal which attached itself to his relationship with the Duchess,[46] forced her to send him to India. The panache of Soubise's life made a sharp contrast to Sancho's more sedate existence. The publicly pious Sancho had little sympathy for Soubise's cavortings,[47] but he nonetheless wrote to friends in India, telling of Soubise's impending arrival and warning of his failings. 'I do strictly caution you against lending him any money upon any account, for he has everything but principle.'[48] Sancho tried to keep the wayward Soubise informed of events in London, urging on him the rewards of diligence, work and worship. He offered to help him in any way possible, 'but whatever commissions you send over to me – send money'.[49] Whatever his reservations about Soubise's shortcomings he still felt obliged to help him. In a similar vein, he used his influential contacts to find employment for other Blacks, even when he had little personal knowledge of them.[50]

Ill health continued to haunt him. His activities had been strictly limited for many years by his obesity and crippling gout. He began to feel the advance of old age before his time. 'I feel myself since last winter an old man all at once – the failure of eyes – the loss of teeth – the thickness of hearing.'[51] As the winter of 1780 drew on Sancho's letters recorded the painful details of his deteriorating physical condition. 'My cough is pretty stubborn; my breath very little better; body weak as water – add to this, a smart gout in both legs and feet.'[52] By the middle of 1780: 'The gout has used me like a tyrant – and my asthma, if possible, worse – I have swelled gradually all over.'[53] Desperately turning from one doctor to another Sancho failed to find comfort or relief, and died on 14 December 1780. He was buried at Westminster Broadway.[54]

Two years later his letters were edited and published.[55] Their sales were enormous; the subscription list for them was claimed to have been longer than for any other publication since the first edition of the *Spectator* fifty years before.[56] But the immediate popularity of the letters was insignificant compared to their long-term importance. Sancho's writing was ideally suited to the abolitionist cause of the later 1780s. It seemed to offer tangible proof of black attainments and black perfectibility and was adopted by the humanitarian campaign as evidence and proof of their arguments. By 1803 the letters had appeared in five editions, the last one prepared by Sancho's son, William, librarian to Sir Joseph Banks.[57] Thus long after his death, Sancho had an audience and exerted an influence which he could never have envisaged in his lifetime.

Most of his letters were of little consequence. They were grandiloquent missives about the trivia of family life and Sancho would have been surprised and perhaps a little embarrassed to think that letters penned for private reading had been seized on by a readership anxious to find traces of African abilities. For this was the key to the posthumous success and political influence of Sancho's letters. But the late 1780s he had come to belong to a triumvirate of African writers, with Equiano and Cugoano. Abolitionists were fond of pointing to these men and to their limited literary achievements. In answer to the assertions of the slave lobby that the Negro was at best merely the last link in the Chain of Being, and at worst subhuman, abolitionists could use the pseudo-Augustan prose of Sancho as a striking refutation. His weaknesses were writ large – he was in fact a failure in almost everything he tried – but by virtue of his blackness, his limited talents were elevated to the lofty plain of creative ability. In his letters during his lifetime Sancho, when pleading for the black cause, was simply preaching to the converted. Paradoxically, in the years after his death he was greatly influential in reaching the unconverted. The deceased Sancho was effectively the first African in England to plead with a white audience on behalf of the Blacks.

Sancho's successor, Olaudah Equiano (or Gustavus Vassa) continued the written campaign to which Sancho's letters made such an important contribution. Unlike Sancho, however, Equiano threw himself energetically into the politics of England's black community.[58] His autobiography, an immediate best seller when published in 1789, was designed as part of that wave of abolitionist literature which had welled up since the death of Sancho.[59]

The life which Equiano described was much more complex and varied than Sancho's. It covered a remarkable range of experience. He was born an Ibo in Biafra in 1745, and was enslaved along with his sister when only ten years old. Thus he had vivid memories of his African childhood. Despite some obvious flaws of retrospection,

Black and White

Equiano's account of his own transmutation from free African into white man's slave provides an indispensable insight into a process which altered the lives of millions of Africans. His reaction for instance to the first sight of Europeans forms an interesting comparison to the sixteenth-century accounts of English travellers confronted by black Africans for the first time. 'I was now persuaded,' he wrote, 'that I had gotten into a world of bad spirits, and that they were going to kill me. Their complexions too differing so much from ours, their long hair and the language they spoke . . . united to confirm me in this belief.'[60] Experiences on the slave ship did little to alter this judgment.

Part of the standard process of de-Africanization through which the slaves had to pass, was the procedure of renaming. In Equiano's case he was called first Jacob, later Michael and finally Gustavus Vassa, the name by which most contemporary Englishmen came to know him.[61] His career did not follow the conventional pattern, for although still technically a slave, he was not put to work on a plantation but was employed as a sailor, spending long spells ashore in England and North America. Placed with a decent master he 'began to consider myself as happily situated',[62] but he was to learn the bitter lesson that loyalty and kindness in no way undermined the master's legal right or determination to treat or sell the Black as a slave. Equiano, like thousands of others, was plunged back into the worst despair of bondage when he had begun to feel confident in his limited freedom.[63]

During the first eight years or so of his bondage he underwent a slow but distinct process of acculturation. Of his first voyage to England, he later wrote, 'I could smatter a little imperfect English'.[64] Three years later his mastery of the language was greatly improved when some London ladies sent him to school,[65] to complete a process of education which, like that of Job ben Solomon many years before, had begun on board a ship in mid-Atlantic. At about the same time Equiano turned to spiritual affairs, initially out of curiosity but later from a determination to insure himself for the world hereafter. He was baptized at the age of fourteen at St Margaret's Westminster in 1758[66] but, contrary to popular belief, baptism in no way altered a slave's status. He had to wait a further eight years before he was able to purchase his freedom, when he was twenty-one years old.[67] Once freed, he continued to ply the trade he had acquired as a slave, travelling as a sailor between the far-flung limits of England's mid eighteenth century empire, and even venturing as far afield as the Arctic.[68]

Long after his baptism, Equiano became a zealously devout Christian, but was for long undecided about which sect to join.[69] He passed through a phase of mental and spiritual torment, consulting the Bible at every step before finding spiritual satisfaction.[70] Sancho too had been a devout Christian and his letters are riddled with Christian exhortations and warnings; 'let me, as your true friend, recommend seriously to you to make yourself acquainted with your Bible. Believe me, the more you study the word of God, your peace and happiness will increase the more with it.'[71] To Equiano the Bible was equally important, particularly in the later phase of his life. 'Now the Bible was my only companion and comfort; I prized it much, with many thanks to God that I could read it for myself, and was not left to be tossed about or led by man's devices and notions.'[72] Such piety on the part of both men must have greatly helped Englishmen to accept and treat them as equals. Job ben Solomon on the other hand had made no effort to turn to Christianity, although his commitment to his own religion – a religion moreover which was closer to Christianity than any other in West Africa – won the admiration of those Englishmen who met him.[73] In all three cases, religion brought the African closer to the understanding and sympathy of the white host society.

When the African approximated in his religious life to the ideal demanded or expected by white society, he had a better chance of equal treatment by the English. But the tolerance of a society cannot be measured by its treatment of those minorities who try to assimilate; rather must it be gauged by the reaction to those who cling to their own religious or cultural values. Among the Blacks, baptism was the most sought after religious benefit of white society,[74] and that largely from the mistaken belief that it would confer freedom, but examples of black piety of the intensity displayed by Sancho and Equiano are rare. It is more than likely that large numbers of free Blacks in London (where both these men lived) had no religion at all, like the poor whites around them. Their lives and circumstances placed them beyond the limits of daily Christian practice and beyond the reach of the feeble religious probes into poor urban communities. Not until the rise of Methodism were the poor to be brought within the embrace of organized religion. Negroes in a position to enjoy full religious experience were, by definition, in a superior social position, or closer to a white master, than the subterranean mass of rootless, poor Blacks. Religious experience tended to compound rather than create social advantages. Nonetheless, where it existed, black Christianity formed a bridge between the black believer and white society.

Equiano's religion was unmistakably tinged with other-worldliness and was a last refuge from the tribulations of black life in a white world. He frequently retreated into the shell of his beliefs, surrendering all earthly effort in the hopeful knowledge that all would turn out well in the world hereafter. On one occasion, unable to convince his captors of the evil of their actions in enslaving him, Equiano 'told them that as I could not get any right among men here I hoped I should hereafter in Heaven'.[75] Frustrated by the sins of Englishmen, he took his 'punishment' stoically. 'I considered that trials and disappointments are some times for our good, and thought that God might perhaps have permitted this in order to teach me wisdom and resignation.'[76] His open confession that he sublimated earthly cares in the balm of religion must have sounded like sweet music to planters and all those who feared the encroachment of religion among the Blacks. Far from disturbing the peace of mind of the converted Black, Christianity, if carefully administered, could easily become a palliative and induce a drugged acceptance of life's brutalities.

Equiano's hopes for future salvation did not preclude him from striving for change. In the 1780s he actively involved himself in black politics, campaigning against slavery and the slave trade, volunteering for missionary work in his native Africa and finally becoming the spokesman for the black poor in London. In all these activities he emerged as a link between the Blacks and their white friends who belonged to a different social world. In this crucial political period of his life Equiano made contact with the pioneer of humanitarianism, Granville Sharp, forging a relationship which was to have profound political repercussions for the Blacks in England. On 19 March 1783 Sharp recorded in his diary: 'Gustavus Vassa a Negro called on me with an account of 130 Negroes being thrown alive into the sea from on Board an English Slave Ship.'[77] With a thoroughness and zeal born of indignation Sharp turned his unwavering attention to the details of this appalling case, ordering his solicitors to unravel the facts and, if possible, to bring a private prosecution. Ultimately the affair surfaced in an English law court, but not in the form of a murder trial. Instead, the legal argument, stemming from the calculated killing of some 130 Africans, was concerned purely with the issue of compensation for the loss of such valuable property. Having come before the courts, it was inevitable that the humanitarians would hear about the case sooner or later. But in fact the issue had first been brought to their attention by an African – Equiano – who had evidently heard of the case on the African grapevine.

The facts of the case were simple, but repellent and horrifying. An English slave ship, the *Zong*, sailing from Africa to Jamaica with a cargo of 440 slaves, found itself rapidly running short of water. The captain therefore decided that, rather than run the risk of a total commercial loss, by large numbers of slaves dying from 'natural' causes, he would jettison a number of them and claim the loss against insurance. He decided 'to lessen the consumption of it [water] in the vessel by throwing overboard one hundred and thirty-two of the most sickly slaves'.[78] Ironically, when the contested issue of the insurance claim came to court it was heard by Lord Mansfield, who had presided (if such a word adequately describes his feeble control) over the famous slave case in 1772.[79] Sharp hoped that the legal point would be much broader than one of mere compensation, and even tried to persuade the Admiralty to prosecute the offenders for murder.[80] He was unsuccessful and the case simply revolved around the question of the validity of the compensation claim. Mansfield himself asserted 'they had no doubt (though it shocks one very much) that the case of the slaves was the same as if horses had been thrown overboard'.[81] Spurred on by indignation at this and other inhumanities, Equiano and his white friends intensified their efforts for the black cause.[82]

Equiano incessantly petitioned friends urging them to continue their work on behalf of 'those captived, oppressed, and afflicted people' of whom he counted himself one.[83] He confronted the humanitarians with outrages committed against Blacks; he campaigned up and down the country on behalf of abolition, speaking in Birmingham, Manchester, Sheffield, Nottingham, Belfast, Durham, Hull and the West Country.[84] When in the summer of 1786 he returned to

Black and White

England from another voyage it was logical that he should be recruited by the new London committee formed to solve the problem of the 'black poor'.[85] He was an obvious choice; he was well known to white humanitarians and a prominent man in the black community.

Appointed as commissary to the expedition designed to ship the Blacks to Sierra Leone, Equiano immediately raised a series of objections about their treatment on board the vessels waiting to carry them 'home'. Fortunately for himself, his part in the proceedings lasted only for the first leg of the tiresome journey. He was dismissed from his post and put ashore at Plymouth. The complaints about his incitement to unrest among the Blacks were undoubtedly accurate, but so too were his bitter complaints about the open exploitation of the hapless – and by this stage helpless – black emigrants. The treatment he received at the hands of the organizers of the scheme merely succeeded in driving him into a more uncompromisingly aggressive position. He even went to the extent of petitioning the Queen 'for millions of my African countrymen, who groan under the lash of tyranny'.[86]

Hemmed in by a series of tightly interlocking injustices, Equiano, like Sancho before him, was brought to the sad realization, despite his own favoured circumstances, of the inevitable isolation of the Black in white society. He was forced to speak up, not solely for himself, but mainly for his less fortunate fellow Africans whose experiences he had shared and whose fate he had narrowly escaped. In his great range of occupations, as slave, sailor, domestic, commissary, princely African and black Englishman and friend to the new 'popular' London radicals,[87] Equiano was able to speak with greater authority and assurance than Sancho, whose life had been, in black terms, relatively sheltered. This range of experience ideally equipped him to be spokesman for black society.

An accident of time, too, guaranteed Equiano a wider and more attentive audience than Sancho had been able to command, but there is nonetheless an unmistakable continuity of purpose between the two men. Equiano was politically active at precisely the time when Sancho's letters were making such an impact on the reading public. Seven years after the first publication of Sancho's letters, Equiano's autobiography appeared and fed the same appetite for evidence of black attainments. While there is a startling stylistic contrast between the writings of the two Africans, their books neatly spanned a decade and appealed to a similar reading public to whom the issue of black politics had become both familiar and important. Their contribution in adding to this ground swell of political interest in black affairs has been underestimated.[88] Equiano, like Sancho, was unusual in that he spoke with the free voice of Africa at a time when hordes of his fellows were muted beasts of burden. Even more unusual was the fact that, despite these circumstances, both men were heeded.

Equiano's anxiety to return to Africa was apparently blunted by the experiences of the Sierra Leone disasters, and finally ended in April 1792 with his marriage to a Miss Cullen of Cambridgeshire. The marriage was shortlived, for Equiano died in 1797,[89] attended at his death bed by the ever sympathetic Granville Sharp.

Closely associated with Equiano in the late 1780s was Ottobah Cugoano who had been brought to England in the year of the Mansfield judgment after serving two years as a slave in the West Indies. Born in what is now Ghana, Cugoano, like Equiano before him, was enslaved as a young boy. Soon after arriving in England he was baptized, and later given a new name, John Stuart (or Stewart), as part of the common de-Africanization process.[90] But it is significant that both Cugoano and Equiano continued to use their African names in addition to their new ones. In their published works for instance both used their original names – Cugoano even omitted to use his English name. If the way in which immigrant black slaves continued to view themselves indicates a retention of Africanisms, despite the efforts of their white masters to change their identity, it would appear that Africans brought to England resisted the tendency towards total assimilation. When facing white society Africans were known by and used their new English identities, but their own collective and individual awareness seems to have been firmly rooted in their African background. They kept their own African names among themselves.

When in the 1780s the black community found friends ready and able to press the case for their freedom, Cugoano came to the forefront of black politics. He volunteered, along with his friend Equiano, for the expedition to Africa projected by the African Association. Later, although he did not play as important a role as Equiano, he remained in touch with developments throughout the Sierra Leone scheme.[91] While Equiano expressed the powerful 'back to Africa' mood among London's Blacks, Cugoano reflected rather the reservations about the scheme shared by a majority of the local Blacks. From the first Cugoano had doubts about the plan: 'the wiser sort declining from all thoughts of it, unless they could hear of some better plan for their security and safety.'[92] This caution was to be fully justified.

The extent of Cugoano's activities is difficult to ascertain. Certainly he helped to organize a ginger group from the black community and was in personal contact with the white humanitarians led by Granville Sharp. His main contribution to the abolitionist cause however remains his tract *Thoughts and Sentiments* published under his name in 1787, and a series of political letters to prominent figures, notably Burke.[93] A comparison of the book and his manuscript letters unfortunately reveals an enormous disparity of style. The disjointed and badly spelled letters bear little resemblance to the fluent and educated style of the book. Paul Edwards has convincingly shown that the content of Cugoano's book is largely derived from earlier abolitionist literature, while the actual writing must have been undertaken with the assistance of another highly literate African, possibly Equiano himself.[94]

Whatever the doubts about the authenticity of Cugoano's writing there can be no question about the importance of his activities in London. He had plans to open a special school 'for all such of his Complexion as are desirous of being acquainted with the Knowledge of the Christian Religion and the Laws of Civilisation'. Had this proposal materialized it would have transformed the black community and its relations with white society by bringing a wider black audience to a faith which had active recruits among the prominent Blacks in the capital. Like Sancho and Equiano, Cugoano was extremely pious, at least in his public utterances. His ambition in opening such a school was to spread his own faith wider in the black community, 'to have them educated in the Duties and Knowledge of that Religion which all good Christian People enjoy'. In this, as in most contemporary black affairs, Cugoano found himself unavoidably dependent. He admitted that to accomplish his purpose 'I must wholly depend on the humane and charitable Contributions of those Ladies and Gentlemen who are inclinable to Support this Undertaking'. While Cugoano's ambition was to make the school not exclusively black, he confessed that 'my Design is chiefly intended for my countrymen'.[95]

Like Equiano in the aftermath of his dismissal from the Sierra Leone scheme, Cugoano made direct appeals to the royal family in his campaign against the evils of slavery. He also sent a copy of his book to Burke, hopefully adding that 'a trifle towards the printing will be acceptable'.[96] In common with Sancho and Equiano, Cugoano's efforts for his fellow Blacks were not limited to the problems in London or even in England. He constantly tried to focus the attention of his audience on the global dilemma of the Negro. All three Africans clearly appreciated, in a way only a Black could appreciate it, that to secure freedom for themselves in England offered only a partial victory, as long as slavery held sway in other parts of the British empire. There was little satisfaction – and precious little safety – in being the exceptional African; a free man in a society which treated the Negro as chattel. Cugoano took the fate of his fellow Blacks seriously. He was even prepared to sail to New Brunswick to care for the interests of the Blacks left there in the aftermath of the American revolution. More immediately however he was able to stump the country campaigning against the slave trade.[97]

Most of the sparse knowledge we possess about Cugoano is derived from his abolitionist tract which, for all its flaws, remains a revealing document. At many points it confirms the experiences of Sancho and predicts some of Equiano's published two years later. Cugoano suffered racial prejudice, as had Sancho,[98] but in his capture, reaction to the first sight of white men, conversion to religion and growing literacy his history was practically identical to Equiano's.[99] Whatever the differences of detail and emphasis, the common links between Sancho, Equiano and Cugoano are even more pronounced. All three, for instance, steeped their utterances in biblical terminology. Inevitably, they all turned to influential white friends in their efforts to help the black community and, where possible, all gave personal assistance to other needy Blacks. Throughout their published work there runs a strong and distinct theme of black identity; a striving towards personal and collective identity based on common experiences and commonly shared ethnic pressures. Each had arrived in England via the slave trade, like flotsam on the surface of England's commerce. Each had been a slave, transformed from a human being into an item of trade for the benefit of white society, a

Black and White

fact which pressed painfully on their sensitivities. The unforgettable knowledge that they had been slaves must always have qualified their dealings, no matter how friendly, with whites around them. To a certain extent the rise to prominence of the three men had been fortuitous. But whatever their personal progress, they remained black and thus essentially isolated. Their blackness cut them off from white society, while simultaneously tying them indissolubly to the black community. Their colour obliged them to face the brutal truth of their position and to appreciate their identity of interests with Africans on both sides of the Atlantic. 'We are', wrote one group of London Blacks, 'of those whose minds and bodies are bartered from hand to hand on the coast of Africa, and in the West Indies, as the ordinary commodities of trade.'[100] It was an awareness of this fact which stimulated the three Africans to speak for their fellows, and their achievements have to be measured by their success in countering this chattel status. All three strove to expunge from the African the stigma of commodity and to restore a lost humanity in the eyes of white society.

Fame more than any other quality distinguished the four Africans studied here from the society which spawned them. But in several respects they reflected a range of experience common to thousands of Blacks. In their persons they mirrored the wide personal, tribal and social divisions inside the English black community. Job ben Solomon was a Fulani of princely rank; Equiano was similarly highborn. Cugoano originated from the Gold Coast while Sancho was born on the high seas. Their physical characteristics – in the case of the three men whose portraits survive – differed enormously and presented tangible proof of the African diversity to be found in London. Job eventually moved freely as a respected figure in the upper reaches of English society. Sancho, while eking out an uncertain living at the artisan or shopkeeper level, was graced with the friendship and help of a distinct intellectual group. Equiano and Cugoano remained poor working men, the former primarily as a sailor, the latter as a domestic. In their occupations, the four men virtually span the full range of black life and labour to be found in eighteenth-century England. All had suffered the hell of the slave ships and had emerged from the miseries of black life in the New World; Sancho and Cugoano in the West Indies, Job and Equiano in the mainland colonies. The initial contact with white men had ter-

The Free Black Voice

rified both Equiano and Cugoano; the first taste of English society similarly frightened Job. Ultimately however all became reconciled to the white society into which they had been unwillingly pitched. Each nonetheless remained aware of the serious dangers for all Blacks inherent in white society.

The four favoured Africans present an interesting random sample of the patterns of immigration at the height of the slave empires. They landed in England at very different stages of their lives. Job was a man in his early thirties on arrival but Sancho a child of two. Equiano was twelve on his first visit; Cugoano about fifteen. Linguistically all four present useful case studies of the process of acculturation. English was Sancho's native language but the other three had to learn it as a foreign language. Equiano and Job learned the rudiments of the language on board a ship bound for England and showed great determination in mastering both comprehension and full literacy. Cugoano's use of English on the other hand reveals distinct and unmistakable elements of his native West African language patterns. The use of English was only one factor in the process of acculturation. So too was the renaming process through which most Blacks on both sides of the Atlantic were forced to pass. With the exception of Job, whose stay in England was temporary and whose treatment was exceptionally privileged because of his education and religion, all were renamed. Two of them however retained their African names whenever it proved convenient.

Our knowledge of marriage and mating patterns among the Blacks is hazy. From a purely demographic position it was not possible, in a sexually unbalanced black community, for all Blacks to form steady monogamous heterosexual relations with someone of their own colour. Again, three of the Africans examined here suggest a wide diversity of marital patterns inside the black community. Job's African marriage was sundered by his enslavement. Equiano finally married an English woman, while Sancho, after a sexually successful youth with English women, married a fellow Black. Since black males greatly outnumbered black females in eighteenth-century England, Equiano was perhaps more typical in finding a partner from white society. Evidently there were no institutional barriers preventing the mating of black and white but social restraints would limit the range of sexual choice open to a Negro and restrict his real choice to the poorer sections of white society. To judge from the hostile comments of white observers, sexual relations between black and white were common at both the lower and upper reaches of English society. This, coupled with the noticeable sexual imbalance among the Blacks, was to be ultimately responsible for the gradual collapse of the black community and the absorption into white society of those who mated with whites.

Each of the four Africans mixed freely with different social levels of white society. Sancho, Equiano and Cugoano worked and lived alongside white workers. Sancho's customers – and his neighbouring shopkeepers – were white. Perhaps with the exception of Cugoano, all four were familiar with, and periodically honoured by visits to the houses of the upper-middle class and even ventured into the more rarified atmosphere of aristocratic homes. At the same time, despite these contacts with various levels of English society, the most influential factors in the lives of these men were the memories of Africa and their contacts with their fellow Blacks. Relations between the Blacks in England, particularly inside London, were close and formative. From these bonds of black unity there flowed the self-help, cooperation and internal strength which so characterised the black community. Through the persons of Sancho, Equiano and Cugoano, this independent black society found a means of making political contact with the surrounding white society. Thus the black spokesmen were influential both within the black community and also in forging crucial links with the outside world.

In the middle and late years of the eighteenth century black society in England possessed a dual character. It had on the whole been created accidentally, growing as an offshoot of economic development in the New World. But the shape and structure of black society in England was fashioned by the needs, the prejudices and the uncontrolled reactions of white society. That said, it is still true that *the* most crucial element in the growth of that black society was Africa, and in this it was similar to the development of black society in the plantation colonies. Africa, the black mother, had conceived and brought forth generations of Blacks who lived out their lives beyond her shores but who carried with them the unmistakable marks of their parentage. Of the four Africans examined here (and it is significant that all four were men), all were remembered and known by their African names. Their clothes were English, but their features were African. They were at one and the same time assimilated and yet isolated. Certain areas of their lives remained for ever African and black. In other respects, notably in religion, three of them became distinctively English. Throughout their complex lives they all uttered words learned from the English, but their collective voice had the intonation of Africa.

Notes

CHAPTER FIVE: *The Free Black Voice*

1. Job ben Solomon (1702–73); Douglas Grant *The Fortunate Slave,* Oxford University Press, London, 1968; P. D. Curtin 'Ayuba Suleiman Diallo of Bondn', in *Africa Remembered, Narrative by West Africans from the era of the slave trade,* ed. P. D. Curtin, University of Wisconsin Press, 1967, 17–34.
2. Grant, 66–8.
3. ibid., 86.
4. Quoted in ibid., 90.
5. ibid., 96–7.
6. ibid., 99–101.
7. Quoted in ibid., 105.
8. ibid., 170.
9. Ignatius Sancho (1729–80). *The Letters of the late Ignatius Sancho,* with introduction by Paul Edwards, London, Dawsons, Pall Mall, 1968.
10. Robin Hallett, *The Penetration of Africa to 1815,* London, Routledge, 1965, 147.
11. *Gentleman's Magazine*, 1782, 438.
12. Sancho to Laurence Sterne, 21 July 1766, Letter xvi, *Letters.*
13. ibid.
14. Edwards, IVN. 4; Grant, 106–7; 116–17; 119.
15. Jeckyll, *Letters,* ii.
16. ibid., iii–iv.
17. ibid., v.
18. *Gentleman's Magazine*, 1773, 437.
19. Jeckyll, *Letters,* v.

Black and White

20. Sancho appears to have married in the late 1750s. See his comments in Letter LIV, *Letters*, 113.
21. Edwards, V; *Letters*, 37.
22. Letter LVI, 20 December 1771. *Letters*, 120.
23. Letter CXIV, 16 November 1779, *Letters*, 231.
24. Letter XIV, 11 October 1772, *Letters*, 33.
25. Letter LXXX, 29 November 1772, *Letters*, 173.
26. Edwards, XII.
27. Letter CV, 7 September 1779, *Letters*, 214.
28. Letter XXXVI, July 1766, *Letters*, 72.
29. Letter LXVI, 3 May 1778, *Letters*, 143.
30. Letter XLIX, 27 August 1777, *Letters*, 101.
31. Letter CIII, 4 September 1779, *Letters*, 209–10.
32. Letter CVIII, 5 October 1779, *Letters*, 218.
33. Letter CXXVII, 5 January 1780. *Letters*, 252.
34. Letter LXI, 4 May 1778, *Letters*, 133.
35. Letter LXVIII, 1778, *Letters*, 150.
36. Letter CXXXIV, 6 June 1780, *Letters*, 270.
37. Letter XIII, 18 July 1778, *Letters*, 30.
38. Jeckyll, *Letters*, IV.
39. Letter LVIII, 27 January 1776, *Letters*, 125.
40. Letter LXXXI, 1 January 1779, *Letters*, 174–5.
41. Letter CXXIX, 17 January 1780, *Letters*, 259.
42. Letter CXXXIII, 20 May 1780, *Letters*, 268.
43. Letter XXV, 12 August 1775, *Letters*, 52–3.
44. ibid., 52.
45. *Reminiscences of Henry Angelo*, London, 1828, 2 vols, i, 446–52.
46. Predictably, the Duchess and Soubise were the subject of a popular caricature by Rowlandson. Caught in a fencing scene, Soubise's sword pressed to the Duchess's breast, Soubise (or Mingo) was seen to exclaim 'Mingo here, Mingo dere, Mingo everywhere, above and below Hah! Vat you Gracy tink of me Now', in C. Paston, *Social Caricature in the Eighteenth century*, London, 1905.
47. Letter XIV, 11 October 1772, *Letters*, 31–33.
48. Letter I, 14 February 1768, *Letters*, 5.
49. Letter LXXX, 29 November 1778, *Letters*, 173.
50. Letter CXXIV, December 1779, *Letters*, 246.
51. Letter CXLII, 27 June 1780, *Letters*, 288–9.
52. Letter CLV, 5 November 1780, *Letters*, 304.
53. Letter CLV, 18 November 1780, *Letters*, 305, (this is mistakenly numbered by the editor).
54. Letter CLVIII, 9 December 1780, *Letters*, 309–10; Edwards VIIn.
55. Edwards, I.

56. Hallett, 148.
57. *Equiano's Travels*, London, 1967 edition; introduction by P. Edwards, XIV. (Hereafter, *Travels*.)
58. Equiano (1745–97); Where I quote from Equiano it is from the first edition, *The Interesting Narrative of the Life of Olaudah Equiano or Gustavus Vassa, the African, written by Himself*, 2 vols, London, 1789.
59. Edwards, *Travels*, IX–X.
60. Equiano, i, 70–1.
61. Equiano, i, 95–6.
62. Equiano, i, 131.
63. Equiano, i, 176–9.
64. Equiano, i, 95.
65. Equiano, i, 133.
66. Equiano, i, 105; 133–4.
67. Equiano, ii, 12–19.
68. Equiano, ii, Chapter IX.
69. Equiano, ii, 116–18.
70. Equiano, ii, Chapter X.
71. Letter LXXX, 29 November 1778, *Letters*, 173.
72. Equiano, ii, 150.
73. Grant, 95–6.
74. Sir John Fielding, *Penal Laws*, 144–5.
75. Equiano, i, 178.
76. Equiano, i, 182.
77. Diary, 1783–98, 19 March 1783, Sharp Papers, Hardwicke Court, Box 56, Book H.
78. Hoare, 237.
79. Chapter Seven below.
80. Hoare, 241–4.
81. Hoare, 241.
82. Equiano, ii, 226–7.
83. Equiano, ii, 227–8.
84. Edwards, *Travels*, XIII.
85. Equiano, ii, 230–1; Chapter Nine below.
86. Equiano, ii, 243.
87. *Memoirs of Thomas Hardy*, London, 1832, 15.
88. I think Paul Edwards underplays the degree of black consciousness to be found in Sancho's *Letters*. Edwards, i.
89. Edwards, *Travels*, XIV–XV; *Gentleman's Magazine*, 1792, 384.
90. Ottobah Cugoano (1757–1790s?); *Thoughts and Sentiments on the Evil of Slavery*, London, 1787: new edition with introduction by P. Edwards, London, Dawsons, Pall Mall, 1969; Cugoano, IV;

Edwards, *Thoughts*, V–VII.
91. Edwards, *Thoughts*, VI.
92. Cugoano, 141.
93. Edwards, *Thoughts*, IV–V.
94. Edwards, *Thoughts*, VII–XI.
95. Cugoano, XIII.
96. Letters to Burke, 1787, Edwards, *Thoughts*, XX; for other letters see XIX–XXI.
97. Letter to Granville Sharp, Edwards, *Thoughts*, XXI–XXII.
98. ibid., XXII.
99. Cugoano, 5–10; 11–13.
100. Letters to Granville Sharp, Hoare, 333.

CHAPTER SIX

The Legal See-Saw: Slavery and the Law to 1772

The number of important factors in the evolution of any society is enormous. In the case of an immigrant society, the overall picture is complicated further by the historical and social legacies introduced into the host society from other parts of the world. Thus to understand the historical nature of black society in England, we must strive to understand the context of West African and West Indian history, in addition to studying English society itself.

The African – or African-descended – Black in eighteenth-century England owed his unfortunate position to the peculiar economic development and the slave foundations of the New World empires. But the English domestic response to Africans was not stimulated solely by economic factors. It is true that the dehumanization to which the African had been – and continued to be – subjected, was largely a function of the need to explain and justify a system based on slave labour. But there were nonetheless certain English responses to the Blacks which proved equally influential in defining the contours of black society, and English relations with that society, and which were only marginally economic in their origins. Nowhere was this more clearly the case than in the far-ranging debate about the blackness of the African. But the most crucial non-economic factor in the shaping of English black slavery was the historical precedent of slavery in England itself. Slavery as an institution was not new in England nor was it created by the introduction of black slaves in the mid-sixteenth century.

The institution of slavery was much more than a simple creation of economic factors and of *post hoc* justifications. Slavery was an estate of man common to many civilizations long before the rise of the British empire – and indeed long before the rise of English society itself. In England however slavery, like freedom, was not simply an abstract notion. Both had a shape and a definition in statute and common law which were quite separate from, though related to, the contours of slavery etched in by economic usage. England, in common with most other areas of the British Isles, had sustained various degrees of human bondage for centuries. By the late fifteenth century the most common form of bondage, villeinage, was extinct. From the mid-sixteenth century the English became enmeshed in the development of a new form of bondage: black slavery on the West African coast and in the New World. In the course of the seventeenth century, as the English settled and developed their West Indian and mainland American colonies, the new form of slavery which evolved owed its inspiration to the Spanish and Portuguese, but its details and special characteristics emerged from the fusion of English legal traditions, the new legislative structure of the empire and, of course, the crude economic needs of the plantations.

The fabric of society which slowly evolved in the New World colonies differed from one colony to another. Generally, however, it grew from the confused intermingling of social and legal practices introduced by the white settlers, the efforts of the metropolitan government to exercise an overriding influence over colonial growth and, most important, from the need to justify in legal terms, the new economic relationships within the colonies. In the tropical colonies, the plantations which became the economic backbone of the new societies, had been copied from the Spanish and Portuguese. The rapid expansion of plantation society in the seventeenth century was paralleled by an expansion of the English slave trade, like all other areas of maritime trade, closely supervised and regulated by Parliament in London. Similarly, as the legal framework of colonial slavery emerged, closely suiting the economic needs of the white settlers who framed the colonial laws, the metropolitan government, as the centre of the web of empire, exercised a supervisory and often paternal role. Thus the growth of slavery in the empire was constantly refined, qualified and directed by legal supervision from London. The nature of English slavery on the high seas and in the plantations owed as much to London as it did to Kingston, Bridgetown or Charleston.

Three aspects of legal control were influential in moulding the social characteristics of black slavery. First, and perhaps the most important, were the laws which came from the colonial legislatures and received approval from the Privy Council. Secondly there was parliamentary legislation governing the trading and sailing conditions of the slavers – generally through Navigation Acts. Finally there were the precedents of common law, some of which stretched back to the Middle Ages and the era of English villeinage. It was this last area of English law which slave owners, when importing black slaves from the colonies into England, exhumed and tried to employ as a legal defence for their tenure of slaves in England.

As the social and economic identity of the colonies grew more distinctive, the imprecise legal relationship between mother country and colony became an issue of great political contention, more so as the economic interests of both sides diverged and sometimes clashed.[1] The State Papers are filled with details of quarrels between the colonies and London about the respective limits of each other's legal jurisdiction. This is particularly noticeable in relation to the sugar colonies where home governments faced the difficult task of transforming the legalized plantocratic brutality towards slaves into something more humane. Early on there was a sharp divergence between the two sides on the subject of slavery itself – or rather about the more grotesque brutalities introduced by planters sitting in their other capacity as colonial legislators. In 1683 a Jamaican law ordered a fine to be levied against anyone found killing a slave. The law was refused by the Privy Council who told the Jamaicans that 'The King will not confirm this clause, which seems to encourage the wilful shedding of blood. Some better provision must be found than a fine to deter men from such acts of cruelty.'[2] The English however were caught in a cleft stick, since a series of monarchs had approved the development of a trade which specifically treated the African as commodity.[3] The English, no less than the colonial settlers, had been instrumental in casting the African in his subhuman role. It was logically and legally impossible to maintain on the one hand that Blacks were chattels, and on the other, that they ought to be treated as humans. As long as slavery continued to exist throughout the empire, the English were never able to escape the logic of the position they had created. A report from the Committee of the Privy Council for Foreign Plantations in 1664 had put the case succinctly. 'The Blacks are bought by way of trade ... [and are] the most useful appurtenances of a plantation.'[4] When in 1672, the Royal Charter was given to the African Company, Negroes were specifically designated as commodity.[5] Five years later the Solicitor-General asserted 'that Negroes ought to be esteemed goods and commodities'.[6] In the face of this definition and the weight of practice, it was, to say the least, difficult for the English government to complain to West Indian assemblies, via the governors, of excessive cruelty towards the Blacks.

The contradictions in the confused relationship between English law and slavery had emerged long before black slaves began to gather in England in appreciable numbers. In view of the enormous wealth which flowed into England by profit from the slave trade, the English could scarcely claim that the status of the Negro was purely a colonial issue. As if to prove the point, as more and more Blacks settled in England, the question of their legal position cropped up with increasing frequency. The law courts became the exposed nerve of the imperial system, for in them the contradictions within English law, and between certain areas of English law and economic reality, were periodically revealed. Courts were required to adjudicate on the particulars, and the general concept of black slavery in a series of major cases from the seventeenth to the early nineteenth century. Throughout, the courts were the scene of unhappy indecision and contradiction as they sought to reconcile the irreconcilable.

The issue of slavery placed English courts in an embarrassing quandary for it demanded a choice between two legal traditions which had come to characterize English law and which, in general, were not contradictory. The one tradition was the powerful defence which English law gave to property rights. The other, which was given new shape and direction in the course of the seventeenth century, was designed to safeguard basic human rights. Central to this latter tradition was the writ of *habeas corpus*, 'the protector of the liberty of the subject'.[7] Evolving painfully in the political struggles of the seventeenth century, the use of the writ of *habeas corpus* was perfected by the famous Act of 1679. On the basis of this Act, *habeas corpus* became the major safeguard of liberty, preventing arbitrary arrest and improper extradition, and hastening criminal proceedings. The Act which proved so vital to the security of English liberties was clearly applicable to Blacks, for it made no distinctions between men of different colours. For the Negro, the most important section was clause 12 which forbad the arbitrary expulsion of any-

The Legal See-Saw: Slavery and the Law to 1772

one from the country against their wishes. It was stated that 'no Subject of this Realm that now is, or hereafter shall be an Inhabitant or Resident of this Kingdom ... shall be sent Prisoner into Scotland, Ireland, Jersey, Guernsey, Tangier, or other parts, Garrisons, Islands or Places beyond the Seas'.[8] More than a century was to elapse before the English realized that the growing practice of shipping Blacks *back* to the colonies was in defiance of *habeas corpus*. The Act remained for so long inoperable in black interests for the simple reason that to secure a writ of *habeas corpus* demanded both knowledge of the procedure and financial resources to put it into operation. Since the Blacks lay beyond the reach of legal assistance, remedies which were theoretically available, went unused. Not until the white humanitarians, led by Granville Sharp in the late eighteenth century, made efforts to bring legal redress within the reach of the black community, did the existing legal machinery begin to operate in black interests. Until that time most of the slave cases which came before English courts produced victories for the legal tradition which defended an Englishman's rights to his property, even when that property consisted of human beings.

The problem of slavery as a legally debatable issue was revived in English courts in the mid-sixteenth century. In 1569, in a case involving a slave brought from Russia, it was held 'that England was too Pure an Air for Slaves to breathe in'.[9] Such a clear, general statement was not limited in its application to any race or ethnic group. But although the case was noted in later slave cases involving Blacks, it failed to set a precedent. A century later, by which time the number of Blacks living in England had become noticeable, the opposite principle was enunciated: 'Negroes being usually bought and sold among Merchants, so Merchandise, and also being Infidels, there might be property in them.'[10] In 1687 this view was given greater strength when an English court gave compensation for the value of 'the fourth part of a negro'.[11] Ten years later the process of legal contradiction began in earnest, as courts found themselves pulled between the two traditions. In 1697 an English court held, contrary to earlier views, that the Black was *not* to be regarded as chattel, 'for he is no other than a slavish servant'.[12]

Different courts took different criteria into consideration to arrive at their contradictory positions. The legal opinion consigning the Black to the level of property for instance drew great strength from the alleged paganism or 'infidelity' of the African (a fact much stressed by early explorers and later exponents of the slave-lobby). But a corollary to this view was that baptism and conversion of the Black would automatically make him a free man.[13] As we have seen, belief in this became a powerful myth among the Blacks from the late seventeenth century onwards and held sway well into the nineteenth century. Theologically the view had a great deal to commend it, and was first propagated by George Fox and the Quakers.[14] But, were it accepted, there was no logical reason why the power of conversion to Christianity should be restricted to Europe. Should it gain ground in the plantation colonies it would undermine the very basis of the economy. Not surprisingly, the colonial legislatures were swift to arrest the corrosive threat of Christianity. A Virginian Act of 1667 provided that 'the conferring of baptisme doth not alter the condition of the person as to his bondage or freedome'.[15] English courts were similarly forced to grapple with the problem posed by black baptisms. Did they, or did they not, confer freedom? 'If baptism should be accounted a manumission,' it was decided in 1697, 'it would very much endanger the trade of the plantations, which cannot be carried on without the help and labour of these slaves; for the parsons are bound to baptise them as soon as they can give a reasonable account of the christian faith; and if that would make them free, then few would be slaves.'[16] While the Church seemed to hold out the key of freedom to the black slave, colonial legislatures and English courts abruptly snatched it away.

By 1700 three distinct areas of legal debate had defined themselves from the slave cases heard in English courts. First, there was the issue of whether the air of England was too pure to sustain slavery; second, whether baptism conferred freedom, and finally, whether a Black was merely property or commodity. Inevitably there was no clear division between these three areas of debate. In the first thirty years of the eighteenth century the prevailing common law view in each of these areas was overruled or altered. Nor did the process of contradiction end there, for all three areas continued to be open to legal scrutiny until full emancipation in 1833.

When in 1706 the case of *Smith v. Gould* was heard before Lord Chief Justice Holt sitting in the Guildhall, the judgment seemed to overthrow all the previous rulings and come down firmly on the side of black freedom. The 'common law takes no notice of negroes being different from other men. By the common law no man can have property in another ... there is no such thing as a slave by the laws of England'.[17] In one terse statement the development of English chattel slavery seemed to have been arrested. Freedom beckoned – but in reality the judgment made not the slightest impact on the daily practice of slavery in England. As Holdsworth, the modern historian of English law, noted, such statements 'are of little avail unless means are provided to assert them'.[18] By this time, slave cases had made no appreciable impact on public opinion, a fact which makes a sharp contrast to the period during and after the case of 1772, when the fate of the slave Somerset became a *cause célèbre* hotly disputed in public and throughout the press. The early lack of public interest and publicity stemmed from the fact that most cases before 1729 were only marginally concerned with slavery. Courts were called on to resolve various legal complications posed by black slaves, only as part of a wider legal problem. Most cases for instance centred on a question of compensation or damages and the more delicate question of slavery arose from a discussion about whether the Negro, owned by one or other of the feuding parties, ought to be treated as property for assessment purposes.[19] In the seventeenth century, slavery in England was not sufficiently developed to produce legal cases which had profound social repercussions. But with the growth of a black community in the eighteenth century, coupled with the publicly expressed uncertainty of the slave owners, it was but a matter of time before English law would have to face directly the problem of chattel slavery in England, rather than defining its legal status haphazardly and tangentially.

An opportunity for a comprehensive review of slavery and for a definitive opinion of its legality occurred in 1729. West Indian merchants and planters anxious to secure a favourable legal opinion which would justify their possession of black slaves, approached the Attorney-General, Philip Yorke, and the Solicitor-General, Charles Talbot.[20] Both men had a great deal of political experience and must have been acutely conscious, not simply of the legal niceties, but also of the political and economic implications lurking behind the planters' request. The West Indians went away happy for, as Mansfield said in 1772, Yorke and Talbot 'pledged themselves to the British planters for all the legal consequences of slaves coming over to this kingdom or being baptised'.[21] Their opinion, which was not given in court, or in response to a specific case, was the most important English legal interpretation of slavery up to that time. It was, furthermore, the first to be drawn up specifically to cope with the problem of a growing black community in England. Their opinion was terse and clear: 'We are of opinion, that a slave coming from the West Indies to Great Britain or Ireland, with or without his master, doth not become free, and that his master's property in him is not thereby determined or varied; and that baptism doth not bestow freedom on him, or make any alteration in his temporal condition in these kingdoms. We are also of opinion, that his master may legally compel him to return again to the plantations.'[22]

This held out little hope for the Blacks who were landing in the country in increasing numbers. The opinion has been explained simply as an accurate interpretation of what was, already, accepted common law.[23] Against this has to be set the equally strong opposite tradition which was given its best expression by Holt in 1706. Unlike the judgments tending towards black freedom, the Yorke–Talbot opinion was given wide publicity in the years which followed.[24] Thus it was both the first direct interpretation of domestic slavery and the first to be publicly accepted as the law of the land.[25] Naturally enough, slavery continued to flourish despite, rather than because of, the prevailing state of legal opinion.

Twenty years after the Yorke–Talbot pronouncement, Yorke (now Lord Hardwicke) pronounced his detailed views on black slavery. In so doing he gave strength and support to the chattel status of the Negro who, he claimed, 'is as much property as any other thing'. As to Holt's contrary judgment of 1706, Hardwicke found that it 'has no weight with it, nor can any reason be found, why they [Negroes] should not be equally so [free] when they set foot in Jamaica, or any other English plantation'. He took the view that England lay at the heart of an imperial system which would collapse if exceptions to general economic and legal practice were given approval by an English court. He spelled out in crude detail his opinion of the Blacks, who 'wear out with labour, as cattle or other things ... they are like stock on a farm'.[26] As a statement of colonial reality, Hardwicke's 1749 judgment was accurate. But he was not simply describing a colonial system; he was defining a legal status. No Jamaican planter could have done more than Hardwicke to

The Legal See-Saw: Slavery and the Law to 1772

advance the plantocratic cause. On the other hand the growing black community in England was dealt a blow more severe than the one administered by the same man in 1729. It must have seemed that the legal tradition defending equality and human rights had been permanently abandoned in relation to the black community. The lesson was clear. Freedom in England could only be secured by escape from white masters, and self-help, and only safeguarded by combined effort. Thus the fabric of black society was woven partly in reaction to the Blacks' inability to secure a legal safeguard for their very humanity.

Hopes for freedom returned yet again in 1762, in the form of a judgment by Lord Chancellor Henley. The case *Shanley v. Harvey*, was bizarre and illustrates the convoluted channels through which the issue of slavery came to the attention of English courts. Joseph Harvey was a black slave, imported by his master Edward Shanley, and given to Shanley's niece, Margaret Hamilton. She promptly had the Black baptized and gave him an English name. On her early deathbed she called the slave to her side, giving him a purse saying, 'Here, take this, there is £700 or £800 in bank notes, and some more in money, but I cannot directly tell what, but it is all for you, to make you happy: make haste, put it in your pocket, tell nobody, and pay the butcher's bill.' The former master Shanley brought his action against the Black in order to recover the money, only to be rebuffed by the Lord Chancellor who totally reversed previous slave case judgments. 'As soon as a man sets foot on English ground he is free.'[27] Henley's statement was a complete denial of the legal view which had held sway since 1729 and went back for its inspiration to the earliest slave case of 1569. Once again one searches in vain for evidence that the new legal position in any way altered daily practice, with the pleasant exception of Joseph Harvey of course, who was allowed to keep the change from the butcher's bill.

Generally stated, the institution of slavery was so antithetical to the way English society functioned by the mid-eighteenth century that the law was consistently unable to cope with the translation of that alien institution from the colonies into England. Black slavery touched on a series of delicate legal points which could not be resolved without a prior judgment on the legality (or illegality) of slavery. But by the 1760s the confusion in legal circles had become so obvious that the need for a legal solution became pressing. Any solution, however, could only come from what contemporaries called positive law, that is parliamentary legislation. Freedom based on mere common law precedent was, as had already been shown, ephemeral. In the 1760s legislation aimed at outlawing slavery had scarcely been considered, even by those white friends of the Blacks who sought a termination of slavery. Still more remote was legislation designed to legalize slavery in England. Any such legislation was too fraught with legal, social and even philosophical implications for any government willingly to embark on such a programme.

When after 1767 Granville Sharp launched his personal campaign against English slavery, he did so, in the first instance, through the courts, using legal apparatus already in existence. Five years earlier Lord Chancellor Henley had suggested that this line of approach might be tried, by asserting that a Negro 'may have a *habeas corpus* if restrained of his liberty'.[28] Friends of black freedom in the late 1760s felt that this offered the best chance of success. But it was to take a further twenty years of frustration before the same people realized that the question of black freedom could not be satisfactorily answered in isolation. To guarantee freedom in England, while permitting slavery in the colonies, was both inconsistent and impractical. But to fight for black freedom throughout the colonies in addition to England involved a political struggle of daunting dimensions. As long as the colonies continued to flourish on a slave basis, and as long as a small group of Englishmen sought to use English legal traditions to defend the Blacks in England, there was bound to be a conflict of two legal attitudes, the one rooted in freedom, the other in slavery. The movement of people from the slave colonies of the New World to the relatively free society of the old increased in the course of the century. Importations of slaves into the metropolis and the consequent legal confusion brought home to the imperial authorities, both legal and political, a central dilemma which was to face the British empire, in different forms, well into the twentieth century, namely the impossibility of running the political and economic fabric of empire as a unity. London had already effectively conceded, because it could not resist, the rights of the colonial governments to legislate in their own interests in certain areas. Where the two sides, metropolitan and colonial, violently diverged about these respective rights, there was a danger that the colony would split away. By the mid-eighteenth century these diffi-

The Legal See-Saw: Slavery and the Law to 1772

culties of empire found no better expression than in the legal clash played out in various guises inside English courts of law. The courts were given the impossible task of arbitrating between the economic realities of empire and the tradition of English liberties. A resolution of this problem could only come from Parliament, not from a court, for it was in the last resort essentially a political question.

Confusion about the legal ramifications of slavery extended even to William Blackstone, the foremost commentator on English law in the eighteenth century. In the first two editions of his classic *Commentaries on the Laws of England*, Blackstone sided with Henley's view of 1762. The 'spirit of Liberty is so deeply implanted in our constitution, and rooted in our very soil, that a slave or a negro the moment he lands in England, falls under the protection of the laws and so far becomes a freeman'. Between 1767 and 1772 however Blackstone became aware of the complexity of the issue, and from the third edition of his book onwards, he added the crucial qualification, 'though the master's right to his service may possibly continue'.[29] A brief glance at newspaper advertisements would have reminded Blackstone of the daily reality, as opposed to the legal mythology, of slavery.

> Judge Blackstone made a learned book
> On subjects, and on kings,
> And many reasons sage he gave
> For many foolish things.[30]

The foremost legal experts, as well as the judges, were hopelessly but understandably, confused about English slavery. But in 1772 a case was heard which seemed at the time to change dramatically the lot of the black community. Under careful scrutiny however it will be seen that the famous Somerset case, far from simplifying the matter, actually compounded the legal difficulties by adding misunderstanding to the decades of legal indecision.

Notes

CHAPTER SIX: *The Legal See-Saw*: Slavery and the Law to 1772

1. The most obvious and extreme illustration of this point is the sequence of events leading to the American Revolution of 1776.
2. 17 February 1683, *Cal.S.P. Col, Am W.I.*, 1681–85, 386.
3. See Chapter Three above.
4. Report of the Committee for Foreign Plantations, 1664, *Cal.S.P. Am.W.I.*, 1661–68, 229.
5. Charter of the Royal African Company, September 1672, *Cal. S.P.Am W.I.*, 1669–74, 412.
6. 24 July 1677, *Cal.S.P.Am.W.I.*, 1677–80, 120.
7. W. S. Holdsworth, *A History of English Law*, London, 1926, ix, 112.
8. 31, Ch. II, 6, 2, Clause 12.
9. 'Cartwright's Case, 1569', Catterall, i, 9.
10. 'Butts v. Penny, 1677', ibid., 9.
11. 'Noel v. Robertson, 1687', ibid., 10.
12. 'Chamberline v. Harvey, 1696/7', ibid., 11.
13. 'Butts v. Penny, 1677', ibid., 9.
14. H. Apetheker, 'The Quakers and Negro history', *Journal of Negro History*, xxv, 1940, 352.
15. Catterall, i, 3, n. 16; *Cal.S.P.Am.W.I.*, 1661–68, 500.
16. 'Chamberline v. Harvey, 1696/7', Catterall, 10, n.3.
17. 'Smith v. Gould, 1706', ibid., 11–12.
18. Holdsworth, vi, 265.
19. Catterall, i, 9–11.
20. Philip Yorke (1690–1764); Charles Talbot (1685–1737).
21. 'The Case of James Sommersett, 1772', *Howell's State Trials*, xx, 81.
22. 'The Yorke–Talbot Opinion, 1729', Catterall, i, 12.
23. Philip C. Yorke, *The Life and Correspondence of Philip Yorke*, Cambridge, 1913, 2 vols, ii, 473.
24. *Gentleman's Magazine*, xi, 1741, 186.
25. Yorke, ii, 472.
26. 'Pearce v. Lisle, 1749', Catterall, i, 12–13.
27. 'Shanley v. Henley, 1762', ibid., 13.
28. ibid.
29. William Blackstone, *Commentaries on the Laws of England*, 3rd edn, Oxford, 1773, i, 217. For the details of his changes see P. Hoare, 91n.
30. George Cruikshank's, *Comic Almanack, 1835–43*, London, n.d., 124.

CHAPTER SEVEN

The Somerset Case, 1772

The case of James Somerset[1] the Negro, heard before Lord Chief Justice Mansfield, intermittently between December 1771 and June 1772 is England's most famous slave case. The details which slowly unfolded in those months received as much attention from contemporaries as historians have since given to the case. What seemed at first sight to be a simple application for a writ of *habeas corpus*, developed into a legal epic. The Lord Chief Justice was presented with a case filled with immediate and long-term social and political implications. It was partly to avoid these that he procrastinated, allowing the proceedings to splutter from one postponement to another; by so doing he simply gave scope and time to the Negro's lawyers to expand the range of their case. Throughout, the press, and the white humanitarians behind Somerset, kept public attention riveted. The Somerset case has all the ingredients, backed by copious manuscript material, of a historiographical classic. Unfortunately historians have only added misunderstanding and misinterpretation to the inherent confusion.

To understand the case, we need to go back seven years, to 1765. In the winter of that year a black youth found his way to the surgery of Dr William Sharp in Mincing Lane, London. The boy's condition was desperate, 'having almost lost the use of his Legs and Feet, being at the same time extremely ill of an Ague and Fever; and to compleat his misfortunes afflicted with so violent a disorder in his Eyes that there appeared to be the utmost danger of his becoming totally blind'.[2] These frightful complaints had resulted from a series of savage beatings, the last of which 'he received upon his Head with a Pistol till the Barrel and Lock were separated from the Stock'.[3] While the boy – Jonathan Strong – waited for treatment, the Doctor's brother, Granville Sharp, saw him, a confrontation which was ultimately to prove decisive for the black community in England. Sharp's prickly sensitivity was outraged by what he saw and heard.

He immediately took Strong to St Bartholomew's Hospital, where he was detained for four months. On recovery he was found employment as a chemist's messenger.[4]

Strong enjoyed his work and proved to be a good employee but in September 1767 Granville Sharp received a letter from the terrified Negro, claiming that he was about to be sold back into slavery in the colonies. Strong's former owner, David Lisle, who had originally brought the boy from Barbados, had chanced to see him and promptly had the youth seized and placed in the Poultry Counter prison[5] before 'selling' Strong to James Kerr, a Jamaican planter. On hearing this news, Sharp moved swiftly, dashing to the prison to order the keepers not to release the Negro before a magistrate had heard the case. Sharp followed this up with a visit to the Lord Mayor. Despite the latter's instructions to the keeper to release the Black, Kerr's representatives tried forcibly to seize him in Sharp's presence. Sharp personally prevented them from doing so by threatening them with a private prosecution for assault. In return a writ for trespass was issued against Sharp by Strong's former owners, but technical flaws in the writ ruined the planter's case.[6]

Sharp sought friendly legal advice, only to make the discovery that in the view of Sir James Eyre, Recorder of London (who had privately consulted Lord Chief Justice Mansfield) the Yorke–Talbot opinion of 1729, giving the planters permission to ship their slaves back to the colonies, was binding. Sharp was appalled, but instead of conceding the legal point, he flung himself into his own legal research to prove the lawyers wrong. Within a year he had produced a paper, based on the most exact scholarly and legal research, which not only answered the immediate charges still levelled by Kerr, but even paved the way for a redefinition of legal attitudes towards chattel slavery in England. The manuscript paper was read by Blackstone and circulated among twenty or so eminent lawyers until Kerr's counsel were intimidated by the weight of legal opinion swinging behind Strong's case, and they dropped the prosecution. (Strong's freedom was short-lived, for he died on 19 April 1773.[7]) In 1769 Sharp published his seminal paper, *On The Injustices and dangerous Tendancy of tolerating Slavery, or even of admitting the least Claim to private Property in the Persons of Men, in England*.[8] By this time he had become totally engrossed in the battle against slavery and his tract proved to be a turning point, for it brought public and

The Somerset Case, 1772

legal attention to bear both on the issue of slavery in England and on the legal indecision and weakness towards slavery.

By 1768 Sharp was accepted – by both black and white alike – as the principal white defender of black interests in England. Following the Strong affair increasing numbers of Blacks took their problems to Sharp in the hope that he could secure their freedom as he had Strong's. Even while the Strong case was proceeding, Sharp became involved in another slave case. Thomas John Hylas and his wife Mary were Negro slaves, born in Barbados and brought to England as domestic servants to Miss Judith Alleyne and John Newton respectively. When in 1758 the two slaves were married in England, Thomas Hylas was released from his bondage. In 1760, however, despite the wishes of the husband, Newton sent the slave wife back to the West Indies. With the advice and help of Sharp, Hylas prosecuted Newton for damages. The plaintiff was awarded the derisory amount of one shilling but his main object was to see his wife again. The inhumanity of the court hearing and the preposterous attitudes displayed in court towards the Negro can be gauged from the question put to him. 'The poor Man indeed was asked in Court whether he would have his Wife or Damages? He replyed he desired to have his Wife.'[9] Ultimately the defendant was ordered to return the woman by the first available ship or, at the latest, within six months.[10] The trial, which Sharp attended throughout, was yet another triumph for the pioneer of white humanitarianism, won through a combination of black doggedness and white technical assistance.

No sooner had Sharp impressed his anti-slavery cause on the public than he was drawn into another legal battle for a black slave, during which he came face to face with Lord Chief Justice Mansfield, whose view of the validity of the Yorke–Talbot opinion in the Strong affair had proved influential in pushing Sharp into action. Sharp had developed a deep unhappiness about Mansfield's handling of, and attitudes towards, slave cases, and his experience with the Lord Chief Justice in 1771 was to be of enormous value in the Somerset hearing the following year.

On 3 July 1770 a Mr Banks called on Sharp 'about a Negro Thomas Lewis who had been kidnapped'.[11] A familiar unhappy story was unravelled. Lewis had been the slave of a certain Mr Stapylton in Chelsea and had been later sold to a ship's captain bound for

Jamaica. Lewis naturally resisted, but was forcibly put on board the vessel. By the time Sharp was able to secure a warrant for Lewis's release the vessel had sailed, but was delayed in the Downs, giving Sharp time to send the writ of *habeas corpus* to Spithead and to effect Lewis's release. Once the Negro was safe, Sharp – persistent and angrier than ever – undertook a prosecution of Stapylton in Lewis's name. Eventually the case came before Mansfield in February 1771.

By this time such cases had become something of a regular event, and it was increasingly apparent that a court of law was singularly ill-equipped to deal with the issue of black slavery in England. No one was more aware of this than Mansfield himself. He made it abundantly clear that he wished to avoid making a decision which might have far-reaching social repercussions. It was largely for this reason that he had come down firmly on the side of the Yorke–Talbot opinion. On the first day of the Lewis case he reaffirmed this view; 'that negroes continue to be Slaves in England' and, continued the Lord Chief Justice, 'he had many times granted Writs of Habeas Corpus to take Negroes that had been pressed into the publick Service and restored them as *Private Property* to their respective masters'.[12] Throughout the hearing, Sharp quietly seethed with anger at Mansfield's handling,[13] and the only favourable point he could make in the Lord Chief's favour was that he was anxious to 'avoid bringing the issue to question'. The Jury were less reluctant than Mansfield, and they returned a verdict favourable to the Blacks. 'We don't find he was the defendant's property' – a judgment which drew shouts of 'No property, No property' from the agitated public galleries filled with Negroes.[14] Lewis had indeed won the point, but in June 1771 Mansfield refused to follow up the jury's verdict with adequate compensation, claiming that since the Negro had won his freedom, the central issue had been decided and compensation was not called for. Mansfield had made clear his line of reasoning in the main question: 'Perhaps it is much better that it should never be finally discussed or settled. I don't know what the consequence may be, if the masters were to lose their property by accidentally bringing their slaves into England. I hope it will never be finally discussed; for I would have all masters think them free, and all Negroes think they were not, because then they would both behave better.'[15] Mansfield was preoccupied with the wider social issues, almost to the exclusion of the legal niceties, a feature which was to occur again in his handling of the Somerset case in the following year.

Mansfield's hopes that both sides would 'behave better' was a daydream in the teeth of Sharp's determination to clinch the legal argument for black freedom. For the third time in as many years Sharp had engineered a legal clash between the daily practice of slavery and the precedents of human freedom. On each occasion he had been successful, but each time the victory was slightly hollow and partial. Nonetheless humanitarian determination backed by black resolution was pressing on the weaknesses in the legal structure. The contradiction which lay at the heart of the legal struggle was, by the summer of 1771, apparent to anyone who read the newspaper coverage of the slave cases. Sharp, spurred on by Mansfield's lack of firm leadership, was on the look-out for a suitable case with which he could finally shatter the legal pretensions of the slave owners.

The ideal opportunity arose on 13 January 1772, when, as Sharp recorded 'James Somerset a Negro from Virginia called on me this morn. to complain of Mr Charles Stewart'.[16] Somerset's case was practically identical to Lewis's. Brought to England in November 1769 by his master Charles Stewart, the slave promptly ran away. Recaptured by his master, Somerset was placed on board the *Ann and Mary*, under Captain Knowles, for transportation and sale in Jamaica but was released on a writ of *habeas corpus*. Even before Sharp was drawn into the case, Somerset had already come face to face with the Lord Chief Justice, who dealt with the preliminaries, granting a writ of *habeas corpus* for Somerset.[17] Over the next six months Mansfield was to preside uneasily over the various stages of Somerset's case. Behind Stewart and Knowles lay the admitted wealth and influence of the West Indian lobby;[18] behind Somerset lay the efforts and schemes of Granville Sharp and his humanitarian friends.

Between the first application for a writ on 3 December 1771, and Mansfield's decision on 22 June of the following year, the Somerset case had no fewer than eight separate hearings. From one adjournment to another, the legal army expanded, and the basic issues at stake in the case were warped in translation from the court to the streets. But the man whose persistence in the previous three years had made such a legal climax possible, failed to attend a single hearing. In all the previous cases Sharp had been in court. In 1772 he again organized the slave's case – but from a distance – deciding that his presence in court might irritate Mansfield.

Sharp's first decision was to place all his personal papers used in previous cases in the hands of Somerset's counsel, Serjeant Davy. On 24 January 1772 Davy presented Somerset's case for freedom under *habeas corpus* to Mansfield, asking for a deferment in view of the importance of the case and of the need to prepare himself. Mansfield also expressed the need to consult his fellow judges – an indication of the seriousness with which both approached the case.[19] At this point, Francis Hargrave, a young lawyer of rising promise, volunteered his services. Already Hargrave had made his personal views public. He now combined his legal talents with zealous moral commitment in order to fight the slave's case.

The case reopened on 7 February 1772 before Mansfield and three other judges Ashton, Willes and Ashurst.[20] Davy opened for Somerset with a speech of two and a half hours. No one believed that what was about to unfold was simply an ordinary *habeas corpus* proceeding. The whole exercise was, it was generally thought, largely designed 'with a view of trying the point, how far a Negro, or Black, is a slave in England and consequently at his Master's Disposal'.[21] Certainly this was the issue which Sharp wished to see settled. But following Davy's inordinantly long speech Mansfield felt the case too complex for immediate resolution and ordered a further adjournment.[22]

From the first it was obvious that there was a bias against Somerset. Indeed his treatment by Mansfield was little short of scandalous. Stewart the former master, was the defendant and yet Somerset, the plaintiff, was obliged to produce sureties for his appearances, 'as if he had been Summoned to answer before the Court, *as an Offender or Defendant*'.[23] When the request for a writ was first brought before Mansfield, the Lord Chief Justice 'advised the poor widow who had been at the expense of the Writ, to purchase the plaintiff of the defendant'.[24] But Mansfield was no longer able to side step the issue, as he had in the Lewis case, for Somerset's supporters wanted a comprehensive review of the principles involved and were not to be fobbed off with suggestions that they should connive in the ownership of slaves, which principle they so contested.

The argument for Somerset's freedom was heard again when the court reconvened on 9 May and was completed by Mr Mansfield,

The Somerset Case, 1772

Francis Hargrave and Mr Alleyne, all of whom refused any fee for their services. The master's case was put by Mr Wallace and Mr Dunning – the latter having been the vigorous defender of the Negro Lewis the year before. In that case, Dunning had waved Sharp's tract in front of Lord Mansfield, boldly asserting that he would maintain 'in any court of Great Britain, that no man can be legally detained as a slave in the Country'.[25] In the Somerset case, with remarkable infidelity to consistency of principle, Dunning presented a strong contradictory case before the same judge.

On 21 May Dunning completed Stewart's case. More than six months had already elapsed since the first hearing, and still Mansfield held out hope that a private compromise could be arranged between the two sides. Twice he suggested that the 'master might put an end to the present litigation by manumitting the slave'.[26] The public at large were similarly given the impression by the press that even at this late stage a mutual agreement could be reached. A further postponement was arranged, reported a Bristol newspaper, 'to give the Parties an opportunity of compromising it'. Were it to continue, however, 'it is generally thought, [it] will go in favour of the Negro'.[27] When he adjourned the case for the last time, the Lord Chief Justice paid warm tribute to the men who had argued both sides. But he said, concluding with a clear hint about the way his own mind was working, 'the rule for deciding will lie in a very narrow compass. We know every thing, and it will not stand on a large field.'

From the first hearing of January through to June, the court had been packed by interested parties, supporters and reporters. When the audience gathered for the last time on Monday 22 June 1772 to hear Mansfield's long-awaited verdict, the courtroom was once again brimming over. The atmosphere was tense partly because, as the court sat, a commercial panic swept through the City creating a frenzy of rumour and speculation that a major economic crash had hit the market. But by the end of the day it was clear to all in the court that a drama of greater significance had been played out before them.

Mansfield took great pains to spell out the limits of his task.

The question is, Whether the Captain has returned a sufficient cause for the detainer of Somerset? The cause returned is that he had kept him by order of his master, with an intent to send him abroad, there to be sold. So high an act of dominion must derive its force from the law of the country; and if to be justified here, must be justified by the laws of England. The exercise of the power of a master over his slave, must be supported by the laws of particular countries; but no foreigner can in England claim a right over a man : such a claim is not known to the laws of England.

Immemorial usage preserves a positive law, after the occasion or accident which gave rise to it has been forgotten; and, tracing the subject to natural principles, the claim of slavery never can be supported. The power claimed never was in use here, or acknowledged by the law. Upon the whole, we cannot say the cause is sufficient by the law; and therefore the man must be discharged.[28]

Somerset was therefore a free man and Sharp, though happy with the decision, had reservations: 'Slavery is (I hope) happily excluded from this Island.' [29] The black contingent in court was overjoyed. They 'bowed with profound respect to the Judges, and shaking each other by the hand, congratulated themselves upon their recovery of the rights of human nature, and their happy lot that permitted them to breathe the free air of England'.[30] Naturally enough the planters were furious, and desperately sought to bring a new Bill into Parliament which would give them unrestricted control over their black property.[31] Nonetheless many of the West Indians felt that the result had been a draw rather than a total defeat.[32]

Historians have displayed even greater confusion about the result than contemporaries. The most commonly held view is that Mansfield's decision freed all slaves in England.[33] It is true that in the course of the proceedings, Mansfield underwent a personal change of heart. His 'established modes of thinking on the subject were completely overthrown, and the views and bias of his mind totally changed'.[34] It was even rumoured that Mansfield's own black maid had nagged him towards a more favourable view.[35] But what, precisely, had been decided?

Cutting through the welter of propaganda and misinformation it is possible to distinguish the factors which, at the time and in the intervening years, have bedevilled a clear understanding of the case. First there was Mansfield himself. His display of perplexed indecision to a certain extent simply reflected the legal quandary about slavery. He was aware on the one hand that slavery was contrary to English traditions, but on the other hand he had to take cognisance of the

The Somerset Case, 1772

plethora of statutes which implicitly sanctioned it. His main effort seems to have been persistently to try to persuade both parties to settle out of court and thus remove the burden from his shoulders.

But Mansfield's most serious failing was in allowing counsel for both sides latitude to distort the basic issue. Reading through their arguments, particularly that put forward by the fiery young Hargrave, it is difficult to believe that the principle at stake was any other than slavery versus freedom. Hargrave's argument was a brilliant and convincing legal and historical indictment of slavery, the research for which had been greatly assisted by access to Granville Sharp's papers. He took the court through the minutiae of historical precedents and presented a tight resumé of the intellectual case against slavery in England, drawing on a wide spectrum of learning, ranging from classical to contemporary thought. In response to Hargrave's performance, presented on 14 May,[36] counsel for Stewart had to shift ground; they too began to argue about the general principles of slavery and freedom. Dunning, duller and less convincing than Hargrave, realized that he faced an up-hill task. 'It is', he began, 'my misfortune to address an audience, the greater part of which, I fear, are prejudiced the other way.' [37] He set out to sway his audience by challenging Hargrave's general indictment of slavery, but as early as 14 January Mansfield had noted: 'The now question is whether any dominion, authority or coercion can be exercised in this country on a slave according to American law.'[38] Four months later counsel were wrestling with the general principles of slavery in England – quite a different task from the one originally demarcated by Mansfield. Thus the words of counsel were largely influential in misleading contemporaries, and historians, into believing that their arguments were an accurate reflection of the principle at stake.

A third element in the process of distortion was the length of the proceedings. Somerset was held in suspense for seven months, as the case jolted from one hearing to another. It was so protracted because of the inflation of the proceedings. As time passed Sharp, who handled Somerset's defence, added more men and more evidence to the battle. Thoroughness of preparation and length of presentation demanded more and more time. As winter turned to spring and spring to summer, Somerset's case blossomed from a simple application for a writ into a major legal event. It was perfectly reasonable that contemporaries should see a legal epic unfolding before their gaze.

As the case progressed, Sharp set up a major campaign parallel to the hearing and purposely designed to recruit support to Somerset's side. When for instance Sharp sent messages in London, he used Somerset himself as a messenger,[39] a shrewd move designed to evoke immediate sympathy. He also employed a shorthand writer in court to keep an accurate record of the proceedings. As soon as the minutes were written up, copies were dispatched to sympathetic, influential figures, notably the humanitarian Quakers Dr Fothergill and Anthony Benezet and the Archbishop of York.[40] Sharp sent out abolitionist tracts in all directions, aiming at the powerful. Lord North, First Lord of the Treasury, received one; so too did Mansfield, delivered by a Negro.[41] Sharp had already adopted the tactics of the wide-fronted pressure group in the Lewis case,[42] but in 1772 there was an added urgency. Suitable new publications were immediately passed on to counsel to enliven and bring Somerset's case up to date,[43] and gradually under Sharp's thorough and remorseless direction, Somerset's case grew in size and, apparently, in importance.

The press in London and the provinces found the proceedings increasingly gripping, and in the process the fourth element of distortion – contemporary coverage – began to play its part. Both the daily hearings and the final verdict were misinterpreted by newspapers and periodicals, even as far away as the American colonies. Again, this was scarcely surprising if they took their cue from the tone of the debate in court. 'The Cause of the Trial', said the *Bristol Journal* on 14 February, 'was to know how far a black servant was the Property of the Purchaser by the Laws of England.'[44] Later that month the same newspaper claimed that the point of the case was 'how far a Negro or Black, is a slave in England, and consequently entirely at his Master's Disposal'[45] – a claim repeated by the *Scot's Magazine*.[46] Newspapers in general gave very wide coverage to the case,[47] but they tended to focus attention on the great clash of principle along the lines laid down by counsel. By so doing they simplified and distorted the proceedings for the public at large. Not surprisingly, well before judgment was pronounced 'the great cause depending between Mr Stewart and Somerset the negro [has become] one of the principal topics of conversation'.[48] The result naturally was given great prominence, again often inaccurately. Mansfield, alleged the *Middlesex Journal*, had said 'every slave brought into this country ought to be free'. The *Boston Gazette* informed its readers that all of England's 14,000 slaves had been freed.[49] But one searches in vain in the text of the trial for any supporting evidence.

If anything, historical discussion of the case has been even more confused than contemporary opinion. In part this is due to the apparently reliable details, later enshrined in law reports. The standard report of the Somerset case is in volume xx of *Howell's State Trials*, published in 1814. Unfortunately this is a very unreliable source of information, but that has not prevented the legal profession and historians from regarding its report as an accurate account of the proceedings. Substantial parts of the report, particularly the central section dealing with Hargrave's speech, were taken, not from the trial, but from a written account of that speech drawn up after the event by Hargrave himself and published as an abolitionist tract.

Even more significant is the reliance of Howell's version on a notoriously untrustworthy report, published by Capel Lofft in 1776. At the time there was no organized, objective reporting of legal proceedings. Reports were casual and generally drawn up by interested parties who may or may not have had legal training, and though Lofft was called to the bar in 1775 this in no way guarantees the accuracy of his reports.[50] Lofft's report of the Somerset case picks up the proceedings in May, months after the case had begun. Consequently it was inevitable that he should concentrate on the attack on the principle of slavery launched by Somerset's counsel. Even more startling is the summary of the case which Lofft imputes to Lord Mansfield. The words which he put into Mansfield's mouth were indeed uttered in court, but they were spoken by Hargrave, and not by the Lord Chief Justice. Lofft's version of Mansfield's summing up differs from the brief, and accurate report which was quoted in the *Annual Register* for 1772.[51] Lofft and his later imitators gave the false impression that Mansfield specifically abolished slavery in England. Thus at three distinct but related levels – as the case proceeded, when it was reported four years after the event, and in historical analysis – confusion has been heaped on confusion.

Many contemporaries realized the limitations of Mansfield's verdict. England, wrote Benjamin Franklin, 'piqued itself on its virtue, love of liberty, and the equity of its courts, in setting free a single negro.'[52] Thirteen years later, Mansfield himself went out of his way to explain his 1772 decision. The public, he claimed 'were generally mistaken in the determination of the court of King's Bench, in the case of Somerset the negro, which had often been quoted, for nothing more was then determined, than that there was no right in the master forcibly to take the slave and carry him abroad'.[53] If anyone needed further proof of the reality, as opposed to the mythology of Mansfield's judgment, they had only to glance at the large number of slaves in England long after 1772. In 1774 John Wilkes, sitting as a London magistrate, heard the case of a poor woman who 'was married to a black, who was a slave to a merchant in Lothbury'.[54] Runaway slaves continued to be sought through the medium of newspaper advertisements long after the alleged emancipation of 1772.[55] As late as the 1820s English courts discussed the question of slaves in England.[56] Illogically enough, in 1778 a group of humanitarians purchased an enslaved African chief in order to manumit him. Had English slavery genuinely been outlawed by Mansfield in 1772 such a step would have scarcely been needed.[57]

Even in its strictest sense, Mansfield's ruling was flouted. Kidnappings and forcible repatriation to the colonies, so clearly prohibited in 1772, continued to haunt the black community for years. At the very least, after 1772 Negroes faced by a kidnapping threat could always claim legal immunity. But how could any such theoretical legal backing be translated into a genuine social right? After 1772 the kernel of the black dilemma remained precisely the same, namely that common law decisions designed to improve the Blacks' conditions remained practically inoperative. There had after all been decisions of an even wider importance earlier in the century but it is doubtful whether they had in any real way helped to guarantee the freedom of the black community. Legal freedoms were mere points of law as long as a climate of opinion prevailed in which violations of those freedoms were possible and easy.

News of Mansfield's verdict must have percolated swiftly into London's black community, yet there is no evidence of a rush to freedom. The poor Blacks were beset by social and economic problems which made Hargrave's performance largely academic. Those, measured perhaps in their thousands, who had already seized their freedom by escaping, found their insecurity in no way diminished. When the immediate euphoria had died down few Blacks, with the obvious exception of Somerset who had been spared a return trip to the colonies, could have felt any better for Mansfield's decision. Furthermore Somerset's was not the last slave case to come before an English court. In the years to come Negroes were to find themselves suffering further blows administered by English law. They consequently had to care for their own interests without the positive backing of legal freedom and equality. This situation prevailed until the emancipation of all slaves in 1833.

Notes

CHAPTER SEVEN: *The Somerset Case, 1772*

1. I have chosen to use this spelling of 'Somerset' rather than other variations used by contemporaries.
2. 'The Case of James and Granville Sharp so far as they are concerned with James Kerr', Granville Sharp, *Letter Book, 1768–1773*, 195.
3. Sharp to Dr Findlay, 14 August 1772, ibid., 93.
4. 'An account of the Occasion which first impelled Granville Sharp to study law and undertake the Defence of the Negro Slaves', Sharp Papers, Box 54.
5. 'The Case of James and Granville Sharp', *Letter Book*, 198–9.
6. ibid., 203–9.
7. Sharp Papers, Box 56, Book G, 26.
8. Hoare, 36–40.
9. 'Copy of the Trial before Lord Chief Justice Wilmot, 3 December 1765', *Letter Book*, 18.
10. Hoare, 47.
11. Sharp's Diary, 1772–82, Sharp Papers, Box 56, Book G, 10.
12. 'An account of the Occasion', Sharp Papers, Box 54.
13. Sharp to Sir Joseph Banks, 20 February 1772, *Letter Book*, 80.
14. Hoare, 60.
15. ibid., 61.
16. Extracts from Diaries, 1772–82, Sharp Papers, Box 56, Book G, 12.
17. 'The Case of James Sommersett a Negro', 1771–1772, *Howell's State Trials*, xx, 1–2.

18. Hoare, 89.
19. ibid., 70–1.
20. ibid., 72–3.
21. *Felix Farley's Bristol Journal*, 15 February 1772.
22. Hoare, 77–8.
23. 'Memorandum concerning the Case of James Somerset', *Letter Book*, 185.
24. ibid., 186; 59.
25. Hoare, 54.
26. ibid., 88.
27. *Felix Farley's Bristol Journal*, 30 May 1772.
28. *Howell's State Trials*, xx.
29. Sharp to Benezet, 21 August 1772, *Letter Book*, 61.
30. Quoted in Hecht, 48.
31. Sharp to Dr Fothergill, 27 October 1772, *Letter Book*, 51.
32. Edward Fiddes, 'Lord Mansfield and the Sommersett Case', *Law Quarterly Review*, l, 1934, 508.
33. ibid., 499n; M. D. George; Richard West; See also R. A. Fisher, 'Granville Sharp and Lord Mansfield', *Journal of Negro History*, xxviii, 1943.
34. 'A Briton', *Considerations on certain Remarks on the Negro Slavery and Abolition Question* . . . , London, 1827, 16.
35. Hecht, 41.
36. Hargrave's speech was delivered after three other speeches for Somerset (Hoare, 75–83) but the State Trial only records Hargrave (*Howell's State Trials*, xx, 23).
37. *Howell's State Trials*, xx, 71.
38. Quoted in Fiddes, 505.
39. 26 January 1772, *Letter Book*, 43.
40. ibid., 43; Hoare, 81.
41. Hoare, 81.
42. *Letter Book*, 24; 31–2.
43. Letter to Dr Fothergill, 8 February 1772, *Letter Book*, 48.
44. *Felix Farley's Bristol Journal*, 1 February 1772.
45. ibid., 15 February 1772.
46. *The Scot's Magazine*, xxxiv, 1772, 297.
47. J. Nadelhaft, 'The Somerset Case and Slavery', *Journal of Negro History*, 1966, li, 193–208 : 199.
48. *The Scot's Magazine*, xxxiv, 1772, 301.
49. Quoted in Nadelhaft, 194.
50. ibid., 200–1.
51. ibid., 201; *Annual Register*, 1772, 110.
52. *The Works of Benjamin Franklin*, ed. J. Bigelow, 1887, IV. 507.

53. Quoted in *A Letter to Philo-Africanus* . . ., 1788, 39.
54. *The Scot's Magazine*, xxxvi, 1774, 53.
55. *The Bristol Gazette and Public Advertiser*, 4 November 1773.
56. Chapter Eight below.
57. Fiddes, 509; Hoare, 93.

CHAPTER EIGHT

From Mansfield to Emancipation. Slavery and the Law, 1772-1833

One immediate consequence of the widespread coverage given to Mansfield's judgment was to stimulate similar proceedings in a Scottish court. Despite the differences between the legal systems of the two countries black slaves were employed, bought and sold in Scotland as they were in England, though evidently in smaller numbers.[1] The *Edinburgh Courant* for 30 August 1766 for example offered for sale 'A NEGRO WOMAN, named Peggy . . . [and her] young CHILD A NEGRO BOY'[2]. Opponents of slavery hoped that the Somerset case would finally put an end to 'the disposal of negroes by auction and sale, like other property', in Scotland as well as in England,[3] but as we have seen, it failed to achieve this even in the latter. One man quick to realize the implications of Mansfield's words was Joseph Knight, an African slave brought to Scotland via Jamaica by his owner John Wedderburn. 'In 1772 he read in a newspaper the report of the decision in the Somerset Case', after which he firmly resolved to leave his master's house and assert his freedom.[4] This determination led, in January 1778 to the case of *Knight v. Wedderburn*. Although the case is less well known than Somerset's, it deserves wider prominence because it had much more important and far-reaching results.

It had seemed likely that Scottish law would resolve the slavery question many years before the English, for as early as July 1757 a major slave case had come before a Scottish court which in many respects closely resembled that of Somerset. A Negro brought to Scotland from Virginia was baptized and promptly asked for his freedom, only to be put on board a vessel bound for Virginia. The principle at stake was not resolved in that year, for the Negro died in the middle of the court hearing, with the result that the 'respective claims of liberty and servitude by the master and the negro' were not resolved.[5] Twenty years later a similar sequence of events took place. Joseph Knight ran away from Wedderburn, but was arrested and ordered by the justices to return to his master. Knight appealed to the sheriff of Perthshire who overruled the magistrates, asserting, perhaps with Somerset's case in mind, 'that the state of slavery is not recognised by the laws of this kingdom'. Wedderburn in his turn appealed to the Court of Sessions, which upheld the Black's freedom. Their opinion was that 'the dominion assumed over the Negro, under the law of Jamaica, being unjust, could not be supported in this country to any extent: [and] that therefore, the defender had no right to the Negro's service for any space of time, nor to send him out of the country against his consent.'[6]

It was immediately apparent that this judgment, though obviously restricted in application to Scotland, was more far-reaching than Mansfield's. James Boswell wrote that Knight's case 'went upon a much broader ground than the case of Somerset . . . being truly the general question, whether a perpetual obligation of service to one master in any mode should be sanctified by the law of a free country'.[7] Boswell, puffing up with that northern patriotism which so irritated Dr Johnson, preened himself on Scotland's achievement. In fact the victory was a close run thing. A minority of four judges had opposed freeing Knight,[8] and much of the credit for it was due to the Lord Advocate, Henry Dundas, whose speech 'generously contributed to the cause of the sooty stranger'.[9]

South of the border, in the years following Mansfield's judgment there was no similar immediate loosening of the slaves' legal shackles. In fact new slave cases, far from following Scotland's exemplary lead, produced a positive worsening of the already poor legal position of England's Negroes. The situation following Mansfield's ruling was confused for slaves and owners alike. While Negroes could not be shipped back to the colonies against their wishes, freshly imported slaves certainly were not emancipated simply by landing in England. Negroes could still be bought and sold, and courts were still prepared to underwrite a master's rights to property in his slave, providing it did not entail a gross violation of common law.[10] But of all the legal disabilities which affected the Negroes in England, the one which brought home to the black community their highly vulnerable position was the legal disregard for the mass murder of Negroes on board English ships. The case of the ship *Zong*, heard before Mansfield in 1783, in which compensation was sought for 132 slaves thrown overboard, concerned itself not with the act of murder, but solely with the technical questions of insurance and compensation. Humanitarians and Blacks alike fought to widen the issue – but in vain. Mansfield was shocked by the facts of the case, but nothing was done to bring the murderers to trial.[11] The *Zong* affair raised, in a peculiarly acute form, the inevitable clash of principle between human rights and the simple but dreadful logic inherent in the chattel status of the Negro. But the case was successful in illustrating to an increasingly sensitive public the monstrous inhumanities latent in such a status.

It was Mansfield's greatest misfortune (with the possible exception of having his house picked out for demolition by the Gordon rioters) to have been Lord Chief Justice at the critical juncture in legal history when slavery severely tested the fabric of the legal structure. Try as he might he was never able to escape the shadow of black bondage which periodically cast itself across his court room. In the 1780s he presided over two major slave cases, that concerning the *Zong* and, in 1785, *Jones v. Schmoll*.[12] Both simply concerned the issue of financial compensation for dead slaves, and each was a classic example of the legal dilemma which stemmed from the overlap of two distinct social systems. England, a free country, sustained an Atlantic empire based on slavery and yet found great difficulty in accommodating the transplanting of colonial problems and institutions into the mother country.

Mansfield himself pinpointed the continuing problem in 1785 when he noted that 'the court has never decided that a negro brought to England is there under an obligation to serve,' an admission which in itself is enough to destroy some of the more fanciful myths about his 1772 decision. In the same year he was responsible for a further worsening of the Black's position, for he decided to deny a poor Black the minimum benefit of parish relief on the grounds that it could only be given to persons who had originally been hired for work in the parish.[13] Thus, once again, the Blacks found the law to be an obstacle, rather than a defence, in their search for full rights and equality in English society.

Nor were they alone in the sense of insecurity resulting from their uncertain legal position. Slave owners too were faced with legal uncertainty about their hold over slaves. After 1772 therefore, the owners devised a new procedure which would legally bind a slave to a master. Before leaving the colonies the slave was simply obliged to sign an indenture, promising to work for his master under specified conditions. On arrival in England the slave's status was technically transmuted from bondage to indentured worker. Thus the slave-cum-indentured worker was shackled to his owner-cum-employer by terms of employment which would receive the full backing of English law.[14] Under these new conditions, English courts rigorously enforced the terms of the indenture. If a slave ran away, or refused repatriation to the West Indies, he was in breach of his agreement and liable to prosecution. Thus paradoxically the lessons learned by the planters from the Mansfield judgment led to a worsening of the legal position of freshly imported slaves.

To add insult to injury, an English court decided in 1799 that no master was obliged to pay wages to his 'indentured' black servant, unless a wage clause had been specifically included in the original indenture signed before leaving the colonies.[15] From the slave's viewpoint, this was asking for the impossible, for in the slave societies no slave was in a position to dictate terms of employment to his master. He or she was simply given the task of signing, or marking, an indenture placed before them by an all-powerful master. Furthermore no master would have thrown away his money by unnecessarily promising the slave more than life's basic essentials. Thus, after 1799 the slave owner was legally empowered to bring his slaves to England and employ them under what were virtually West Indian terms of employment, knowing that the terms of the indenture obliged the slave to return to the colonies.

In the last twenty years of the century, while it is true that there was a powerful ground swell of pro-black public sympathy, it must have been a difficult task to convince the black community that their best interests lay in seeking their freedom and rights through the process of law. The only route open to the slave was, as before, escape into the black community. While on the surface it may seem that the law came to the help of the slave owners, the practical results of court decisions in many cases were counterproductive and led to a swelling of the ranks of the black poor. Certainly between 1772 and 1789 people were alarmed that black immigration seemed

Black and White

to be growing faster than ever.[16] Technically the majority of newly arrived Negroes were slaves, but the major white fear was that increasing numbers would escape and thereby seize their freedom. English courts, far from preventing this, actually made it more likely, though this was certainly against their conscious wishes.

During the last thirty years of the existence of slavery in the empire, English law found itself drawn into an increasingly complex, and at times farcical situation. Many of the slaves who became the objects of legal attention in these years were tragic figures, caught in a process of law which sanctioned a metamorphosis of their status by crossing from one side of the Atlantic to the other. Thus the runaway slave who had freed himself by escaping from the slave colonies to England often found that his freedom was a temporary status. If he returned to the colonies he reverted to his earlier bondage. Naturally enough this absurd situation had serious consequences for any slave wishing to work as a sailor.[17]

Where precisely did the two legal systems, colonial and metropolitan divide? A slave who was legally enslaved in the West Indies was freed by escaping to England. But what of his status en route, on the high seas? This abstract question was put to the legal test, in a case which had Gilbertian overtones. In 1815, sixty-two slaves fled from a Florida plantation owned by an Englishman, scrambled on board a vessel of the Royal Navy and promptly claimed their freedom. The officers in charge gave the planter the opportunity to speak to his slaves and, not surprisingly, none of them took up his invitation to return. Later transferred to other vessels, the slaves were moved to Bermuda, but it was a full year before they were finally allowed to land as free men. The delay, in which time they were held, like present-day East African Asians in stateless limbo, was due to the government's uncertainty about their legal status. The former slaves were both stateless and statusless, caught between two societies and two conflicting legal systems. Nine years elapsed before an English court heard the case of the aggrieved planter against the naval officials involved. The decision went against the planter but in the process further complications were added to the legal complexity surrounding slavery. It was decided that when the fugitives '... went on board an English ship (which for this purpose may be considered a floating island) ... they became subject to the

English laws alone'.[18] Mr Justice Best pronounced that 'the instant they get beyond the limits where slavery is recognised by local law, they have broken their chains, they have escaped from their prison and are free. These men when on board an English ship, held all the rights belonging to Englishmen.'[19] Evidently those rights evaporated into the tropical air once they stepped ashore in a plantation society and became slaves again.

It was thus possible in the early nineteenth-century for a slave to pass through a number of estates of man within a matter of weeks. If a slave in the West Indies, he was freed by effecting an escape; he became a free Englishman on board an English ship outside colonial territorial waters. In England he was free but constantly had to guard his freedom against those who wished to profit by shipping him back to the slave colonies. Were he to return to his former colony he immediately fell subject to its laws and thus reverted to slavery. But what of those slaves, and there were apparently large numbers of them, who passed through England without claiming freedom by escape? Were they freed simply by breathing the English air?

This was perhaps the most commonly believed source of manumission quoted, and misquoted, in English slave cases from the sixteenth century onwards. As often as not it was misunderstood by judges and legal commentators alike[20] and was only finally resolved – and that with a crushing blow – in 1827, in the case of the slave Grace. In 1822 a Mrs Allan came from Antigua to England with her slave, Grace, returning in 1823 without the slightest sign on the part of Grace that she wished to stay in England or to become free. In 1825 however, after an inexplicable delay, Grace was seized by the local customs officials who alleged that she had been brought into Antigua as a slave and therefore contrary to the abolition of the slave trade Act. Hearing the appeal from the local Vice-Admiralty Court, Lord Stowell passed a judgment which was as uncompromisingly behind the slave-owners as any since the 1729 opinion. Stowell guaranteed the slave-owners' possession of their property. He referred to all the major eighteenth-century slave cases, superciliously dismissing Hargrave's attack on slavery in the Somerset case. Stowell took as his basic point that a Black returning to a colony from England was not entitled to retain any freedoms or liberties acquired or exercised in England. Grace's freedom 'had totally expired when that residence [in England] ceased and she was imported into Antigua'.[21]

It was not clear moreover just how free Grace had been simply by living in England. In reaching his decision, Stowell had to scrutinize this point and in so doing severely criticized Lord Mansfield for failing to make clear the precise limitations and nature of his 1772 judgment.[22] Unlike Mansfield, Stowell was an abolitionist, but there was precious little pro-Black sentiment in his verdict, for he felt that he had to make his decision solely on the technical legal issue. In studying the Acts governing the slave trade, and the precedents set in previous cases, Stowell came to realize the impossible task facing anyone wishing to reconcile two contradictory systems of law. He was not the first to realize this, but he was the first judge to admit the dilemma openly. 'How the laws in respect of that trade made in England and enforced by our courts of law, the King's Privy Council, and the Court of Chancery, to their utmost extent, can consist with any notion of its entire abolition here, is, in my view of it, an utter impossibility.'[23] The essence of his final verdict was that a slave's residence in England merely suspended the state of slavery which revived on return to the New World colonies.

Grace was exceptional, as were all those slaves whose cases came before an English court of law. Behind every slave whose situation was subjected to legal scrutiny and public attention, there marched a silent army of anonymous Negroes who had to look to themselves and to their friends, rather than to an English court, for justice. But for those whose cases were discussed in court after 1772, the legal results were scarcely encouraging. As we have seen, conditions of employment were actually changed to the slave's disadvantage, while the oppressive relationship between master and slave was not improved simply by calling the latter an indentured worker. 'I knew I was free in England,' said one slave, Mary Prince, brought to England in the 1820s, 'but I did not know how to get my living; and therefore I did not like to leave the house.'[24] Driven to despair by the cruelty of her owners, Mary Prince finally fled, seeking refuge in a Moravian church, which was the only institution recognizable from her Antiguan past. 'The case of Mary Prince,' added an abolitionist, 'is by no means a singular one; many of the same kind are daily occurring.'[25] Many slave-owners knew that in England they did not need to threaten their slaves into obedience. Escape into freedom was an unhappy prospect, involving a constant struggle for survival in an alien and unfriendly world. That generations of slaves did in fact escape speaks for their desperation.

Such escapes, where they involved the breaking of an indenture by the slave, were illegal in the eyes of the English law right up to the eve of emancipation. The law put the slave into a position where, to seize the rights enjoyed by Englishmen, he had to break the law. When a slave escaped from a slave colony to England, the law would guarantee his freedom, but, equally, it would sanction his punishment on his return to the colonies. 'With what system of ethics can we reconcile the holding out of so great a temptation to crime, and sanctioning the punishment, not for the commission, but because the culprit has failed to consummate his guilt?'[26]

In the absence of a written constitution, basic human rights could only be safeguarded by open and readily available access to the courts. But this 'equality before the law' was a mere chimera for the black community. Judges felt impelled to uphold the economic basis of the empire, and to do this they had to concede the legality of property in slaves. In England itself there were no slave codes, as there were in the colonies, to uphold slavery, and judges were forced to look at other areas of legal practice to find sanctions for slavery. It proved impossible to use the precedents of England's long years of villeinage, for that would equally endanger the rights of white Englishmen. When therefore English judges looked for legal precedents to justify slavery, they were forced to turn to imperial situations, and to the statutes and cases which resulted from the growth of empire. But when colonial practice was imported into England it often transgressed a number of fundamental principles of English law. It was precisely this dilemma which faced all English judges who were obliged to deal with slave cases, but no one was prepared to admit it until Stowell did so in 1827.

Between the Somerset case and emancipation the legal status of the imported Black was more complicated and, if anything, worse than it had been in the eighteenth century. Complete freedom, or total bondage, were the only viable alternatives for the Negroes throughout the empire. Yet black freedom was bitterly resisted as an economic disaster by the planters, while any attempts to introduce legalized slavery into England would have proved fruitless in the face of a mounting crescendo of humanitarian propaganda. The battle for black freedom was thus a political battle, won, after more than fifty years, by the humanitarian cause. Until that time the law existed as a no-man's-land between the two feuding sides in which had to be resolved and reconciled the equally powerful but mutually exclusive claims from both sides. That no single case, and no single judge, was ever able to satisfy both sides is an indication of the impossible quandary in which slavery placed English judges.

The 'Act for the Abolition of Slavery throughout the British Empire' passed in 1833[27] made the Negro in Jamaica as free as the Negro in England. But the relationship between freedom and slavery on a global scale still remained unresolved, for the simple reason that England's emancipation was exceptional. Large areas of the world continued to depend on slave labour and as late as 1860 it was, for instance, perfectly legal for a British subject to own slaves in a country where slave-owning was still legal.[28] The overlap of legal systems, between free and slave-owning economies, continued to cause embarrassment to England until late in the century, but the problem of the Negro's legal status inside the British empire had been resolved in the only way possible – by total emancipation.

One of the key problems facing the Negro in the eighteenth and nineteenth centuries had been not simply the legal hostility towards black freedom but the general inaccessibility of the legal machinery. Negroes were able to bring their cases to court in greater numbers, from the 1760s, thanks to the efforts of, and opportunities created by white humanitarians, but there is no way of knowing of the others who were never able to gain access to the legal process.

Until 1833 the black community in England was influenced by English law in two distinct ways. Firstly, the law was weighted preponderantly on the side of the slave-owners. Rarely did it interpose itself between the Negro and his bondage. At this level, the legal process was clearly an adjunct and a reflection of the imperial economic system. Secondly, the fundamental legal safeguards of human rights, notably *habeas corpus*, were (until the late eighteenth century) generally beyond the awareness and reach of the black community. Thus even where the Negro could technically use the process of law to his own benefit, it was largely unavailable.

The subtleties of legal discrimination against the Negro, so common by the mid-twentieth century, were not in evidence in the eighteenth and nineteenth centuries. There was no need for subtlety

From Mansfield to Emancipation, 1772-1833

in a society which consigned him to the level of subhumanity. In this process, the law played a crucial role. For more than two centuries of black history in England the law was instrumental in relegating the Negro to a status far below that of any other minority in the country. Unfortunately this crucial fact has been overlooked. More recently, particularly since 1945, English judges have gone out of their way to extol the virtues of the colour-blindness of English law.[29] If this is true (and there is an abundance of evidence to suggest that it is not), it is a recent phenomenon, and forms a startling contrast to the situation which prevailed for more than 200 years. In the period which separates the emergence of England's slave empire and English involvement in the slave trade from emancipation in 1833, English law was far from colour-blind. It was instead a vital factor in the subjection, dehumanization and enslavement of generations of Africans. Statute law made possible the growth of the slave trade; the King in Parliament supervised the evolution of colonial slave laws; generations of English judges denied the black community any meaningful legal protection. Of course this situation changed, but it did so painfully, slowly and only under the alternating blows of economic change and abolitionist propaganda. It is no mere coincidence that by the time the Negro was accorded the full status of a free man, he was no longer economically important.

Slavery, racial discrimination and exploitation of the most grotesque form were not simply the offshoots of economic growth. The law, mirroring economic fact, in its turn paved the way for further oppression of the Negro, yet no historian has so much as mentioned the deep historical roots of legal discrimination against the Blacks. In 1949 Lord Denning asserted: 'It is a cardinal principle of our law that (persons of all races) shall not suffer any disability or prejudice by reason of their race and shall have equal treatment under the law.'[30] This 'cardinal principle' was hard won, for the law reports and statute books groan with evidence of a different kind; of a legal system committed to the preservation and defence of racial exploitation. One might indeed go so far as to claim that with the obvious exception of the West India lobby, no single section of English society proved more influential in moulding the abject experiences of England's black minority than the legal fraternity.

Notes

CHAPTER EIGHT: *From Mansfield to Emancipation. Slavery and the Law, 1772–1833.*

1. The evidence of Blacks in Scotland is sparse. Colleagues more familiar with the peculiarities of Scottish history have been unable to help satisfy my tentative enquiries as to why Scotland's major towns and ports failed to develop a black minority. This is clearly a study in itself and I will not presume to deal with it here in anything but a tangential fashion.
2. Quoted in *The Scot's Magazine*, xxviii, 1766, 445.
3. Quoted in *The Scot's Magazine*, xxxiv, 1772, 299.
4. *Boswell's Life of Johnson*, Oxford University Press, 1934, iii, 214, n.l.
5. 'Sheddan v. a Negro, 1757', Catterall, i, 18.
6. 'Joseph Knight v. Wedderburn, 1778', Catterall, i, 18.
7. *Boswell's Life of Johnson*, iii, 212.
8. G. W. T. Ormond, *The Lord Advocates of Scotland*, Edinburgh, 1883, ii, 67. See also *An Introduction to Scottish Legal History*, The Stair Society, Edinburgh, 1958.
9. *Boswell's Life of Johnson*, iii, 213.
10. Fiddes, 506.
11. See Chapter Five above.
12. 'Jones v. Schmoll, 1785', Catterall, i, 19-20.
13. 'King v. Inhabitants of Thames Ditton, 1785', Catterall, i, 33.
14. 'Keane v. Boycott, 1795', Catterall, i, 21.
15. 'Alfred v. Marquis of Fitzjames, 1799', Catterall, i, 22.
16. G. Francklyn, *Observations on the Slave Trade*, xi.
17. 'Williams v. Brown, 1802', Catterall, i, 23–5.
18. 'Forbes v. Cochrane, 1824', Catterall, i, 33.
19. Quoted in H. G. Tuke, *The Fugitive Slave Circulars*, London, 1826, 13.
20. Lord Campbell, *Lives of the Lord Chancellors*, 3rd edn, London, 1874, 293.
21. 'The Slave Grace, 1827', Catterall, i, 34.
22. ibid., 35.
23. ibid., 37.
24. *The History of Mary Prince*, London, 1831, 20.
25. ibid., 40.
26. *Negro Emancipation Morally and Politically Considered*, London, 1824, 20–1.

27. *Public General Statutes*, lxxiii, 1833, 913.
28. Bob Hepple, *Race, Jobs and the Law in Britain*, Penguin Books, 2nd edn, 1970, 61.
29. ibid., 143.
30. ibid.

CHAPTER NINE

Back to Africa

In the years immediately following the American war the black poor in London became a serious social problem. Discharged black sailors and soldiers swelled the forlorn ranks of black beggars who already haunted the capital. By the spring of 1786 the 'great number of Blacks and People of Colour, many of them Refugees from America and others who have by land or sea been in His Majesty's service, were from the severity of the season in great distress'.[1] Almost two centuries earlier, the embryonic black population had been singled out by Elizabeth's government as a social grievance for the simple reason that they were the most easily isolated foreign element in a society already sorely taxed by famine and over population. In the 1780s a new generation of Negroes found themselves falling victim to a similar chain of events.

Throughout the nation as a whole, the indices of social unrest – population increase, the consequent pressure on food and employment, and general economic dislocation – took a dramatic upward swing as the nation lurched into the early, painful spasms of industrial change. London had always been a sensitive barometer for social changes in the country at large. Crowded into its offensive and often pestilential streets were some of the wider social problems of the nation as a whole, adding to those peculiar to the metropolis itself. The city housed a poor population whose marginal existence bears a close resemblance to the lot of the poor urban dwellers of present-day developing nations. Society's ability to contain the social tensions inherent in the capital was delicately balanced. Occasionally it collapsed completely, as for instance in the Gordon Riots of 1780.[2]

From the late 1760s public scrutiny focused ever more searchingly on the special problems posed by the black minority. After 1783 this scrutiny became more concerned as the Negroes came to symbolize, in isolated and immediately recognizable form, the general problems of the capital. They were largely poor, unwanted, unskilled and friendless, at the heart of one of the world's greatest urban areas, where poverty and related crime already strained the sinews of authority to breaking point.

Granville Sharp became as familiar with the problems facing the black poor as anyone in London. Inevitably his role in the slave cases of the 1760s and 1770s and his charitable work for Negroes had won for him an unrivalled reputation. As his fame grew, so too did the number of Negroes who flocked to him in search of relief. Eventually Sharp found himself swamped by the weight of their numbers. By the time his 'pensioners' and 'orphans' reached a total of 400, he realized that a more organized basis for black relief would have to be devised.[3]

What guided Sharp's thoughts towards Africa as a dumping ground for London's surplus black population remains a mystery, but in the summer of 1783 he drew up a rudimentary memorandum planning a resettlement of London's Negroes on the African coast. From the first, he envisaged his plan both as a means of transplanting London's social problems into an African setting and as an exercise in social and human perfectibility. 'The proposal for a Settlement on the coast of Africa will deserve all encouragement if the settlers are absolutely prohibited from holding any kind of property in the persons of Men as slaves.' Government and society were to be based on 'the Israelite commonwealth under the Theocracy, purified and improved by the precepts of the Gospel'.[4] Grafted on to this were to be those Anglo-Saxon institutions which the enlightened radical Englishman of the period so cherished and struggled for.[5] The African settlement was, in brief, to be an ideal society, shedding the imperfections of historical and contemporary society while creating a new social organization in which man's strengths, rather than his weaknesses, would flourish.

Sharp's train of thought had been stimulated by the plight of London's Negroes. The Negroes were equally to be responsible for unleashing a chain reaction of political events which fundamentally affected two continents. In the first place, black destitution forced a variety of Englishmen to see the evils of slave-trading. It was no mere coincidence that the same men who set out in the 1780s to assist the black poor in London also turned their talents and energies to the early campaign against the slave trade. The collective strength and individual talents of the humanitarians provided a base for the initial attacks on the slave trade, and, as a by-product of these meetings, the first organized efforts were undertaken to relieve London's poor Negroes. Discussions among like-minded men about the principles of slave-ownership led to the formation, early in 1786, of a committee which included Sharp, Wilberforce, Ramsay, Clarkson, Wedgwood and Jonas Hanway.[6] Later that same year another committee sprouted from the first, under the chairmanship of Hanway 'for the Relief of the Black Poor'.

In many respects Hanway was very similar to Sharp. A champion of the under-dog, of prostitutes and chimney-sweeps, Hanway fought for public recognition of, and assistance for, social outcasts.[7] Now his first task was to raise money for the needy Blacks. Contributions from friends, and from the public following a newspaper appeal, brought in some £800 in a few months.[8] With this as capital, daily distribution of relief began at two taverns, *The Yorkshire Stigo* in Paddington and *The White Raven* in Mile End.[9] A special hospital was opened in Warren Street which cost a weekly average of £10 to run. By mid July 1786 some nineteen Negroes, all 'in a miserable state', suffering from a number of complaints, ranging from abscesses and fever to consumption, were cared for in the hospital.[10] Those admitted there were the most desperate of all the destitute black poor. Many arrived for treatment virtually naked; it was 'a common practice with these People to pawn or dispose of their Shirts before they come in the Hospital'.[11] Others, anxious to return to the colonies or to find berths at sea, were given financial assistance by the Committee. But this charitable work could not keep pace with the demands placed on it by the poor Blacks. By mid summer some 700 Negroes were regularly receiving sixpence a day from the two distribution points at opposite ends of the city.[12] So great was the pressure that even the regular payments towards relief work from the Treasury were immediately soaked up.[13] Within a year of the original scheme for helping the Negroes, almost 1,000 of them had turned to the relief offered jointly by the government and the philanthropists.[14] The Committee administering the funds discovered, as Sharp had before them, that charity was an inadequate solution to the diverse problems of the black population. Despite the sixpence a day given to any Negro in need, there were still large numbers 'in a perishing Condition, by diseases contracted through the severity of the late season and other causes'.[15]

A new solution was suggested to the Committee in May 1786

Two of the many black sailors on British ships in the 18th and 19th centuries

Two graphic comments of sexual relations between black and white

Back to Africa

by one Henry Smeathman, whose basic idea closely resembled Sharp's earlier plans for repatriation to Africa. The great attraction of Smeathman's scheme was that it offered to remove the Negroes (and their problems) completely. Furthermore the scheme possessed the added attraction of profitability. Any proposal to repatriate hundreds, if not thousands, of Negroes was clearly going to involve enormous expense and Smeathman's suggestion that the scheme could actually finance itself clinched the issue with the Committee. Unfortunately, his proposals were wildly optimistic. He was something of an eccentric; a man of great ambition and few talents. He had already spent some time in Sierra Leone, collecting botanical specimens (in the process picking up the nickname 'Flycatcher'), and later in Paris where he had turned to ballooning. In January 1786, giving evidence to a committee examining the possibility of establishing a convict colony in West Africa, Smeathman had asserted that any such scheme would cost 100 lives a month. Only weeks later he wrote to the Committee for the Relief of the Black Poor extolling the virtues of the same region as a place to deposit London's Negroes. This he offered to do for a mere £4 a head. By the charm of Smeathman's words Sierra Leone was converted from a fatally pestiferous land into one flowing with milk and honey.

'Such are the mildness and fertility of the climate and country, that a man possessed of clothing, an axe, a hoe, and a pocket knife, may soon place himself in an easy situation. All the clothing wanted is what decency requires; and the earth turned up of 2 or 3 inches, with a light hoe, produces any kind of grain.'[17] Smeathman's picture of this African pastoral ideal at first completely deceived the Committee; by the time they came to realize the truth, the Negroes in London took up the scheme with a zeal that made it difficult to resist. Both sides realized that Smeathman was lying only when the first wave of settlers stumbled from one disaster to another. But even then, some in England remained convinced by Smeathman's argument. How could anyone fail to prosper in the setting he described? The trusting Sharp, gullible to the end, when faced with the sad truth from Sierra Leone, could only comment: 'I cannot find that the Climate has been at all to blame; nothing but the intemperance of the people, and their enervating indolence in consequence of it.'[18]

The early enthusiasm of the Committee and the Blacks themselves was soon reinforced by support from the Treasury, who agreed to provide financial and logistic help with the settlement. That the government was prepared to commit itself to so expensive an undertaking is suggestive of their concern about the problems of the black community. The total cost was enormous, involving, in addition to the expense of equipping a migration of some hundreds, the allocation of Royal Navy vessels. In 1791 the cost was to rise further when the government undertook the transportation of Blacks from Canada to the embryonic settlement of Sierra Leone.[19]

Smeathman originally reported that among London's Negroes there was 'an anxious desire, of getting on board the Ship that may be appointed to carry them to the coast of Africa'.[20] As preparations for the expedition gathered momentum this eagerness became less pronounced. The Negroes, like the organizing Committee, had been beguiled by Smeathman. Since he died in July 1786 he was not on hand to answer the growing volume of criticism levelled against him. He had, said the Committee 'the art of telling his story very well and represented things in the most favourable light'.[21]

The most serious of the worries troubling prospective black emigrants was, as they claimed in a petition to the Committee, that 'it appears that there is no Place on the whole Coast of Africa where there can be any solid Security against Slavery'.[22] It was for this reason that the government eventually agreed to provide the settlers with arms. But to compound the doubts in the black community about the scheme, the Negroes got wind of the real intention of the government which was, to put it crudely, to dump the Negroes in the most convenient spot. Africa was only one of a variety of sites considered for the location of England's black population. In July the Treasury made it clear that the government was willing to countenance the transportation of the Blacks to any part of the empire. Accordingly, the Committee received proposals to dispatch them to New Brunswick, Great Inagua in the Bahamas,[23] Gambia,[24] and Nova Scotia.[25] The first rumours of these alternative proposals filtered down into the black community and 'gave them considerable uneasiness, as no Place whatsoever would be so agreeable to them as Sierra Leone'.[26] Having already had second thoughts about the scheme, the Negroes, when faced with the authorities' obvious determination to ship them out of the country at all costs, swung back behind Smeathman's mirage of an African paradise. The Committee had little alternative but to commit itself to the Sierra Leone scheme, which it knew to be faulty in conception and doubtful in potential.

In all these transactions the role of Granville Sharp was distinctive. While the government set out to give the settlers the wherewithal to survive, Sharp tried to provide them with a new social and political awareness needed in the new 'Province of Freedom'.[27] Sharp was very much a man of the Enlightenment. But the theories which he sought to introduce into Africa were not mere abstractions. Only one week after the settlers landed in Sierra Leone the Convention in Philadelphia began to wrestle with precisely the same problem; how best to reconstitute society and ultimately human behaviour. But even before the Americans had begun the task of erecting the delicate fabric of democracy, Sharp's *Short Sketch of the Temporary Regulations*, had laid down similar guidelines for London's emigrant Negroes.[28] His optimism may, in retrospect, seem enormously naive. But his was a distinctively eighteenth-century radical vision of man's basic rationality and perfectibility. Moreover it was a vision shared by many men on both sides of the Atlantic and so inspired events in Philadelphia that same summer. Two years later similar visions were to sweep all before them in France. Oddly enough, in 1787 it was felt that the first major reconstruction of human society could be achieved by former slaves transporting the idea of the European Enlightenment back to Africa. But the practical details of settlement were to prove much more prosaic, or sordid, than Sharp's regulations allowed.

In October 1786 three Royal Navy transports, the *Atlantic*, *Belisarius* and *Vernon*, arrived at Deptford to pick up the intended settlers. The government hoped, by cutting off relief to the Negroes, to oblige them to join the vessels, and were expecting some 750 to step aboard. Whatever the numbers, the Committee felt that embarkation could prove difficult, 'considering the disposition of the Blacks and their want of discipline'.[29] Those who arrived were in a shocking condition. Instructions were passed to the captains of the vessels that, on sailing, they were 'to give the new Cloaths to each of the Blacks and that their old ones be thrown overboard to prevent any infections'.[30] But neither government nor the Committee could persuade more than a fraction of the Negroes on relief to join the ships. After almost four months of waiting in the Thames, only 459 people had boarded the vessels, and of these only 344 were black (290 men, 43 women and 11 children).[31] Over the past few months 965 Negroes had been in receipt of help, some 20 per cent of whom were women.[32] In both groups there was a pronounced sexual imbalance but an even smaller proportion of local female Blacks was prepared to take the risk of resettlement.

While the overwhelming majority of Negroes who entered the ships remains anonymous, one of their company stood out. In the previous summer the Committee had thought itself lucky when Equiano had returned from yet another voyage and was prevailed on to join the undertaking as commissary for supplies.[33] From November 1786 to March 1787 he worked on board the three vessels and was immediately struck by the blatant abuses already in operation. Food, clothing, bedding, all ordered and paid for, had failed to reach the emigrants, but had instead simply gone to line the pockets of officials and speculators.[34] Equiano raised strong and persistent objections to the agents, to the naval authorities, to the government and to the newspapers. Naturally his complaints affected the black emigrants. On the first leg of the voyage, from the Thames to the south coast, Equiano, the captain reported, had been 'turbulent, and discontented, taking every means to actuate the minds of the Blacks to discord; and I am convinced that unless some means are taken to quell his spirit of sedition it will be fatal to the peace of the settlement'.[35] Predictably, Equiano was dismissed following this complaint and was put ashore at Plymouth, a fact which almost certainly saved his life. Sharp unfortunately was willing to believe the worst of Equiano, writing to his brother John that 'all the jealousies and animosities between the Whites and Blacks had subsided, and that the discontented persons had been left on shore at Plymouth'.[36]

The Government and the Committee were too deeply committed, both politically and financially, to allow Equiano's accurate allegations of corruption to interfere with their advanced scheme. Already some £10,000 had been invested in the expedition; the final figure was to be £15,000.[37] In February 1787 the convoy finally set sail for Africa, only to be battered by a Channel storm. While the *Vernon* underwent repairs in Torbay, the other two vessels waited in Plymouth. More than fifty of the original emigrants had already died on the ships; a further twenty-three ran away in Plymouth, much to the chagrin of local magistrates who complained to the Admiralty that 'a number of Black Men are come on shore'.[38] More Negroes were sent from London to fill the gaps, but when on 8 April the convoy finally set sail for Sierra Leone there were only 411 people on board; 459 had left London. The demoralizing events in British waters between October and April were an omen of things to come.

As the disastrous news from Africa filtered back to London, Sharp refused to accept the truth of the matter. 'I have had, hitherto, but melancholy Account of my poor little ill thriven swarthy Daughter, the unfortunate Colony to Sierra Leona. But I have however discovered that most of the Events have arisen from the Allowance of Rum.'[39] The truth was much more complex, and yet could have been predicted long before the settlers left England. The peace and prosperity which had never been theirs in England proved to be even more illusory in Africa. Landing on the eve of the rainy season, the Negroes wilted before an unusually heavy season. Within three months of arrival, one third had died from dysentery and fever,[40] a mortality rate which could stand comparison with the middle passage and West Indian 'seasoning', or acclimatization periods. Leaderless and, literally aimless, the prime concern of the Blacks, so recently languishing on the streets of London, was simple self-survival. In this most of them were unsuccessful. Early in September 1788 a mere 130 settlers were alive, as death, flight and, ironically, employment with the slave-traders, drastically reduced their numbers.

The white organizers in London were not the only people to hear of the settlers' plight. The Blacks who remained in England – those who had been wiser than the emigrants in their reservations about the scheme – were swift to draw their own conclusions. Ottobah Cugoano recorded the fear 'that they never will be settled as intended, in any permanent and peaceable way at Sierra Leone'. Rum apart, the reason was straightforward. The plan 'has neither altogether met with the credulous approbation of the Africans here, nor yet been sought after with any prudent and right plans by the promoters of it'.[41] In principle London's poor Blacks evidently supported the Sierra Leone scheme, but the initial doubts, now compounded by hard news of disasters from Africa, confirmed them in the wisdom of staying in England. 'Many more of the Black People still in this country,' claimed Cugoano, 'would have, with great gladness, embraced the opportunity, longing to reach their native land; but as the old saying is, A burnt child dreads the fire.'[42]

To settle in Africa was to expose oneself anew to the whole risk of enslavement. European traders and sailors, continued Cugoano, 'have such a prejudice against Black People that they use them more like asses than men, so that a Black Man is scarcely safe among them'.[43] Everyone involved in the scheme was acutely aware of the dangers. For this reason every emigrant was equipped with a parchment certificate in a tin box, certifying the bearer 'to be a good and faithful Loyal Subject of His said Majesty' and to be entitled to 'all the Emoluments, Liberties and Privileges appertaining to a Freeman of the Colony of Sierre Leone, or the Land of Freedom'.[44] Despite such obvious safeguards, fear, more than any other factor, had turned London's Negroes against the scheme: 'The wiser sort declined from all thoughts of it, unless they could hear of some better plan taking place for their security and safety.'[45] But short of total and effective abolition of the slave trade, what could be done to make their position safer?

The support of William Pitt's government was vital to the Sierra Leone scheme, yet its position was ambivalent. Encouragement and finance had been given to the settlement of a free black colony on the coast of Africa which was located only miles from slave-trading posts. The government made no efforts to discourage slave-trading in the region; indeed it had a vested interest in such trading, though the youthful Pitt was known to be personally opposed to it.[46] The apparent contradiction between these two policies of the same administration can be resolved by remembering that the government's prime object in encouraging resettlement was, as far as possible, to rid London of its black population. It was not noticeably over-anxious about what happened when the Negroes landed. Cugoano and his fellow Africans realized the government's real intentions. 'For can it be readily conceived that government would establish a free colony for them nearly on the spot, while it supports its forts and garrisons, to ensnare, merchandize, and to carry others into captivity and slavery.'[47]

Surprisingly, despite the fate of the first wave of settlers, Sharp was approached by others ready to leave. 'Numbers of people, both white and Black are daily applying to me to go there. . . . I have many of them on my hands', he reported to his brother John.[48] Late

Back to Africa

in March 1788 Granville Sharp was ready 'to send out a small ship with about 60 more Settlers'.[49] But once again the miniature settlement failed to go according to plan. Only thirty-nine settlers finally departed, of whom sixteen failed to reach Africa. When the new arrivals were added to the truncated first batch, fewer than 200 settlers comprised the total population. Since the prime purpose had been to remove one of London's social problems, the crucial consideration for both government and the Committee was that fewer than 400 Negroes had actually left England. At a cost in excess of £15,000, almost £40 a head, Smeathman's self-financing conjuring trick, designed to make the black community vanish, had turned into a prohibitively expensive fiasco. By the middle of December 1788, the first settlement – suitably named Granville Town – had been burnt to the ground by local Africans, and its population dispersed, after a confused dispute involving the settlers, slave-traders, the Royal Navy and the indigenous Africans.[50] So ended the first painful efforts to create a free African colony from the displaced English Negroes.

In 1791 the Sierra Leone Company was incorporated by Act of Parliament; a more organized start was made, and new vigorous leadership set out to piece together the fragments of the first community.[51] In the spring of 1792, when English attention had been forcibly diverted to France, more than 1,000 new black settlers descended on the colony. They came, not from Paddington or Mile End, but from Nova Scotia and New Brunswick.[52] The shaky foundations of the new colony, designed to solve London's black problems, were thus precariously laid by immigrants from North America, whose problems in many respects paralleled those of their London fellows. 'When all had arrived, the whole colony assembled in worship, to proclaim to the dark continent whence they or their forebears had been carried in chains:

> The day of Jubilee is come;
> Return ye ransomed sinners home.'[53]

The reluctance among England's Blacks to step forward was only partly related to the weaknesses of the scheme itself, news of which soon spread via the West Indies to mainland America.[54] But the most tantalizing question about this emigration is, why should Canadian Blacks, who had shared similar loyalist experiences in the American war with many of England's Negroes, come forward so promptly and in three times the numbers? At an obvious level, extremes of climate did not aggravate the hardships of English Blacks to quite the same extent as those of the Canadians. In fact it was climatic factors which led to the abandonment of plans to ship England's Negroes to Canada.[55] Moreover the Canadians were scattered among the bleak villages and rural settlements of the maritime provinces; the English were largely concentrated in a densely packed urban area which had a clearly defined black community long before the loyalists arrived after 1783. It was into this existing community structure in London, with its traditions of cooperation, sense of identity and self-reliance, that the newly arrived loyalist Negroes moved. No such facilities for assimilation into a local black subculture existed for those Blacks forced to settle in Canada.[56] A majority of London's Negroes was evidently happier to live as members of this poor community rather than face the serious challenge of African settlement. Rumours of alternative government plans must have simply added to the latent black reluctance to leave.

The self-awareness and self-confidence among England's Negroes, noted so regularly by white contemporaries, proved to be a great disadvantage for the Sierra Leone plans. After 1791 the new Company required tough, hardworking but obedient and malleable settlers. But English Negroes showed signs of truculent resistance to the words of their white leaders. When John Clarkson, brother of the more famous Thomas, went to Canada to recruit black settlers for Sierra Leone, he wrote back to the Company 'to request that no Blacks from England be sent lest they should hurt the morals of the rest'.[57] This was of course the traditional and most prominent complaint levelled at Negroes in England. Their experiences and life style in England affected their behaviour and induced personal and collective qualities which white men took to be subversive, particularly when they settled in the West Indies and Africa. It has to be remembered that the white humanitarians were looking for qualities which must have been rare among their fellow Englishmen and even more unusual among the Blacks. The religiously zealous Sharp, for example, wished to see his repatriated Africans lose all semblance of their native customs and behave instead like English gentlemen. Sharp lectured one emigrant with accusations 'that you are much addicted to the Company of bad Women : and that you could not be restrained from admitting them to your Chamber, even when you were living under the Governor's Roof.'[58] Sharp demanded exemplary behaviour, for the emigrants were, in his eyes, more than settlers; they were the living substance of a daring social experiment. In reality however they were largely desperate refugees, cast from one alien society to another. They asked of Sierra Leone little more than peace and security, and the chance to salvage a decent life from the fragments of past brutal experiences.

Apart from the lack of security against re-enslavement the most obvious flaw in the Sierra Leone scheme was the belief that the colony was 'home' for London's Negroes. 'Back to Africa' lost its appeal given the geographical reality of West Africa and the diffuse origins of the emigré black population. The projected area of settlement occupied a minute patch of land on the vast West African coastline. Moreover for many, Sierra Leone was very far from their home. By the middle and late century slaves were recruited along some thousands of miles of coastline and a network of paths and rivers which fanned eastward deep into the interior of the continent.[59] To many Negroes living in England, Sierra Leone was one step nearer home, rather than home itself. Cugoano admitted that many of his fellow Blacks wanted to go back,[60] but such a return remained pointless and positively dangerous if the home region was still plagued by slave-traders. Furthermore, since many of the Negroes had suffered the trauma of family separations, on board ship or in the New World, the prospect of returning alone to a place of miserable memories must have been painful.

What proportion of England's Negroes were born in Africa remains unknown, but a sizeable number were non-Africans. Creoles born in the colonies or those, like Sancho's children, born and bred in England and knowing only English society, would have had little reason to heed the call to Africa; still less those born in exile of racially mixed families. Blacks more closely assimilated to English society were nonetheless influenced by their African heritage, particularly since they lived side by side with native Africans. But Africa was not 'home'. Neither was England – or the West Indies – in any meaningful sense. It was to be years before the Negro could live as a truly free man in the West Indies, while in England the rejection by white society of the black minority lay at the very heart of the Sierra Leone scheme. England's Negroes were thus trapped

Black and White

in a social vacuum. They were, by and large, homeless people, living as unwelcome guests in a house of bondage. But even that was preferable to recapture or a miserable death, on the equally foreign shore of Sierra Leone.

Notes

CHAPTER NINE: *Back to Africa*

1. 17 May 1786. Memorial of Henry Smeathman, T.I. 631. 1304, (P.R.O.).
2. For fuller details of 18th century London see M. D. George, *London Life in the Eighteenth Century*; George Rudé, *Hanoverian London*, London, 1971; L. Radzinowicz, *History of English Criminal Law*, 4 vols, London, 1948–68.
3. Hoare, 260.
4. Sharp Papers (1783?), Cupboard 6, drawer 13.
5. See in particular E. P. Thompson, *Making of the English Working Class*, Gollancz, 1963; G. S. Veitch, *The Genesis of Parliamentary Reform*, London, 1913; Caroline Robbins, *The Eighteenth Century Commonwealthman*, Harvard University Press, 1959.
6. Johnson V. J. Asiegbu, *Slavery and the Politics of Liberation, 1787–1861*, London, Longman, 1971, 3.
7. Fyfe, *History*, 14.
8. ibid.; Asiegbu, 3.
9. 17 June 1786, Minutes of the Committee for Relief of the Black Poor (hereafter, Minutes), T.I. 632, 1513.
10. 10 July 1786, Minutes, T.I. 633, 1707.
11. Hospital Expenses, 20–26 May 1786, T.I. 632, 1623.
12. 28 June 1786, Minutes, T.I. 632, 1623.
13. Accounts, T.I. 631, 1359.
14. 'Alphabetical List of Blacks.' T.I. 638.
15. 17 May 1786, Memorial of Henry Smeathman, T.I. 631, 1304.
16. Fyfe, *History*, 14–15.
17. Henry Smeathman, *Substance of a Plan of Settlement*, London, 1786.
18. Granville Sharp to John Sharp, 19 January 1788, Sharp Papers, Cupboard 6, drawer 11.
19. Winks, 91.

20. 17 May 1786, Memorial of Henry Smeathman, T.I. 631, 1304.
21. 9 August 1786, Minutes, T.I. 634, 2012.
22. ibid.
23. 15 July 1786, Minutes, T.I. 633. 1707.
24. 28 July 1786, Minutes, T.I. 634. 1964.
25. ibid.
26. Petition, 15 July 1786, T.I. 633. 1815.
27. For details of this, and everything else on Sierra Leone, see Christopher Fyfe's masterly book; *History*, 16.
28. ibid.
29. 24 October 1786, Minutes, T.I. 638.
30. 1 December 1786, Minutes, T.I. 638.
31. 27 February 1786, Navy Office to the Treasury, T.I. 643.
32. List of Negroes, T.I. 638.
33. Equiano, 1789, ii, 231–2.
34. ibid, ii, 234–5.
35. 21 March 1786, Capt. Thompson to Admiralty, T.I. 643.
36. Granville Sharp to John Sharp, 23 June 1787, Sharp Papers, Cupboard 6, drawer 11.
37. Fyfe, *History*, 18; Navy Office, 26 April 1787, T.I. 645.
38. 2 April 1787, Navy Office to Treasury, T.I. 644.
39. Granville Sharp to John Sharp, 31 October 1787, Sharp Papers, Cupboard 6, drawer 11.
40. Fyfe, *History*, 20.
41. Cugoano, 139.
42. ibid., 141.
43. ibid.
44. Certificate, T.I. 636, 2430.
45. Cugoano, 141.
46. 21 April, 1788, Sharp Papers, Box 56, Book H.
47. Cugoano, 142.
48. Granville Sharp to John Sharp, 18 January 1788, Sharp Papers, Cupboard 6, drawer 11.
49. Granville Sharp to John Sharp, 22 March 1788, Sharp Papers, Cupboard 6, drawer 11.
50. Fyfe, *History*, 24–5.
51. ibid., 26–31.
52. ibid., 31–7.
53. ibid., 37.
54. Samuel Hopkins to Granville Sharp, 15 January 1789, Sharp Papers, Box 54.
55. Winks, 62.
56. ibid., 29–47.

57. Quoted in Granville Sharp to John Sharp, 14 January 1792, Sharp Papers, Cupboard 6, drawer 11.
58. Letter, 18 January 1800, Sharp Papers, Box 54.
59. See for example Curtin, *The Slave Trade*, ch. 4.
60. Cugoano, 141.

CHAPTER TEN

Black Caricature: The Roots of Racialism

Negroes were a favourite target of graphic cartoonists in the eighteenth century. The physical features, social characteristics, verbal intonations and the alleged 'natural' abilities or inabilities of the Blacks were frequently reduced to a grotesque shape by English caricaturists from Hogarth to Cruickshank. The mythology of the Blacks – as a species and as individuals – was perpetuated by cartoonists who added to and exaggerated some of the existing stereotyped images.

Another generally unconsidered type of caricature was even more influential than the graphic school in moulding a popular image of the Negro in the English mind. This was to be found in the literary tradition during the four centuries separating early travel narratives from modern racialist writing and thought. Hundreds of books, tracts, newspapers and magazines have dealt with the Negro to produce a cumulative image so absurd, so removed from reality that it belongs more to caricature, calumny and lampoon than it does to descriptive analysis. To quote the most obvious example, at the zenith of eighteenth-century graphic caricature, a flood of literature about the Negro emerged from the plantocratic writers which was the literary counterpart and complement to the work of the artists. But literary caricature, while reaching a peak during and immediately after the campaign for abolition and emancipation, had roots which went back to the pre-colonial world, and exerted an influence, in an uneven but unbroken line to the present day.

The purveyors of racialist thought in the eighteenth and early nineteenth centuries drew much of their inspiration from 'factual' material, from travel accounts dating from the sixteenth century. In their turn these accounts, as we have seen, had been profoundly influenced by speculative writing of an even earlier date. The literary caricature of the central period 1770 to 1860 in its turn influenced the emergence of more modern racialist thought. The caricatured writing of that period thus occupies a crucial role in the growth of English racialist thought, for it employed traditional and, in some cases, ancient ideas about black humanity, and put them in a more coherent form.

The Negro is possessed of passions not only strong but ungovernable; a mind dauntless, warlike and unmerciful; a temper extremely irascible; a disposition indolent, selfish and deceitful; fond of joyous sociality, riotous mirth and extravagant shew. He has certain portions of kindness for his favourites, and affections for his connections; but they are sparks which emit a glimmering light through the thick gloom that surrounds them, and which, in every ebullition of anger or revenge, instantly disappear. Furious in his love as in his hate; at best, a terrible husband, a harsh father and a precarious friend. A strong and unalterable affection for his countrymen and fellow passengers in particular seems to be the most amiable passion in the Negro breast. ... As to all the other fine feelings of the soul, the Negro, as far as I have been able to perceive, is nearly deprived of them.[1]

This description of the Negro, in the *Gentleman's Magazine* of 1788, perhaps the most popular and influential periodical of the day, contains all the major themes. The Negro was held to be peculiarly sexual, musical, stupid, indolent, untrustworthy and violent. This view was not original or even extreme, for its basic ingredients can be found scattered through numerous publications from the mid-sixteenth century. Similar sentiments were to appear until the mid-nineteenth century, finding their apotheosis in the racialist writing of Carlyle and Trollope.

While the Negro became the object of particularly acute enquiry in the late eighteenth and early nineteenth centuries, he had intermittently occupied a special place in the attention of English writers and thinkers since the first European explorations in West Africa. The African's physical, social and 'natural' characteristics were described, explained and remembered. By the mid-seventeenth century, as the English New World colonies underwent an economic revolution made possible by black labour, the English literary treatment of the Negro concentrated on the relationship between the African and slavery. In order to justify both the growth of the slave trade and the development of slave societies, writers continued to focus

Black Caricature: The Roots of Racialism

their interests on the African and his homeland. By elaborating on, or inferring from, what was known of African life, supporters of slavery were able to present apparently convincing arguments in favour of black slavery. Much of their argument, based on anthropological or even biblical evidence, was selective, apologetic and, as often as not, totally inaccurate. Whatever its origin and degree of accuracy, the case of the slave lobby was important in keeping the African in the public-political eye. In the years after 1770 the African was subjected to even closer attention by the two powerful interest groups, the humanitarian and slave lobbies, in their respective efforts to win public support. Although emancipation finally dispelled the bitterness of political debate from the discussion about the Negro, the fate of the sugar colonies in the 1840s and 1850s maintained English interest in the role, and in the very nature, of the black African and his descendant. When Carlyle and Trollope, for example, told their armies of readers about the collapse of the West Indies, much of their analysis took as a point of departure and as a fundamental explanation, the alleged natural and immutable features of the Negro. Trollope's visit to the West Indies took place a mere six years before the violence of the Jamaican revolt of 1865 and its bloody aftermath. The subsequent controversy about the role of Governor Eyre in the butchery of the Jamaican Negroes became a political *cause célèbre*, which sharply divided society and revived, in a particularly virulent form, many of the traditional arguments used by the slave lobby about the Negro.

Only seventeen years separated the Eyre controversy from the re-entry of the African into English domestic politics, with the invasion of Egypt in 1882.[2] Thereafter as vast tracts of land turned an imperial red, the Negro once again became a subject of intense political and intellectual debate. The need to justify and explain the new empire, coupled to the development of Social Darwinism and newer more 'scientific' approaches to the study of race, led to a far-ranging debate about the Negro and other non-white peoples. In many respects the late nineteenth century debate about race, which found a particularly acute focus in the Negro, was similar to that of the eighteenth century. While both debates were separated by a century of enormous change in racial thinking, they are nonetheless linked by common factors. My purpose here is to illustrate some of the prime elements of the caricature image which cut across chronological divisions and which act as links in the continuing process of misunderstanding of the Negro.

Unable to understand the different and varied nature of West Indian tribal societies, Englishmen in West Africa from the sixteenth century placed great stress on the sexuality and 'immorality' of the African. Remembering too that African nakedness loomed large in the early English impressions of Africans, it can be appreciated why importance came to be attached to the concept of black sexuality. The view of the Negro as endowed with great sexual powers was later exaggerated by the development of slave society in the West Indies, where demographic factors led to patterns of morality which seemed to fit no moral order recognized by the English.

The authoritative work of the Arab Leo Africanus, translated into English in 1600, brought home to the English the peculiar morality of West Africans. 'They have among them great swarmes of Harlots among them; whereupon a man may easily conjecture their manner of living.'[3] This view, coupled with the idea of the African as an uncivilized being, occurs time and again in early English writings on Africa. Another contemporary Englishman alleged that the Africans 'are very greedie eaters, and no less drinkers, and very lecherous, and theevish, and much addicted to uncleanliness: one man hath as many wives as hee is able to keepe and maintaine.'[4] Sexual immorality among Africans, according to another English source, bordered on the perverted. 'They are beastly in their living for they have men in women's apparel whom they keep among their wives.'[5] English writers continually found an explanation for sexual activity among the Africans in the alleged size of the African penis. Mandingo men, wrote Richard Jobson in 1623 were 'furnist with such members as are after a sort burthensome unto them'.[6] From that day to now, this particular belief has been commonplace and has proved influential in moulding relations between black and white. Its widespread acceptance can be seen in Shakespeare's use of black sexual imagery.

West Indian planters later added to the myths about black sexuality with stories gleaned from their partial experiences of slave society.[7] One such man, Bryan Edwards, Jamaican planter and English politician, was among the most influential and, odd as it may sound in the light of his writings of the 1790s, one of the least extreme planters when writing about the Negro. But he too dealt with the subject more in terms of caricature than reality. 'The Negroes in the West Indies, both men and women, would consider it as the great exertion of tyranny, and the most cruel of all hardships, to be compelled to confine themselves to a single connection with the other sex. Their passion', Edwards continued, 'is mere animal desire, implanted by the great Author of all things for the preservation of the species. This the Negroes, without doubt, possess in common with the rest of the animal creation, and they indulge it, as inclination prompts, in an almost promiscuous intercourse with the other sex.' [8]

Plantocratic literature tended to be infused with the paranoia which resulted from their style of life in the colonies. The fearful hate which they openly manifested towards their black property reached new heights in the late eighteenth century under pressure from the humanitarians. In the process no one expressed more fully and bitterly the plantocratic caricature of black sexuality than Edward Long, friend and associate of Bryan Edwards and himself a Jamaican planter. Long's *History of Jamaica* (1774) has always been viewed as a classic analysis of colonial society, but rarely has it been seen in its other equally important role, as a landmark in the evolution of English racialist thought. The Negro's 'faculties of smell', according to Long, 'are truly bestial, nor less their commerce with the other sexes; in these acts they are libidinous and shameless as monkeys, or baboons. The equally hot temperament of their women has given probability to the charge of their admitting these animals frequently to their embrace. An example of this intercourse once happened, I think, in England.' [9] Throughout his writing, Long went out of his way to equate the Negro with the animal kingdom; to show that in appearances and responses they belonged more to the animal kingdom than to humanity. As far as black sexuality is concerned Long merely added a new, more bitter twist to myths which were already widely believed in the English-speaking world.

By the early nineteenth century the English took it for granted that Negroes were promiscuous and strongly sexed. One even explained the low life expectancy among slaves by 'the premature intercourse of the sexes and the very early and excessive debauchery'.[10] In reality the causes of slave morality were rooted not in black 'immorality' but in the appalling physical conditions which dominated enslavement, transportation and life on the plantations.

By this time however English writers who concerned themselves with black affairs sought an explanation for black social problems not in social terms but solely in terms of the African's individual 'characteristics'. Moreover the English tended to view these alleged characteristics as universal qualities, possessed by Negroes everywhere. This was perhaps the most damaging legacy of the process of black caricature; generations of Englishmen came to see Negroes as a species undifferentiated by time or place.

Caricatured images were largely responsible for the emergence of stereotyped roles for Negroes in white society. The English treated the Negro in such a way that he had no alternative but to behave in a way expected of him; to live up to the role imposed on him. Thus on plantations slaves rarely settled down to stable monogamous relationships, not because they were by nature promiscuous, but for the basic reason that sexual imbalance and the movement of slaves between different properties made such stable relationships virtually impossible. Similarly among Negroes in England, shifting relations with poor white women were more common than stable relations with women of their own colour. Once again, the reasons were primarily demographic. But in dealing with both situations Englishmen explained black social behaviour in terms of the Negro's alleged natural qualities, in this case his 'promiscuity'.

An equally pronounced theme has been the emphasis on black indolence. Physical conditions both in West Africa and the West Indies, so inimical to sustained work by white men, were assumed to induce an uncontrollable lethargy. Moreover Englishmen tended to believe that the natural richness of tropical soil and vegetation could be tapped with little human effort. Negroes, it was thought, had little more to do than eat what grew naturally around them. It was this particular myth which proved so tempting a proposition for would-be emigrants to Sierra Leone in 1787.[11] Geophysical conditions were equally fruitful on the other side of the Atlantic and visitors to the West Indies were staggered, as the casual visitor still is, by the luxuriant growth of fruit and vegetation. In both regions nature had evidently endowed the Negro with bountiful riches – or so it was thought. The Negro, Thomas Carlyle wrote in 1849, 'by working about half-an-hour a day ... can supply himself, by aid of sun and soil, with as much as will suffice'.[12]

While the natural conditions of the two areas might provide a

Black Caricature: The Roots of Racialism

plausible setting for the myth of black indolence, its greatest strength was drawn from the need to justify slavery. Without the rigours and restraints of slavery it was felt that the Black would revert to his natural sloth. They 'do no more work, in general, than they are compelled to do by the terrors of punishment'.[13] Edward Long predictably put the point in his usual extreme fashion. 'A planter would as soon expect to hear that sugar-canes and pineapples flourish the year round, in open-air, upon Hounslow Heath, as that Negroes when freed would be brought into the like necessity or disposition to hire themselves for plantation labour. . . . Idleness, it has been well observed, is the sure consequence of cheap and easy living; and none will labour, who have the means of idleness in their power.'[14] Long took as proof of his case the fate of the freed slaves in London. The view that a 'dissolute, idle, profligate crew repose themselves here in ease and indolence',[15] seemed to give living testimony to the belief in black indolence.

Another of Long's contemporaries commented on London's Negroes that 'not one in a hundred of them would apply steadily to labour'.[16] Once again Englishmen simply refused to look for the social origins of black behaviour but were satisfied to accept surface appearances without looking for underlying causes.

Soon after slaves had been emancipated throughout the empire the ailing West Indian sugar economy collapsed; all the worst fears and predictions of the planters seemed to have been fulfilled. Black freedom coincided with (and therefore, in the minds of Englishmen, caused) West Indian ruin. While this correlation is beguilingly simple, it ignores the complex structural economic changes already in train long before the granting of black freedom.[17] Like their eighteenth century predecessors, nineteenth century commentators on the West Indies looked not to the social-economic roots of the problem, but to black characteristics. Indolence among Negroes, for long used as political ammunition by the planters, was now used to explain the collapse of the sugar system. Carlyle, whose voice was heeded in a variety of circles in Victorian England, put the blame for the West Indian collapse firmly on the Black. He conjured up the vision of a 'black gentleman', 'with rum-bottle in hand . . . no breeches on his body, pumpkin at discretion, and the fruitfulest region of the earth going back to jungle around him'.[18] Even the dignified rebuttal of this view by Carlyle's former friend John Stuart

Mill, was insufficient to correct the impressions left by one of the most nakedly racialist tracts to be laid before the English reading public. After the Morant Bay revolt of 1865 it was scarcely surprising that Carlyle should lead the gadarene rush of English writers who supported Governor Eyre's butchery of the former slaves.

Carlyle's racialist views were kept alive by Anthony Trollope who, after a West Indian tour for the Post Office in 1858, similarly conveyed to his white readership a view of black indolence. The West Indian Negro, he alleged, 'is idle, unambitious as to worldly position, sensual, and content with little. ... He lies under the mango-tree, and eats the luscious fruit in the sun; he sends his black urchin up for breakfast and behold the family table is spread. He pierces a cocoa-nut and lo! there is his beverage. He lies on the grass, surrounded by oranges, bananas, and pine-apples.' [19] In the ten years between Carlyle's work and Trollope's the Negro's food had changed from pumpkin to more exotic fruits; a transmutation all the easier because it took place primarily in the author's excitable imagination.

The more grotesque assertions about black indolence will be familiar to anyone conversant with present-day West Indian middle-class society. Furthermore this myth has since travelled the Atlantic and passed into modern Britain. The belief that Negroes are basically lazy is as widely spread as the myth of potent black sexuality, despite an abundance of evidence, from both slave and free societies, to the contrary. In Brazil for example it was the skills of imported Africans, notably in metalwork, which laid the basis for new native industries, while the pioneering bravery of escaped slaves pushed the Brazilian frontiers into the distant interior of the continent.[20] In British colonies it was the blistering work undertaken by generations of Africans which had made possible the transformation of the West Indian sugar colonies. Later, after emancipation, while West Indian black labour was no longer employed in the interests of the masters, the initiative and skills of former slaves were responsible for the emergence of a new Creole agricultural society, despite the appalling conditions which freedom entailed. Jamaican Negroes, wrote William Sewell, a visiting journalist from the *New York Times*, 'are not cared for; they perish miserably in country districts for want of medical aid; they are not instructed; they have no opportunities to improve themselves in agriculture or mechanics; every effort is made to check a spirit of independence, which in the

African is counted a heinous crime, but in all other people is regarded as a lofty virtue and the germ of natural courage, enterprise and progress'.[21] Sewell's analysis was nearer to reality than was the portrayal of the Negroes as indolent beings living off the fruits of nature.

Closely related to this belief in natural indolence was the English conviction that Negroes were basically stupid; so stupid that they failed even to perceive the disastrous consequences of their own indolence. Some self-appointed 'friends' of the Negro were influenced by this view. One early humanitarian wrote that: 'The dull stupidity of the Negro leaves him without any desire for instruction. Whether the Creator originally formed these black people a little lower than other men, or that they have lost their intellectual powers through disuse, I will not assume the province of determining; but certain it is that a *new Negro* (as those lately imported from Africa are called), is a complete definition of indolent stupidity.' The logical deduction from this was clear. 'The stupid obstinance of the Negroes may indeed make it always necessary to subject them to severe discipline from their masters.'[22] Thus evidence of stupidity, like evidence of indolence, was carefully used to reinforce the justice of the slave system.

Evidence for black stupidity was generally drawn from the absence of those achievements, whether in Africa, the West Indies or England, which Europeans recognized as civilized accomplishments. No less a person than David Hume seized on the dearth of black achievements as proof of the superiority of white society. 'I am apt to suspect the Negroes ... to be naturally inferior to the Whites. There never was a civilized nation of any other complexion than white, or even any individual eminent in either action, or speculation. No ingenious manufacturers among them, no arts, no sciences. There are Negro slaves dispersed all over Europe, of which none ever discovered any symptoms of ingenuity.'[23] The Negro as a 'poor blockhead' was a recognizable figure in the English imagination even before Carlyle gave a powerful boost to the flagging dynamic of black caricature.

The myth of stupidity, like most other themes in the English misunderstanding of the Negro, found its origins on the coast of Africa, and in the West Indian slave societies. Hostile white observers took isolated circumstances of black life and expanded them into mistaken generalizations. 'In general', wrote Edward Long, 'they are void of genius and seem almost incapable of making progress in civility or science.' The basis for this claim lay in what he had read about African society. Africans, he concluded, 'are represented by all authors as the vilest of the human kind, to which they have little more pretensions of resemblance than what arises from their exterior form.'[24] To Long and his ilk, black stupidity was self-evident. Had Negroes not been stupid they would have revealed their talents and reached the level of European accomplishments. Of the millions of Africans known to the Europeans, few had been encountered who 'comprehend any thing of mechanic arts, or manufacture; and even these, for the most part, are said to perform their work in very bungling and slovenly manner, perhaps not better than an oran-outang might'.[25]

Edward Long pushed black caricature to a new extreme, in particular giving a new twist to the old belief that Africans were more animal than human. From the first days of the exploration of West Africa Europeans had been particularly fascinated by the animal they knew as the 'oran-outang'. To use the words of Winthrop Jordan, it was a coincidence that 'Englishmen were introduced to the anthropoid apes and to Negroes at the same time and in the same place'.[26] From the sixteenth century to the late eighteenth there was a consequent European curiosity about the possibility of an evolutionary relationship between the African and the ape. At one bizarre level, it was for instance widely believed that sexual relations took place between Africans and apes.[27] English residents in West Africa were largely responsible for the dissemination of this myth. James Houston, medical officer for the African Company on the coast reported of Africans that 'their natural Temper is barbarously cruel, selfish, and deceitful, and their Government equally barbarous and uncivil; and consequently the Men of greatest Eminency among them, are those who are most capable of being the greatest Rogues. . . . As for their Customs they exactly resemble their Fellow Creatures and Natives, the Monkeys.'[28]

The association between the African and the ape was a constant source of speculation in eighteenth century literature; nowhere more clearly than in Edward Long's work which made continual and pointed reference to the physical and social features of the 'oran-outang'. Understandably, Long's argument came to the traditional conclusion – but one tinged with a bitterness peculiar to him. 'Ludicrous as it may seem I do not think that an oran-outang husband would be any dishonour to a Hottentot female.' The 'oran-outang' 'has in form a much nearer resemblance to the Negro race, than the latter bear to white men'.[29] Long undoubtedly believed his own assertions but they also had the much more useful purpose of adding an important new dimension to the slave lobby's propaganda against the abolitionists. Assertions of the animal inferiority of the Negro turned aside the abolitionist question 'Am I not a man and a brother?' In political terms however the abolitionists were able to win more and more support to their side of the argument, convincing increasing numbers of Englishmen that the Negro was indeed a man and a brother.

Yet another school of thought conceded the Negro's basic humanity but tended to regard him as an unmanageable savage who did not deserve the equality of treatment demanded for him by the abolitionists. Sixteenth century accounts of the savagery of African life [30] were added to in the succeeding two centuries. In 1773, for example, John Norris, a slave ship captain from Liverpool, produced a 'descriptive' account of Africa, reprinted in 1789, which added to the view of the savage continent. Norris claimed that Bossa Ahadee, king of Dahomey, was 'absolute master of the life, liberty, and property, of every person in his dominion and that he sports with them, with the most savage and wanton cruelty. Piles of their heads are placed as ornaments before his palace on festival days ... and the floors leading to his apartments are strewed with their bodies.'[31] Few slavers tried to assess their own role in contributing to whatever savagery existed in West Africa; fewer still made comparisons between black savagery and their own inhumanity towards their cargoes. Edward Long, in a vein similar to Norris's, wanted the worst of both worlds; to prove both that the Africans were animal-like and also to prove that African society was uncivilized. 'If no rules of civil polity exist among them, does it not betray an egregious want of common sense ... ? The jurisprudence, the customs and manners of the Negroes, seem perfectly suited to the measure of their narrow intellect. Laws have justly been regarded as the masterpiece of human genius: what are we to think of those societies of men, who either have none, or such only as are irrational and ridiculous?'[32]

The centre of the argument that black society was savage depended upon a portrait of the Negro as a creature in a state of nature, without the romantic gloss of the noble savage. He was, it was alleged, so different from the European, that even his sense and sensibilities were different; 'the feelings quite natural to a Briton are not the feelings of the African'.[33] Furthermore, proponents of the slave trade argued that Africans had benefited by the slave trade, in being moved from a continent where barbarism was a common experience.

> We're the children of Cham! He his father offended
> Who gave him the curse, which to us is descended
> 'A servant of servants' alas! is our curse;
> And as bad as it is, it has saved us from worse.[34]

Both abolitionists and the slave lobby were agreed on at least one point; that slavery had made possible the conversion to Christianity of pagan Africans. Both sides agreed that African heathenism was unfortunate and sometimes abominable. 'They are said to have as many religions almost as they have deities, and these are innumerable,' wrote Edward Long.[35] Nonetheless abolitionists were in a dilemma. While they welcomed the chance to convert the Africans, they could scarcely support the slave trade for this purpose.

Another point of contact between abolitionists and the slave lobby was their joint belief in another area of black mythology, namely that Negroes were peculiarly musical people. By an odd twist of historical progression, this view has now been adopted by the black community on both sides of the Atlantic. But its origins lie deep in the caricature image of the Negro created in the seventeenth and eighteenth centuries. Writing in 1793 Bryan Edwards noted: 'An opinion prevails in Europe that they [Negroes] possess organs peculiarly adapted to the science of music; but this I believe is an ill-founded idea.'[36] Edwards's scepticism was exceptional. Evangelicals for instance saw black musicality as an ideal opportunity for conversion to Christianity. 'The Negroes in general have an ear for music, and might without much trouble be taught to sing hymns.'[37] John Wesley too had noted the opening to religion afforded by black music. 'I cannot but observe that the Negroes above all of the human species I ever knew, have the nicest ear for music. They have a kind of ecstatic delight in psalmody.'[38] Credibility seemed to be added to this myth by the testimony and behaviour of Africans themselves.

Black Caricature: The Roots of Racialism

Equiano told his English readers: 'We are almost a nation of dancers, musicians, and poets. Thus every great event ... is celebrated in public dances which are accompanied with songs and music suited to the occasion.'[39] In this instance Equiano explained African love of music; it was not a natural genetic fact but a socially and culturally acquired quality through which his own people represented their history, military victories and folk-lore. Few English commentators saw black music in these terms, preferring instead the traditional myths. They seemed to be reinforced in this by the emergence in England of black musicians both inside the black community and as entertainers trained for English enjoyment. In the mid-nineteenth century Henry Mayhew calculated that fifty Ethiopian serenaders made a living on the streets of London.[40]

But the presence of black musicians in no way bore out the myth for, believing Negroes to be peculiarly suited to music, the English simply encouraged them to become musicians. In effect Negroes were fitted into a stereotyped role earmarked for them by white society. 'The fondness of the Negroes for music and the proficiency they sometimes make in it, with little or no instruction is too well known to need support.'[41] It was Thomas Carlyle who extended this element in black caricature to the extremes of racial denigration. After fulminating over the condition of the West Indies following emancipation, Carlyle continued, 'Do I then hate the Negro? No; except when the soul is killed out of him, I decidedly like poor Quashee; and find him a pretty kind of man. With a pennyworth of oil, you can make a handsome glossy thing of Quashee, when the soul is not killed in him! A swift, supple fellow; a merry-hearted, grinning, dancing, singing, affectionate kind of creature, with a great deal of melody and amenability in his composition.'[42] For all his hyperbole Carlyle was simply putting in an extreme form a belief which was already commonplace. Anthony Trollope expressed himself with less extremism but his portrait of the Negro was little less caricatured.

Only five years after Trollope's denigration of the Jamaican Negro there occurred in the island a minor black uprising followed by a savage white repression, which constitutes a turning point in the history of English attitudes towards the Negro. In the October of 1865 in the small eastern Jamaican town of Morant Bay local disturbances triggered off wider black unrest. In the military and legal repression which followed some 500 free Jamaicans lost their lives and many more were severely punished.[43] The Royal Commission [44] which followed was extremely critical of the behaviour of the Governor, Edward Eyre, whose actions became the centre of heated political debate. After the events of 1865 English racial antagonisms crystallized more clearly than at any time since the collapse of the slave lobby.

Eyre found enormous support for his legalized savagery, notably from Ruskin, Tennyson, Kingsley, Dickens and Carlyle. Their public utterances and those from sympathetic newspapers revived the very worst English attitudes towards the Negro. Even those who expressed reservations about the handling of the Jamaican revolt often fell back on the old stereotyped views. The *Pall Mall Gazette* for example, generally sympathetic towards the Jamaicans, called the 'poor deluded Negro' 'the most inflammable and unreasoning population on earth'.[45] A missionary spoke of 'the natural tendency of the negro, when free, to sink and drag down those who try to save him'.[46] Negroes, said *The Times*, were 'careless, credulous, and dependent; easily excited, easily duped, easily frightened'.[47] To read the response to Morant Bay is to be pitched back a full century and to imagine that the efforts of the philanthropists to restore the reality of black humanity had been in vain.[48] For the Jamaicans the immediate result was the removal of the franchise from the 'ignorant and irresponsible rabble' [49] and the imposition of Crown Colonial rule.

The political consequence within the growing British empire was the abandonment of any idea of black equality and in its place there evolved a passionately held belief in separate status for colonial peoples. In the process humanitarianism collapsed under the popular resurgence of openly racialist propaganda. Britons, alleged *The Times*, had been deceived by the humanitarians into believing that 'the world was made for Sambo, and that the sole use of sugar was to sweeten Sambo's existence'.[50] Echoes of Carlyle's earlier extremism began to creep into the public utterances of politicians and press. Once again, in English eyes, Negroes were lazy, savage, lustful and domineering and black caricature was raised to the level of acceptable political debate, thereby preventing any reasoned assessment of the black problem.

The revolt of 1865, as Christine Bolt has pointed out, was a major crisis of British liberalism. It was also the catalyst for the revival, though certainly not for the creation, of Victorian racialism. It is only partially true to claim that, by the 1860s 'the upper and middle class of the English people, especially the latter, had come to believe that Negroes were innately inferior beings'.[51] They had felt much the same way a century before, and it has seriously to be asked whether this belief had ever really died. It seems more than likely that under the pressure of philanthropy, the overt racialism of many simply submerged, until brought to the surface once again by the Indian mutiny, the Maori wars and finally the Morant Bay revolt. A similar sequence of events was to unfold again in the mid-twentieth century when black and then Indian immigration tapped hidden springs of English racialism which had long remained invisible.

The racialism revived in 1865 was not absolutely identical to eighteenth century attitudes. Similarly, to claim that the racialism of the late 1860s deeply influenced English attitudes towards the new African empire of the close of the century is not to claim perfect similarity between the two, or even to suggest that a causal link exists. But there are common denominators which make the racial responses of one generation partly explicable in terms of that generation's historical inheritance. From eighteenth-century plantocratic caricatures, to Carlyle and Trollope, through *The Times* of the 1860s to the more 'scientific' apologists for racialism late in the century, common images of the Negro were passed on.

The *Encyclopaedia Britannica* in 1810 had said of the Negro: 'Vices the most notorious seem to be the portion of this unhappy race; idleness, treachery, revenge, cruelty, impudence, stealing, lying, profanity, debauchery, nastiness, and intemperance, are said to have extinguished the principles of natural law, and to have silenced the reproofs of conscience. They are strangers to every sentiment of compassion, and are an awful example of the corruption of man left to himself.'[52] Seventy years later, in 1884, a very different kind of *Encyclopaedia Britannica*, while less harsh, was still repeating the ancient myths. 'No full-blooded Negro has ever been distinguished as a man of science, a poet, or an artist, and the fundamental equality claimed for him by ignorant philanthropists is belied by the whole history of the race throughout the historic period.'[53] This assertion scarcely differed from that written by David Hume a century before.

Philanthropists from the 1770s to emancipation had tried to give the English reading public a corrective to plantocratic legends, but they were never able totally to expel the more grotesque and persistent themes of this caricature. In the short term, the campaign for black freedom was able to silence the racialist propaganda of the planters but it was quite unable to eradicate the more profound subconscious prejudices against the Negro. These prejudices had grown over the centuries; born of curiosity, they had been nurtured and had thrived on economic exploitation. After the development of the plantation societies, the English response to the Negro was dictated largely by economic circumstance, by the need to justify or defend slavery. Simultaneously, white reactions were stimulated and guided by the myths which pre-dated European first-hand knowledge of Africans. These myths were often deliberately transformed by the slave lobby into pure caricature, but sometimes the caricature was simply the product of unconscious selection based on economic interest.

Thus the overtly racialist writings of Long and Carlyle were functions of quite different economic situations. But common elements can be found in the thinking of both and indeed in the wider racial consciousness of their respective generations. Similarly the reactions to the Jamaican revolt of 1865 were quite different from those which greeted the Haitian revolt of the 1790s. But similar stereotyped sentiments echo through both.

Between the English settlement of the New World and the fumbling attempts to reconstruct the colonial government of the former slave societies, successive generations had to cope with the intricate problems of colonial economics and government. Central to all these problems was the person of the imported Black. To justify his importation, his slavery, his freedom and finally his position as a free man, Englishmen conjured up a variety of stereotype images of the Negro best suited to each particular purpose. Almost without exception these images, which made such an impression on the public at large, bore little resemblance to fact. Caricature rather than truth was the hallmark of the English impression of the Negro.

Notes

CHAPTER TEN: *Black Caricature: The Roots of Racialism*

1. Quoted in *Gentleman's Magazine*, 1788, 1093–4.
2. R. Robinson and J. Gallagher, *Africa and the Victorians*, London, Macmillan, 1961, chs IV, V.
3. Leo Africanus, *History and Description of Africa*, i, 187.
4. 'A Description of Guinea', *Purchas – his Pilgrimes*, Glasgow, 1905–7, vi, 251.
5. Quoted in Jordan, 13.
6. Quoted in ibid., 34.
7. For relationship between slaves and planters see M. J. Craton and J. Walvin, *A Jamaican Plantation*, London and Toronto, 1970.
8. Bryan Edwards, *The History, Civil and Commercial of the British Colonies in the West Indies*, 2 vols, London, 1793, ii, 82–3.
9. Edward Long, *History of Jamaica*, London, 1774, ii, 383.
10. Jesse Foot, *Observations*, 1805, 17.
11. Smeathman, *Substance of a Plan of Settlement*, 9–17.
12. Thomas Carlyle, 'Discourse on the Nigger Question, 1849', *Critical and Miscellaneous Essays*, London, 1872, vii, 82.
13. 'A West India Planter', *Consideration on the Emancipation of Negroes*, London, 1788, 4.
14. Long, *Candid Reflections*, 48, 63–4.
15. ibid., 48.
16. *Letter to Philo-Africanus*, London, 1787, 17.
17. Eric Williams, *Capitalism and Slavery*, University of North Carolina Press, 1944.
18. Carlyle, 86.
19. Anthony Trollope, *The West Indies and the Spanish Main*, London, 1859, 56.
20. Basil Davidson, *Black Mother*, London, 1970, 21.
21. W. G. Sewell, *The Ordeal of Free Labour in the British West Indies*, New York, 1861, 178.
22. William Knox, *Three Tracts*, 14; 38.
23. In *Gentleman's Magazine*, 1771, 594.
24. Long, *History of Jamaica*, ii, 351–2.
25. ibid.
26. Jordan, 29.

27. ibid., 28–32.
28. James Houston, *Some New and Accurate Observations*, London 1725, 33.
29. Long, *History of Jamaica*, ii, Book III, ch 1.
30. 'Second Voyage of John Lok', *Hakluyt*, vi, 167.
31. Robert Norris, *Memoirs of the Reign of Bossa Ahadee*, 1789, 157.
32. Long, *History of Jamaica*, ii, Book III, ch. 1.
33. *Observations on the Bill Introduced last session* . . ., London 1816, 18.
34. 'The Negro's Address to His Fellows', *Instructions for the Treatment of Negroes*, 1797, 133.
35. Long, *History of Jamaica*, ii, Book III, ch. 1.
36. Bryan Edwards, ii, ch. 1.
37. William Knox, *Three Tracts*, 37.
38. John Wesley, *Thoughts on Slavery*, 1774.
39. Equiano, i, 10.
40. Hecht, 49: Chapter 4 above; Henry Mayhew, iii, 190. Most of Mayhew's minstrels were however British; an early example of the continuing, bizarre popular taste for 'nigger minstrels'.
41. William Dickson, *Letters on Slavery*, London, 1789, 74.
42. Carlyle, 86.
43. P. D. Curtin, *Two Jamaicas*, Harvard University Press, 1955; M. G. Smith, *Plural Society in the West Indies*, University of California Press, 1965; S. Olivier, *The Myth of Governor Eyre*, London, Hogarth Press, 1962.
44. P.P. 1866, xxxi; 21.
45. Quoted in Christine Bolt, *Victorian Attitudes to Race*, London, Routledge, 1971, 85.
46. ibid., 86.
47. *The Times*, 10 April, 1866.
48. Chapter Eleven below.
49. The words are those of the *Saturday Review*, quoted in Bolt, 91.
50. ibid., 92–5, 98.
51. ibid., 102, 105.
52. *Encyclopaedia Britannica*, Edinburgh, 1810, xiv, 750.
53. *Encyclopaedia Britannica*, 1884, xvii, 318.

CHAPTER ELEVEN

The Voice of Reason: The Restoration of Black Humanity

'I am far from having any particular esteem for the Negroes; but as I think myself obliged to consider them *as Men*, I am certainly obliged also to use my best endeavours to prevent them being treated as beasts.'[1] With these words Granville Sharp, pioneer and pacemaker of English humanitarianism, outlined the prime objective of the English friends of the Negro. Before Parliament, and indeed the English people, could be persuaded of the justice of granting full freedom to slaves throughout the empire, the English had to be converted to the idea that the African and his New World descendants were human.

In the complicated process through which white had become the global master of black, Negroes had been relegated to a position of subhumanity. By the late seventeenth century the legal basis of colonial government and trade, carefully supervised from London, rested precariously on the chattel status of the Negro. English courts of law however were never able totally and convincingly to give approval to this status, but in practice the Negro in English society from the late seventeenth century was more likely to be treated as chattel than a human. The task thus facing Granville Sharp and his friends was to bring about a revolution in English attitudes towards the Negro and thereby 'to prevent them being treated as beasts'. This task is perfectly illustrated by the choice of words etched on the perimeters of Wedgwood's abolitionist plaque; 'Am I not a man and a brother?'

The slave lobby's claim to own slaves in England in the eighteenth century rested on their concept of property rights, upon their 'plea of PRIVATE PROPERTY (the only plea they can alledge with any the least appearance of justice)', according to Sharp.[2] Since such private property was unnatural and contrary to the constitution, slavery was viewed by the abolitionists as merely 'PRIVATE PROPERTY in contraband goods'.[3] Furthermore the institution of slavery had a corrupting effect and Sharp feared that distinctions of colour might not always protect the Englishman's freedom. Thus Sharp set himself the forbidding task of restoring black freedom, partly from anger at the treatment meted out to Negroes and partly from fear of the consequences for English liberties if slavery of any kind were to become a permanent feature of English life.

Sharp came to reflect on the wider philosophical issues of slavery through dealing with some of the social problems of London's growing black population. But the intellectual origins of English philanthropy and abolitionist sentiment predate Sharp's conversion and originate in the upsurge of Enlightment thought which permeated English sensibilities precisely at the time when London's black population began to worry contemporaries.

A simple proof of the influence of French Enlightenment thought on the germination of English abolitionism can be seen in the frequent references to French writers in the works of early English abolitionists.[4] But earlier in the century the flow of influence was the other way. French translations of English travel accounts about Africa directly influenced two of France's pioneer abolitionist writers, Abbé Prevost and Montesquieu,[5] who in their turn exercised a pronounced influence over later generations of French writers and English readers.

Montesquieu's *Esprit des Lois* (1748) contained an ironical but penetrating attack on slavery. 'Were I to vindicate our right to make slaves of the Negroes, these should be my arguments. The Europeans having extirpated the Americans, were obliged to make slaves of the Africans for clearing such vast tracts of land. Sugar would be too dear if the plants which produce it were cultivated by other than slaves. These creatures are all over black, and with such a flat nose, that they can scarcely be pitied. It is hardly to be believed that God, who is a wise Being, should place a soul, especially a good soul, in such a black and ugly body.'[6] Montesquieu was the first philosopher of international reputation to lend his voice to the cause of abolition but the satirical form of his argument was widely misunderstood by the planters, some of whom took his words at their face value, using them as evidence of his support for slavery.

An anti-humanitarian caricature. You can never change a Negro

The Ethiopian Serenaders. A band of London street singers

Molineux. Heavy-weight champion boxer of England c. 1810

Black drummer, Grenadier Guards c. 1790. One of the many black musicians in late 18th-century British regiments

A still-life of an 18th-century Negro

The most direct influence of the *Esprit des Lois* can be seen in the impact it had on Blackstone and Sharp. Blackstone accepted Montesquieu's criticisms of slavery and incorporated them into his enormously influential *Commentaries*,[7] through which legal attention was drawn to the question of slavery. But his reliance on Montesquieu's theoretical attack led him to overlook the daily practice of slavery in England.[8] All the evidence suggests that Montesquieu had a similar impact on the wider English reading public, being read both in the original French and in an excellent English translation by Burke.[9] When in 1769 Granville Sharp, fired by anger at the Strong case, set out to write his definitive tract, *A Representation of the Injustices and Dangerous Tendancy of tolerating Slavery in England*, he based much of his case on the arguments put forward by Montesquieu.[10]

In France itself, Montesquieu exercised great influence over later generations of Enlightenment writers – d'Alembert, Voltaire, the Abbé Raynal, Diderot, Condorcet and Rousseau, all of whom had an enormous English audience, introducing into the elegant parlours of late eighteenth century high society discussion about the morality of slavery. In this galaxy of talents it was Rousseau above all others who captured the intelligent imagination and gave English readers cause to ponder on the issue of slavery.[11] Into the mouth of St Preux, the hero of *La Nouvelle Héloise*, Rousseau put words which roused pity and shame in his English readers. 'I saw Europe transported to the extremes of Africa ... I saw these vast and unfortunate countries which seemed destined only to cover the face of the globe with slaves. At their vile appearance, I turned away my eyes, out of disdain, horror and pity; and on beholding one-fourth part of my fellow creatures transformed into beasts for the service of the rest, I grieved to think that I was a man.'[12]

Rousseau's impact on European thought was seismic. He was extremely important in moulding the romantic imagination on both sides of the Channel, for example, and after 1789 his words became the stimulus for much radical activity, notably in the campaign for abolition. Some indication of his impact on English abolitionism can be gauged from the fact that Thomas Day's abolition epic, 'The Dying Negro', was dedicated to Rousseau.[13] It would be difficult to overestimate the influence of French thought, from Montesquieu to Rousseau, on the flowering of radical and abolitionist sentiment in

Black and White

England from the late 1760s to the years of the Revolution itself. English philanthropists heeded the voice of reason which spoke with a clear but unmistakable French accent.

As if to add physical proof to the already convincing philosophical case against black slavery, the human residue of England's slave empire was accumulating in London at precisely the same time. The evils and inhumanities produced by slavery could be seen in concentrated form in the capital. Awareness of these evils was naturally not restricted to the readers of French thinkers; it was obvious to all whose eyes and senses were open to the changing social problems of London. But to Granville Sharp and his friends, London's Negroes merely added tangible proof to the intellectual case against slavery.

Around Sharp the pioneer there grew up a group of committed philanthropists whose propaganda campaign gathered momentum, wearing down the weakening intransigence of vested interest until rewarded by success in 1806. When Sharp took up the black cause in the 1760s he was politically isolated; all the evidence suggests that at the time humanitarianism was the concern of a small minority. Thirty years later when the first great wave of English popular radicalism shook the foundations of stable government, the issue of black freedom had entered into the considerations and daily political vocabulary of thousands of artisans and working men. Corresponding societies across the country committed themselves to reform of domestic political corruption and to the restoration of black humanity. A sketch on the membership card of the Melbourne (Derbyshire) Corresponding Society, depicted, not the artisan demand for the franchise, but a slaving scene on the coast of Africa. The movement which took Tom Paine's *Rights of Man* as its ideological cornerstone saw its own political disabilities allied to the global dehumanization of the Negro. In the age of the *Rights of Man*, the rights of all men, black and white, were seen to be indivisible. This was a world view which was not the monopoly of propertied and educated men; it swelled up from the grass-roots of English society, both rural and urban. Within the space of thirty years humanitarianism had permeated English sensibilities and opened the way for abolition and later emancipation.

This is not to claim that humanitarianism by itself was responsible for black freedom. Pioneering work by Eric Williams has illustrated

The Voice of Reason

the more complex economic and social factors which made black freedom possible. Humanitarianism paralleled and made use of a series of economic changes which slowly pushed the plantation economies into a position of secondary importance. Equally, economic change alone could not have produced black freedom. The emphasis placed here on the role of philanthropy is not intended to deny or decry the seminal role of economic change.

Economic change was not however responsible for the re-instatement of the Negro to a position of humanity in the minds of many Englishmen. This change was due to a number of men who followed Granville Sharp's early lead. In the last thirty years of the eighteenth century an angry and growing band of writers adopted the issue of black freedom. From all points of the political compass they gathered to heap insult and injury on the slave lobby. While Sharp for example led the Enlightenment attack, John Wesley led a religous assault, successfully pricking the Christian conscience of his wide readership. Wesley's tract *Thoughts on Slavery*, published in 1774, but given enormous circulation in the 1780s, was influential in swinging the vociferous and expanding body of Methodists against the slave trade. His sympathetic portrait of the Negro and his punishing criticism of slavery were largely responsible for the later expansion of Methodist missionary work, but more immediately were invaluable in restoring the human image of the debased Negro. 'Who can reconcile this treatment of the Negroes, first and last with either mercy or justice?'[14]

Wesley was eager to point out that many black characteristics so caricatured by the slave lobby were largely a result of the treatment to which the Negroes were subjected by whites. 'You kept them stupid and wicked, by cutting them off from all opportunities of improving either in knowledge or virtue: And now you assign their want of wisdom and goodness as the reason for using them worse than brute beasts.' To the slave owner and to the slave trader Wesley's message was clear and unequivocal. 'Is there a God? You know there is. Is he a just God? Then there must be a state of retribution; a state wherein the just God will reward every man according to his works. Then what reward will he render to you? O think betimes! before you drop into eternity.'[15]

Wesley spoke on the subject of slavery with authority, for he had personal experience of Negro slaves in America. So too had

James Ramsay who followed up Wesley's religious attack. Ramsay had been a naval surgeon and a West Indian missionary before returning to England to join the abolitionist ranks. Taking Christian egalitarianism as his basic guide, Ramsay set out to demonstrate the essential humanity of the African and thereby undermine the case for slavery. The soul, he claimed, 'is a simple substance, not to be distinguished by squat or tall, black brown or fair'. It was wrong, Ramsay continued, to assume that because the Negro was different, he was therefore inferior. 'A horse and a bull are animals each of a different species, but the superiority has not been established between them.'[16]

Ramsay also attacked the slave lobby's defence of slavery on the grounds of the Africans' barbarism, pointing out that 'vice never appeared in Africa in a more barbarous and shocking garb, than she is seen every day in the most polished parts of Europe'.[17] Like Wesley before him, much of the strength of Ramsay's egalitarian philanthropy stemmed from his personal experience of slavery, while the result of his work was to add to the growing belief, fostered by Sharp and Wesley, that slavery transgressed Christian ethics by treating the slave as subhuman. Christian proponents of slavery continued to produce influential tracts arguing the contrary,[18] but by the last decade of the century it was increasingly difficult to resist the growing body of opinion which sought the elevation of the Negro to the rank of an equal human being.

Of the plethora of philanthropist tracts which came off the presses, few had the political impact of Thomas Clarkson's *On the Slavery and Commerce of the Human Species* (1786). Clarkson's prize winning paper was largely responsible for focusing public attention on the reasons, as opposed to the myths, for black failings. Slave supporters had made great use of the alleged inability of Negroes to rise to the level of white attainments as proof of basic black inferiority. But Clarkson sought to examine the Negro in the context of African society, unaffected by the distortions of slavery. The abilities of Africans, he claimed 'are sufficient for their situations'.[19] This view of the African as a human well suited to his own environment rather than ill-at-ease in the alienating world constructed for him by the white man, offered a fundamental challenge to the planters who simply saw the Negro as a subhuman at worst or, at best, the last link in the Chain of Being.

Supporters of slavery had, in the course of the eighteenth century, seized on the colour of the African as evidence for his inferiority. The colour difference between Africans and Europeans had, naturally enough, struck the early African explorers but it was only in retrospect, with the development of the slave colonies and the slave trade, that colour came to be used as a reason and an explanation for black inferiority.[20] Part of the task thus facing the abolitionists was to convince the public that colour was in no way an indication of inferiority or superiority. The basic explanation for human colouring had been revealed as early as the mid-seventeenth century but the influence of the planters' case was such that, even a century later, philanthropists had still to challenge the popular view.

'I call colour (the principal difference in the varieties of men) a very equivocal mark of superiority,' wrote William Dickson the abolitionist in 1789. Such reasoning, he claimed, was faulty. 'A man may associate his idea of *blackness* with his idea of the devil, or with his idea of stupidity, or with any other of his ideas he thinks proper; but he ought not to reason from such arbitrary associations.' Dickson, like Wesley and Ramsay, had first-hand knowledge of slave societies, having been secretary to the Governor of Barbados. But the strength of his case lay in its cool rationality, much in keeping with Sharp's earlier Enlightenment tract. By what logic, asked Dickson, 'can inferiority be deduced from differences of species?'[21] There was of course no such logic. Those who resorted to this line of argument to defend slavery were merely rationalising their own vested interests.

In attempting to restore the Negro's humanity, the English philanthropists attacked every facet of the caricatured images put out by the slave lobby. Towards the end of the century however, as the early Romantics took up the black cause, a contrary image of the Negro began to emerge which, though conceding the Negro's right to be treated as a human, nonetheless cast him in an extremely unrealistic light. The Negro as a noble savage was a view more sympathetic, but little less fanciful than the crude caricatures of the slave lobby. The origins of the romantic view of the Negro can be traced to the early eighteenth century, but it only gained importance as the question of slavery moved to the centre of the political stage. In the process, poetry became an important vehicle for discussion about the Negro, some of it being sponsored by the Abolition Society.[22]

Black and White

Much of this poetic material was little more than doggerel, often put into the mouth of an imaginary African by a sympathetic and sentimental Englishman.

John Thelwall provides a useful example. The most prominent English Jacobin of the 1790s and the object of attack by government and mob alike, Thelwall fell victim to the romance of the African.

> If while in the slave ship, with many a groan
> I wept o'er my sufferings in vain
> While hundreds around me replied to my moan
> And the clanking of many a chain
> If then, thou but deign'st with a pitying eye,
> Thy poor shackled creature to see
> O, thy mercy apply,
> Afric's sorrows to dry
> And bid the poor Negro be free.[23]

Popular versifiers exploited the growing sympathy for the Blacks, in particular for those they were able to see in London itself.

> In London city once there dwelt
> A poor but honest pair,
> God blessed them with an infant child
> And she was all their care
>
> From Afric's far distant shores,
> To this good land she came,
> Friendless and poor alike unknown
> To fortune and to fame.[24]

Africa as much as the African was the object of vivid romantic imagination, and attempts were made to describe the facts of African life in friendly, but basically unrealistic terms. Nowhere was this more pronounced than in Thomas Day's poem, 'The Dying Negro' which he dedicated to Rousseau in 1773. Day, like Thelwall, transmuted himself into an African for maximum poetic effect, describing the exotic continent in wildly romantic terms.

> Ye streams of Gambia, and thou sacred shade!
> Where in my youth's first dawn, I joyful stray'd,
> Oft have I rouzed amid your caverns dim,
> The howling tiger, and the lion grim,
> In vain they gloried in their headlong force,
> My javelin pierced them in their raging course.[25]

The Voice of Reason

The splendours of Africa, the untamed strength and beauty of the Africans, the abundance and fruitfulness of African nature were themes which emerged time and again as poets, of varying talents, expressed their political views on the question of slavery. Even the powerful abolitionist statements of William Blake were infused with imaginative rather than factual sentiments about the Negro. To Blake the blackness of the African simply hid a whiteness almost English in its purity.

> My mother bore me in the southern wild
> And I am black, but O! my soul is white.

The message he conveyed was beguilingly simple, but it was well worth saying, external appearances were deceptive. Below the surface mankind shared common features which united men of all races.

Of all the poetic fantasies about the Negro and Africa offered to the English reading public, none surpassed James Montgomery's epic *Abolition of the Slave Trade* (1814), for pure imaginative romance.

> In these romantic regions, Man grows wild;
> Here dwells the negro, nature's outcast child,
> Scorn'd by his brethren, but his mother's eye,
> That gazes on him from her warmest sky
> Sees in flexile limbs untutor'd grace
> Power in his forehead, beauty in his face;
> Sees in his breast, where lawless passions rove
> The heart of friendship, and the home of love.
>
> Is he not *Man*, though knowledge never shed
> Her quickening beams on his neglected head?
> Is he not *Man*, though sweet religion's voice
> Never bade the mourner in his God rejoice?
> Is he not man, by sin and suffering tried?
> Is he not man, for whom the Saviour died?[26]

However much one might stress the unrealistic side of this poetry, Montgomery and others like him were committed to a public assertion of a view of the Negro which had been rare only a generation before. 'Is he not man?' was an oft-repeated question, deliberately posed to challenge the view that the African and his New World descendants were brutes or chattels. In making this claim, friends of the Negro, particularly those who expressed their views in verse, frequently overstated or oversimplified their case. They tended to seize on half-truths and inflate them into distorted generalisations about black life. It appears, said a friend of the Negro 'that the natural disposition of the negro is gentle, amiable, grateful, affectionate and docile'.[27] While this view was both overdrawn and unrealistic, it was nonetheless vital in suggesting to a public, long accustomed to vicious distortions about black life, that Africans possessed human qualities, and were capable of social attainments which the English recognised and approved.

Under the impact of romantic portrayal, the Negro became a standard example of a man in a state of nature, unaffected by society or education; a being who was malleable under the pressures of careful education and socialisation. From 'a mental point of view', wrote the *Gentleman's Magazine* in 1816, 'the slaves are but as children'.[28] Like children they were felt to present a *tabula rasa* upon which could be impressed the sophisticated social patterns of white society. It was evidently this vision of the Negro which lurked in the mind of Granville Sharp when he devised his perfect social code for the settlement of Sierra Leone.[29] It was, in fact, a vision little less unrealistic, little less distorted than the caricature emanating from the slave lobby. But the crucial difference lay in the trenchantly advocated belief, no matter how colourfully expressed, in the essential humanity of the Negro. Those men who followed Sharp presented to the public the rounded, recognisable humanity of people who had been long ago stripped of it, physically and by consistent denigration. Thus was the Negro partially restored to manhood, but in the process he was presented as a perfect being, too happy and too good by half to be real. This idyllic view of the noble black savage was to remain well into the nineteenth century.

On the other hand friends of the Negro never succeeded completely in purging the English imagination of its inherited caricatured view. The task of maintaining the human image of the Negro in the face of negrophobic writers posed a continuing problem to white humanitarians. As late as 1850 John Stuart Mill was forced to take up the cudgels against his former friend Carlyle: 'Were the whites born ever so superior in intelligence to the blacks, and competent by nature to instruct and advise them, it would not be the less monstrous to assert that they had therefore a right either to subdue them by force, or circumvent them by superior skill.' Mill looked to the day when slavery throughout the world, notably in America, would be abolished: 'Though we cannot extirpate all pain, we can, if we are sufficiently determined upon it, abolish all tyranny.'[30]

Mill's words may have had an immediate impact. But as we have seen, in the political furore following the Morant Bay rising in 1865, the efforts of the philanthropists were swept aside as all the latent fears and stereotyped views of the Negro erupted once again. *The Times* claimed that it was 'impossible to eradicate the original savageness of African blood ... wherever he attains a degree of independence there is the fear that he will resume the barbarous life and fierce habits of his African ancestors'.[31] In fact, it was the English who had reverted to type, in falling back on hackneyed explanations, long outdated, of black behaviour.

In the years after emancipation, while other nations continued to oppress their black populations, Victorian Englishmen took great pride in the degree of freedom they granted to their once enslaved Negroes. Consequently the Jamaican revolt offended the delicate Victorian pride and made English reaction to the revolt all the more bitter. It was as if all the efforts of the philanthropists, from Sharp to Mill, had been in vain. The voice of reason had been heard, and proved influential, but after 1865, and in even more pronounced manner during the scramble for Africa later in the century, this voice was ignored, as ever more influential figures put forward revived images of the Negro. These new assertions of racialism rooted in the recent past were to be the cornerstone of late nineteenth and twentieth century racialism.

Notes

CHAPTER ELEVEN: *The Voice of Reason: The Restoration of Black Humanity*

1. Granville Sharp to Jacob Bryant, 19 October 1772, *Letter Book*, 159.
2. Granville Sharp, *A Representation of the Injustice*, London, 1769, 75.
3. ibid.
4. This is also true of early American abolitionists.

5. W. Sypher, *Guinea's Captive Kings*, University of North Carolina Press, 1942, 93–4.
6. Montesquieu, *L'Esprit des Lois*, (1748) New York, 1959, 238.
7. F. T. Fletcher, 'Montesquieu's Influence on Anti-Slavery Opinion in England', *Journal of Negro History*, xviii, 1933, 417–20.
8. Chapter Six above.
9. Fletcher, 421.
10. ibid., 415.
11. M. Cook, 'J. J. Rousseau and the Negro', *Journal of Negro History*, xxi, 1936, 298.
12. Quoted in ibid., 300.
13. ibid., 302.
14. Wesley, *Thoughts on Slavery*, 1774.
15. ibid.
16. James Ramsay, *On The Treatment and Conversion of Slaves*, London, 1784.
17. ibid.
18. R. Harris, *Scriptural Researches on the Licitness of the Slave Trade*, Liverpool, 1788.
19. Thomas Clarkson, *On the Slavery and Commerce of the Human Species*, 1786.
20. Jordan, 94–8.
21. William Dickson, *Letter on Slavery*, London, 1789, 61.
22. Sypher, 181.
23. John Thelwall, 'The Negro's Prayer', in *The Vestibule of Eloquence*, London, 1810. I am grateful to Lesley Miller for bringing this to my attention.
24. *The African Widow being the History of a Poor Black Woman*, n.d., 4.
25. Thomas Day, *The Dying Negro*, 1773.
26. James Montgomery, *The Abolition of the Slave Trade*, 1814, 14–15.
27. *Inquiries relating to Negro Emancipation*, London, 1829, 19.
28. *Gentleman's Magazine*, July 1816, 25–6.
29. Chapter Nine above.
30. J. S. Mill, 'On the Negro question', *Fraser's Magazine*, January 1850.
31. *The Times*, 15 November 1865.

CHAPTER TWELVE

Disintegration: Black Society in the Nineteenth Century

In the early years of the nineteenth century the black population of London was large, prominent, and the subject of heated public and private discussion. A visiting American professor in 1805 was struck by relations between black and white in the capital. 'It would seem that the prejudice against colour is less strong in England than in America. ... A few days since, I met in Oxford Street a well-dressed white girl who was of a ruddy complexion, and even handsome, walking arm in arm and conversing very sociably, with a negro man, who was as well-dressed as she, and so black that his skin had a kind of ebony of lustre.'[1] Within less than sixty years such sights had become a rarity on the streets of London. When Henry Mayhew embarked on his massive survey of London's poor in the 1850s and 1860s he found very few Negroes in evidence. Whereas eighteenth and early nineteenth century observers frequently pointed to 'the numbers of poor neglected negroes [who] are constantly seen lamenting in the streets',[2] by 1861 Mayhew reported that 'there are but few negroe beggars to be seen now'. Moreover, by mid-century 'the negro mendicant ... is usually an American negro.' In addition there were bands of black minstrels which sprang up in the middle years of the century. But, as one of the minstrels confessed to Mayhew: 'Some Niggers are Irish. There's Scotch niggers, too. I don't know a Welsh one, but one of the street nigger-singers *is* a real black – an African.'[3]

For American Negroes in mid-century, England was a haven where their freedom was guaranteed and where they could move in a less hostile racial atmosphere. One black American refugee told Mayhew: 'My brother had been living with some Britishers, and he had heard them say that over here the niggers were as good as whites, and that the whites did not look down on them and ill-treat them, as they do in New York.'[4] On arrival however American Blacks were forced on to the streets for survival, like the earlier generations of Negroes who had sought sanctuary in England. For the mid-nineteenth century black refugee however the situation if anything was worse than it had been a century before, for there was no black community on hand to ease his burdens with friendship and help. By the mid-century England's once lively black minority had disintegrated.

In the first years of the century the black population continued to be a noticeable element in the demographic make-up of the capital, and the life style of most Negroes simply followed the depressed patterns established in the eighteenth century. On the whole the black community was still distinguished by its poverty. When in 1815 Parliament looked into the problem of poverty in the capital specific mention was made of black distress. 'In the case of the Africans', asked the parliamentary committee, 'are there any means of taking care of them?' 'I know of none,' answered the witness, 'the only way in which we can dispose of them is to fix them on the parish where they fall, as casualty.'[5] When, in the following year William Wilberforce invited Negroes to a dinner in celebration of the international banning of the slave trade, many of those who attended were 'mendicants, whose faces were recognised, as constantly plying at their respective stands in the public streets'.[6] At one level at least black mendicants were in a more favourable position in the early nineteenth than in the eighteenth century, for they were able to capitalise on the wave of public humanitarian sentiment in the period before emancipation. It became 'a common thing to see a negro with tracts in his hand, and a placard upon his breast, upon which was a wood-cut of a black man, kneeling, his wrists heavily chained, his arms held high in supplication and around the picture, forming a sort of proscenium or frame, the words, "Am I not a man and a brother?" '[7]

To counterbalance any such public sympathy, the planters played on the traditional English fear of expanded black immigration. As part of the rear-guard campaign against emancipation plantocratic writers conjured up for their readers frightening pictures of wholesale black arrivals. Were freedom to be granted to the slaves, argued one planter, 'I think it not unlikely that one in twenty (that is forty thousand) of the black population, would find their way to England in the first ten years'. Most would migrate in the 'hope of bettering themselves', but whatever the cause, the consequences for England would be 'the increase of the poor rates, by half a million per annum', to say nothing of the increased threat of widespread miscegenation.[8]

Tidal waves of black immigrants failed to materialise, and those few Negroes who did settle in England after 1807 (when abolition of the slave trade made Negroes too valuable to be moved in any great numbers from the West Indies) differed little in occupation or fate from their predecessors, but their numbers were markedly lower. Domestic work however continued to offer a special niche for black new arrivals as late as Mayhew's surveys.[9] The English still possessed a special attraction for black servants and loyal servants had no problem in moving between a variety of English employers.[10]

Immediately before emancipation the institution of slavery continued to be in evidence in England, although in much less obtrusive a form. The Abolition Act of 1807 had for instance given colonial masters special dispensation to carry their slaves abroad, without fear of breaking the new law, thus allowing them to travel to England with their slaves. Unless the slave escaped and made a positive effort to regain his freedom his legal relationship with his master continued to operate in England. As late as 1827 Lord Stowell ruled in the case of the slave Grace that any temporary freedom acquired in England by a slave 'has ever been superseded upon return of the slave; and slaves never have been deemed and considered as free persons on their return to Antigua, or the other colonies'.[11]

The slave Grace was exceptional only in becoming the centre of legal attention. Many other West Indian slaves in the first two decades of the nineteenth century were subjected to the same agonising and uncertain process of legal transmutation, as they found themselves torn between the determination of some Englishmen to secure their freedom in England, and the West Indians' intention of maintaining their bondage both in England, and the West Indies. In 1826, vested interests in Antigua 'requested the co-operation of the other islands in resisting the freedom of all such slaves as have been in England but have since returned to the West Indies'.[12] Agents of the imperial government were simultaneously working to the opposite effect. 'The Collector of Customs [in Antigua] has twenty-five Negroes of this description under his care', and was anxious to prevent them falling back into the hands of their masters.[13] Paradoxically the return of Negroes from England to the West Indies assisted the further dissemination of ideas of freedom in the slave colonies. 'Many slaves accompany their owners to England ... where they often remain a considerable time, and acquire an insight of the principles and effects of liberty and knowledge, which on their return to the colonies, they disseminate among their fellow slaves',[14] a communication of ideas that had been feared a century before.[15]

The English involvement with slaves in England became less direct and more subtle as emancipation sentiment and legal restraints made open trafficking both difficult and unwise. Although advertisements of Negroes for sale ceased to appear in English newspapers by the early nineteenth century, it was still possible as late as the 1820s to find advertisements in which slaves were offered for sale as adjuncts to property. In 1829 for example *The Times* offered for sale: 'The Orchard Plantation, Jamaica. – To be sold by auction, at the Auction Mart, in the City of London, the 19th day of February, 1829 ... containing 723 Acres of land or thereabouts ... together with 145 male, and 140 female slaves, and the buildings and stock therein.'[16] Although the slaves never left the colonies it was still possible and legal to buy slaves on the London market on the eve of emancipation. 'Would it not be well', asked one emancipationist, 'to investigate clearly the question how far sales of Slaves, by advertisements and auctions in England are legal?'[17]

Many West Indian slaves, as we have already seen, were tied to their masters in England by the master's use of the indenture, a device which effectively corroded much of the legal protection afforded to the Negro.[18] Furthermore indentured slaves in England were often subjected to treatment little less brutal than that meted out to slaves in the West Indies. One such 'indentured' Negro in London was confined in chains; another was worked to the point of mental and physical collapse.[19] Since English courts accepted the legality of indentures there remained little effective protection for Negroes caught in such vicious situations.

Despite such ill-treatment, England had a reputation for being less severe than other countries. Consequently, in the pursuit of freedom or searching for better treatment, Negroes fled to England from all points of the compass, the hazards they faced en route testifying to their determination to escape. Two slaves for example made good their escape from Brazil, arriving in England by way of

Disintegration

Jamaica and Plymouth. But on arrival they merely faced a life of begging.[20] Before the American Civil War, American Negroes in particular found the prospects of life in England tempting. James Watkins was one American slave who secreted himself on board a vessel bound from New York to Liverpool; 'when we entered the Mersey and came into the docks at Liverpool, I could not help shouting and leaping for joy'.[21] His joy was short-lived for he found 'more than one proof that the "leprosy" [of racial hatred] had affected some on British soil, especially those who came much into contact with American merchants and captains'.[22] Yet another escaped American slave, John Williams, who had similarly exchanged American bondage for English freedom, expressed surprise at seeing in Liverpool, 'a person dressed like a gentleman, with a face black and shiny as ebony – an unmistakable negro – come walking down the street with a beautiful white lady on his arm'.[23] Whatever the reality of English attitudes towards the Negro in mid-century, and they clearly ranged from egalitarian friendship to open racialist hatred, American Negroes believed that they stood a better chance of fair treatment and equality in England than in the United States,[24] and those who fled to England publicly testified to the improvement in their condition.

Other slaves had English freedom bestowed on them without seeking it. Nine African slaves, found on board a Portuguese vessel in Liverpool, were released by local authorities and given employment as free sailors on English ships.[25] In 1815 two African child-slaves, discovered on a French ship brought into Plymouth, joined another African child recently rescued from similar circumstances.[26] Of another batch of five found on a French vessel driven into St Ives in 1826, two soon died, two were sent to Sierra Leone while the fifth, Louis Asa-Asa, stayed in England.[27] Thus as long as the ships of other nations continued to trade in slaves, England took it upon herself to accommodate any Negro who had been inadvertently brought within English jurisdiction.

In the nineteenth, as in the eighteenth century, the freedoms offered by escape to England were accompanied by harsh physical privations. Stowaways to England suffered the harshness of a secret voyage coupled, at least until landfall, with the gnawing fear of discovery and return to the place of origin.[28] More fortunate, if less numerous, were those slaves able to cross the Atlantic as fare-paying passengers, but even they suffered the oppressive anxieties common to all runaways.[29] Travel to England was obviously the most serious obstacle separating the New World slave from English freedom, and the planters' threats of massive immigration were utterly unrealistic in the light of the practical and economic transport problems.

Another serious obstacle to black settlement was institutionalised in 1832 in an Act of Parliament. A new Customs Act of that year specified that 'the master of every Vessel coming from the Coast of Africa, and having taken on board at any Place in Africa any Person or Persons being or appearing to be Natives of Africa, shall ... state in the Report of his Vessel, how many such persons have been taken on board by him in Africa; and any such Master failing herein shall forfeit the sum of one hundred pounds'. When making his report the master was 'required to enter into Bond to His Majesty in the Sum of One Hundred Pounds, conditioned to keep harmless any Parish or any Extra-Parochial or other Place maintaining its own Poor, against any Expence which such Parish or other Place may be put to in supporting any such Persons during their Stay in the United Kingdom'.[30] In the first ten years of the Act's operation the highest annual number of Africans registered as landing was 213 in 1840; the lowest was 94 in 1841.[31]

The Act thus effectively prevented African settlement in England, despite the expansion of maritime trade with Africa, simply by giving ships' masters an incentive to take Africans back to their place of origin. But the motive behind this measure was clearly economic; a determination to prevent black visitors from adding to the already mountainous task of relieving the English poor.

Not all Negroes who arrived in England were considered to be a potential addition to the problems of poor relief, for some came purely in a temporary capacity. In the course of the century an increasing number of Africans and West Indians came to England for education, a process which had in fact first been established when the early merchant-adventurers had Africans instructed in English to assist the trading ventures in West Africa.[32] In the eighteenth century this economic incentive behind the education of Africans was assisted by a growing religious determination to draw as many Africans as possible into the Christian fold. But trade remained the most important stimulus to education. 'The Motives

Disintegration

which principally induce the Natives of Africa, or the resident White Traders, to send their Children to England, are to receive such an Education such as will fit them for trading with greater Advantage.' These children, whether black African or the mulatto offspring of white traders, often returned home with the manners, attitudes and style of the polite Englishman upon a model of whom their education had been based.[33] Assimilation to English standards was the ideal behind the education of the first African students in England although the final product frequently fell short of the ideal.[34]

Assimilation through education was, understandably, more pronounced among West Indians than Africans, because most of them came from racially mixed families whose ambitions and attitudes tended to be those of the lighter skin group. In 1824 for instance a Negro commented that in Jamaica 'the Browns were far above most of us in fortune, and some of them had been educated in a very respectable manner in Great Britain'.[35] In St Lucia in the same period there lived a barrister, 'a young gentleman, the son of a judge of that island by a dark coloured woman, [who] had received from his father a good plain education at Liverpool'.[36] Further south, in Trinidad, one of the island's best known doctors, Dr John Baptista Philip, a mulatto, had been 'sent to England where he performed his first studies in literature. . . . He afterwards entered the university of Edinburgh where he eminently distinguished himself.' [37]

Indigenous West Indian education presented the colonial and metropolitan authorities with perplexing problems, caused in the main by the changing contours of the population. In the nineteenth century freed slaves, mulattoes, Indian and Chinese indentured workers, Arab traders and various combinations of all these groups, produced a mosaic of national, racial, linguistic and religious elements which seemed to defy all possibility of educational uniformity.[38] Moreover, the pathetic educational facilities set up in the black West Indian colonies in the years of freedom were monopolised by the children of the middle class, i.e. the fair or white-skinned.[39] In all the islands 'anyone with the means sent his children to England for all but the most elementary education'.[40] Thus throughout the century English educational institutions, from pioneering elementary schools to the most advanced vocational departments of the universities, received a trickle of West Indian and black African students. Overwhelmingly they came from the West Indian middle class or the upper reaches of West African societies, as indeed they still do.

Negroes – both African and West Indian – were educated in England primarily in the knowledge (or hope) that they would return home. African boys sent by the Sierra Leone Company were expected to return to work for the Company,[41] or to become local school teachers.[42] Even those young Africans who had been rescued from slavery were educated for repatriation. One youth was educated 'in the hope that with proper instruction he might hereafter become useful as a school-master in Africa'.[43] Englishmen appreciated that bilingual Africans were the most useful kind and to this end efforts were made to produce fluency in English while maintaining the student's native language.[44] But through all the educational dealings between the English and the Negro in the nineteenth century ran the assumption that the students were only temporary visitors. Furthermore it was generally hoped that on return to his native country, the educated Negro would prove useful and pliant to English interests.

The trickle into England of black students, freed slaves, domestic servants or sailors was not sufficiently strong to compensate for the steady numerical decline of the local black population. We must look for causes of this decline (as of its rise) to the other side of the Atlantic. Between abolition (1807) and emancipation (1833) planters could no longer refresh their labour force with new purchases of Africans, with the result that Negroes in the West Indies became too valuable to be brought to England as domestics in any great numbers. Furthermore the movement of people between the West Indies and the mother country declined dramatically in the 1830s and 1840s. With emancipation and the equalisation of the sugar duties in 1846 the tottering fortunes of West Indian sugar finally collapsed. Trade to and from the West Indies was reduced to a shadow of its former self as British investments and maritime trade sought new outlets for the commercial energy generated by the march of industrialisation. West Indian planters by the 1840s were generally bankrupt or had already removed themselves to England to enjoy the last fruits of absentee leisure. In either case they had lost the economic base which for so long had sponsored their colourful homecomings, surrounded by bevies of black retainers.

As the plantations fell to ruin there sprang up on the neighbouring land new communities of squatters and farmers, drawn largely from the ex-slaves who had fled their former house of bondage to assert their independence as small producers. Negroes no longer had to escape from the islands to seek freedom; it was theirs as of right to enjoy, or to be endured, as they wished. After 1838 they were free men in their own land.[45] It was in this way that the two main stimuli to black emigration, white prosperity and the related phenomenon of black slavery, ceased to operate.

Like slave populations in the islands at the height of the slave trade, England's black population in the early years of the century was sexually unequal. Males greatly outnumbered females, and future generations of Negroes, in these circumstances, could only be guaranteed either by fresh infusions of Negroes from outside or by a levelling up of the ratio between men and women. After 1807 neither of these alternatives was feasible. As black immigration slowed down, the overall number of Negroes went into sharp decline at a time when the population as a whole was increasing at an unprecedented rate.

The process of disintegration was hastened by the blurring of the edges dividing the black from the white communities. In the absence of adequate numbers of black women, Negroes in England settled down with white women. Their offspring were English, and with further interracial breeding their pigmentation became lighter and increasingly less noticeable. Miscegenation had of course been common in the eighteenth century but in the nineteenth it was not counter-balanced by new arrivals of Negroes. The overall process was thus one of absorption of the Negroes into the poor white communities alongside which they had always lived. The combined process of absorption and decline in immigration rapidly proved to be effective solvents of English black society.

Demographically, Negroes ceased to be significant in England by mid-century. Politically the same process had begun with emancipation, the long-term effect of which 'was to remove them from the centre of the stage as a special category of mankind'.[46] In London, the remnants of the black population were drawn into their local communities, where racial mixing was no longer exceptional. As early as 1817 a magistrate had noted that Shadwell's population consisted of 'foreign sailors, Lascars, Chinese, Greeks, and other filthy dirty people of that description'.[47] Whereas in the late eighteenth century Negroes had been seen as a distinct social problem in the capital, by the 1850s their numbers and conditions posed no more of a serious problem than did many other minority groups. When relief was organised, it was no longer directed primarily at the Negroes.[48] Thus in 1857 there was established in the West India Dock Road 'The Strangers Home for Asiatics, Africans and South Sea Islanders'.[49] In the surrounding East End districts the absorption of black pockets into the local population continued apace. In Stepney they were absorbed by other immigrant groups; in Limehouse they intermingled with Asiatics.[50]

Small groups did however remain distinctively black, although these tended to consist of transient dockland knots of black sailors. Most notably between 1854 and 1873 West African seamen of the Kru tribe traditionally stayed at 'Green's Home' in the West India Dock Road. In Canning Town, where many Negro sailors stayed, relations between black and white were amicable. 'Where the unionjack flies Nigger is well-treated. English sailors do not disdain to drink with him, work with him, and sing with him.'[51] Since black sailors belonged to an occupational group whose history could be traced back to the seventeenth century, if not further, it was perhaps the antiquity of their trade which may have forged friendly relations and made for friendly acceptance of Negroes in ports. Indeed the special position of the black sailor was legitimised by an Act of Parliament in 1823, which stipulated that Negroes were to be 'as much British seamen as a white man would be', while Indian and other non-whites were to be paid less and accorded treatment inferior to that of either black or white.[52]

In maritime communities Negroes may have been more in evidence than in other parts of cities, particularly in London. Nonetheless, by the late century, the Negro was an exceptional sight. The observant Taine glimpsed a Negro fiddler in Shadwell and a mulatto whore in a Manchester brothel,[53] but they were isolated cases. In the same period, Africans were brought to England as exhibits in travelling shows but, again, they were unusual cases and in no way constituted a community. The unusualness of Negroes could be guaranteed to draw crowds of gaping Englishmen. In May 1880 the Rev. C. T. Wilson returned to Bedford from missionary work in Uganda bringing with him four Africans. No fewer than 320 people flocked from the small villages near Bedford to see this rare sight. After being

Disintegration

presented to Victoria the Africans lived peacefully in Bedford until 'one of them bit another's ear off, (and) it was considered advisable that they should return to their native land'.[54]

More organised and lavishly produced exhibitions of Africans proved enormously popular in the last years of the century, particularly to large numbers of English women who bestowed their favours on the visiting Africans. The 'familiarity which exists between certain white women visiting the Kaffir Kraal at Earl's Court Exhibition and the blacks on show there, is a particularly revolting spectacle', moaned a London newspaper in 1889.[55] Similar scenes were common wherever Africans were put on display, and similar cries of revulsion issued from the popular press.[56]

Negro exhibits had been common in the eighteenth century; so had students, sailors and domestics. But while these continued to be elements in the fabric of English society right through the nineteenth century, they existed as isolated elements and not as obvious representatives of a wider black society. In the first years of the nineteenth century in London, black society had been vibrant and organic, even if depressed. Within the space of two generations it had ceased to exist. Black freedom in the colonies, the collapse of the sugar economy and the absorption of the predominantly male population, cumulatively led to the rapid disintegration of black society, and to the resultant view that black society had never existed in England. It was to take the enormously different circumstances of England in the throes of World War I to form a new black community and put it back to the numerical strength it had once had.

Notes

CHAPTER TWELVE: *Disintegration: Black Society in the Nineteenth Century*

1. Benjamin Silliman, *Journal*, i, 272.
2. Beckford, *Remarks*, 96.
3. Henry Mayhew, *London Labour and the London Poor*, Dover Publications, 1968, 4 vols, iii, 191; iv, 425.

4. ibid.
5. 'Report from the Committee on the State of Mendacity in the Metropolis, 1815', P.P., 1814–15, iii, 15.
6. Joseph Marryat, *More Thoughts*, 1816, 105–6.
7. Mayhew, iv, 425.
8. 'A West Indian Planter', *A Letter to the Most Honourable* . . ., 22.
9. Mayhew, iv, 425.
10. *Fifth Report of the African Institution*, London, 1811, 88.
11. 'The Slave Grace, 1827', Catterall, i, 6.
12. *Twentieth Report of the African Institution*, London, 1826, 30.
13. ibid.
14. *An Important Appeal to the Reason, Justice and Patriotism of the People of Illinois*, London, 1824, 4.
15. Fielding, *Penal Laws*, 145.
16. *The Times*, February 1829.
17. *The Principles, Plans, and Objects of the 'Hiberian Negro's Friend Society'* . . ., Dublin, 1831, 9.
18. Chapter Eight above.
19. *Ninth Report of the African Institution*, London, 1815, 69–72; *The History of Mary Prince*, 1831, 18–20.
20. *A Word from the Bible* . . ., London, 1829, 23n.
21. *Narrative of the Life of James Watkins*, Bolton, 1852, 37.
22. ibid., 38.
23. *The Narrative of John Williams*, London, 1855, 23.
24. Mayhew, iv, 425.
25. *Fourth Report of the African Institution*, London, 1810, 25–26.
26. *Ninth Report of the African Institution*, London, 1815, 68–69.
27. 'Narrative of Louis Asa-Asa', *The History of Mary Prince*, 42.
28. Mayhew, iv, 425.
29. *Narrative of the Life of James Watkins*, 36.
30. 2 and 3. Will.4, c.84, ss. 4 and 5. Clauses IV, V.
31. P.P. 1842, xxxvii, 35.
32. 'William Towerson's first voyage', *Hakluyt*, vi.
33. C. Fyfe, *Sierra Leone Inheritance*, London, Oxford University Press, 1964, 102–3; Fyfe, *History*, 11.
34. *Reports of the House of Commons*, x, 1785–1807, May 1807, Appendix, 744–5.
35. Thomas Cooper, *Facts Illustrative of the Condition of the Negro Slaves in England*, London, 1824, 24–25n.
36. J. Jeremie, *Four Essays on Colonial Slavery*, London, 1831, 49.
37. *An Oration Pronounced on the 29th of July 1829*, London, n.d., 9.
38. Eric Williams, *History of the People of Trinidad and Tobago*, London, 1964, Chapter 14.

39. ibid., 205.
40. Philip D. Curtin, *Two Jamaicas*, 57.
41. Robert Thorpe, *A Letter to William Wilberforce*, London, 1815, 4; *Second Report of the African Institution*, London, 1808, 5.
42. Hannah Kilham, *Report on a Recent Visit to the Colony of Sierra Leone*, London, 1828, 6; *Eighth Report of the African Institution*, London, 1814, 24; *Third Report*, 1809, 3.
43. *Ninth Report of the African Institution*, London, 1815, 72.
44. *Sixth Report of the African Institution*, London, 1812, 29; H. Kilham, 10.
45. Their freedom was in many respects negative.
46. Banton, *The Coloured Quarter*, 24.
47. Quoted in ibid., 26.
48. The Sierra Leone scheme is the best example of relief offered primarily for Negroes.
49. Banton, *The Coloured Quarter*, 26.
50. ibid., 27.
51. ibid.
52. 4. Geo. IV, c.80; Bob Hepple, 63–4.
53. H. Taine, *Notes on England*, 33, 304.
54. *Bedfordshire Mercury*, 15 and 22 May 1880; C. D. Linnell, *Old-Time Pavenham*, 1958, 20. Information communicated by Archivist Bedfordshire County Record Office.
55. Quoted in Rogers, *Sex and Race*, i, 206.
56. ibid.

CHAPTER THIRTEEN

Into the Twentieth Century: 1900-1945

Between 1900 and the outbreak of World War I the black population in England was minuscule and fragmented, as it had been for the best part of the previous half century. Negroes in England were, like so many of their unknown ancestors, depressed people, eking out a living on the poverty-stricken fringes of society. In the early years of the century distress was so acute among Negroes and other colonial peoples living in England that governmental and charitable relief workers found the task they posed beyond their means. Accordingly Parliament itself investigated the problem by setting up a committee of enquiry.[1]

Two distinct groups of Negroes found themselves the object of parliamentary scrutiny in 1910: colonial sailors stranded in England, and those, mainly West Indians, who had emigrated to England in the hope of improving their lot. Emigration from the West Indies was common at the time, but normally took the form of inter-island migration, or emigration to Central and North America. Some small numbers of West Indians however tried their luck in England. Two men found their way from the Caribbean, 'work being slack in St Vincent', only to find, not the work they were seeking, but merely local charitable relief. Others, almost in eighteenth-century style, had been brought to England as servants, but had fled from ill-treatment to destitution. Some West Indians arrived as a family group, but they too simply fell into the arms of the parish poor law guardians. Destitute West Indians claimed a great variety of occupational skills in their attempts to secure charitable relief. One claimed to be a 'Music Hall Performer', another a Jamaican planter. Among others were 'a phrenologist and a shoemaker, and one or two nurses and a valet'. It was noticeable that of the destitutes a fair number belonged to the 'domestic serving class, including butlers and nurses', a reminder that the stereotyped economic role imposed on Negroes as far back as the seventeenth century continued into the twentieth.

But the majority of distressed Negroes consisted of unemployed sailors, another black occupational group with well-established traditions in England. Repatriation of men in this position, to most parts of the West Indies and West Africa, was periodically financed by the Colonial Office, more frequently by a charitable concern, but the main obstacle to repatriation was not simply a question of finance. Some West Indian islands refused to readmit men who had come from there. Consequently bands of Negroes in England were suspended in a state of limbo. Desperate black sailors tramped the length of the country seeking work, from Liverpool to London, from London to Cardiff. When they arrived at a new port they usually met queues of other unemployed sailors, including other Negroes, all fruitlessly seeking maritime work. While it is true that the small black community in London was often kind and helpful to the transient unemployed black sailor, resident Negroes could do little to cope with the real problem of black unemployment. Inevitably the unemployed fell upon parish and private charities. In London, at least six parish authorities in addition to private organizations in twelve parishes were presented with the problem of unemployed black sailors. Other major ports around the country were faced with the same problem: Bristol, Cardiff, Hull, Liverpool, West Hartlepool and Glasgow. The overall number of sailors involved was small, in particular when compared to the large number of Indians caught in the same situation. But the consequences were to be important in the evolution of twentieth century black society, for many of those involved settled, and bitterly remembered that their first taste of life in Britain was that of the unemployed worker, shunted from one charity to another.

To make matters worse the black unemployed were confronted with blatant discrimination. Many were unable to secure work because of 'The repugnance of Masters and Engineers to mix coloured seamen and firemen with white.' Discrimination sometimes came from white workers. A West Indian lucky enough to secure work in Tilbury docks was obliged to quit when white workers went on strike rather than work with him. West Indians were also in a worse political position than either Indians and Africans, for the West Indians, who constituted a majority of Negroes in distress, had no London-based representatives from their home colonies. 'Men from the West Indies', noted one charity relief man, 'are very numerous, and cases of distress are often met. They have no home or agency and repatriation is difficult on account of the West Indian Island laws.'

While the London docks and dockside areas seem to have housed the largest number of transient and destitute Blacks, they appear to have been widely dispersed throughout the country. This was a notable change from the patterns of the eighteenth century community which had centred primarily on London. The reason for this was not so much the migration of black labour from London in search of work, but the changing structure of Britain's maritime trade and ports. The explosion of trade in the course of the nineteenth century, the introduction of steamships, and the resultant opening and expansion of many new ports around Britain led to the growth of immigrant or transient colonial minority groups in areas of the country previously untouched by immigration. By 1909 for example Cardiff was as important a home for black sailors as London.

Cardiff's growth to eminence in the nineteenth century was due to a combination of its location and careful planning. It was a crucial coaling and coal-exporting port which benefited from the vast dock and railway developments of the late nineteenth century. Cardiff became the centre of large-scale imports of ore and exports of metal products. In the years before World War I a greater annual tonnage of foreign cargoes was cleared from Cardiff than from either London or Liverpool.[2] Of Cardiff's maritime trade, a substantial part was of the tramp variety, a form of shipping which involved great insecurity of labour. Unlike the liner trade from Liverpool, the Cardiff tramp trade attracted a great deal of casual labour. Thus large numbers of Negroes were deposited in Cardiff by the trade and were also attracted there from other parts of the country in the hope of finding casual tramp work.[3] Black settlement, beginning in the 1890s, was clearly marked in the city by 1900 and gathered momentum in the years up to 1914 but, as throughout the country as a whole, it was even more significant in the course of the war itself.

A similar process of black settlement was evolving in other ports – Liverpool, Bristol, North and South Shields and along Tyneside in general. Most of the black immigrants were men; sailors or unemployed sailors. Once again, as in the eighteenth century, the absence of black women was to have important results in the formation of

Into the Twentieth Century: 1900–1945

relations between the Negroes and the white host community. The immigrants were a mixture of West Africans and West Indians [4] and all tended to settle in the first instance in dockside areas which were invariably slum districts long before the Negroes arrived. Once there they formed a nucleus around which fresh arrivals gathered as they landed, particularly in the course of the war. But it has to be stressed that the deplorable conditions of the embryonic black reception areas were inherited, rather than created, by black immigrants. When the black population expanded in the years 1914–19 it did so in already deprived and blighted urban areas.

World War I produced an enormous increase in Britain's black population. Workers were in a sellers' market as the armed forces drained industry of its manpower. Black seamen left their ships to look for work on land while others travelled from the colonies in search of lucrative employment. Some ships with black sailors on board were requisitioned by the government and their crews deposited in Britain. Other Negroes were recruited into the armed forces and were demobilized in Britain.[5]

The British desperately needed labour to fight the war and turned to the untapped potential of the colonies. But the experiences of large numbers of Negroes during the war give some indication of the prevailing discrimination which continued to operate against them, even when they were considered to be economically vital. Throughout the war the War Office actively resisted the integration of black troops into existing regiments, preferring instead the creation of separate black units. The Army Council opposed commissions for men 'who are not of unmixed European blood', while the 2,500 black West Indian volunteers were, despite their wishes, barred from combat duty. Instead they were formed into labour gangs. Naturally enough, white volunteers from the West Indies were allowed to fight.[6] Even in war, the Blacks were consigned to their age-old role of being the beast of burden for their white masters.

Between 1914 and 1918 the black population expanded rapidly. On Tyneside it was thought to have increased fourfold.[7] Black workers from the colonies found their way into the munition and chemical factories of the North and Midlands. But the boom which brought these men to Britain was temporary. At the end of the war, as industries contracted and the country slid into the depression which came to characterize the interwar years, many of the Negroes whose presence was caused by the war found themselves unemployed. Many began to drift into the older black communities of London and Cardiff looking for work or for a passage home.[8] But they were in a delicate position, for they were easily recognized and isolated as outsiders, competing for jobs in contracting industries with English workers, many of whom had been recently released from the armed forces and resented the competition for work. The trade unions insisted on the employment of Englishmen in preference to Negroes[9] and consequently increasing numbers of the immigrants found themselves unemployed and unemployable. The social and racial tensions which had long simmered below the surface erupted into the open under the pressure of economic unrest. In the summer of 1919 a series of serious race riots, in which groups of poor whites pitched themselves against local black minorities, broke out in a number of British towns and cities; London, Liverpool, Cardiff, Manchester, Barry, Newton and Hull.

The local and national impulses behind the riots are difficult to distinguish but certain characteristics seem to be common to all areas. Liverpool saw the start of a chain reaction of violence which lashed round the country. In May 1919 the Liverpool police fought a running battle with local Negroes in an illegal gaming house.[10] Within three weeks they were busy trying to keep black and white apart. As a result of the wartime expansion in industry, some 5,000 Negroes lived in Liverpool by 1919, but by that time many of them were unemployed. Relations between the Negroes and local white women was one of many bitterly resented complaints levelled at the black community. 'Many have married Liverpool women,' wrote *The Times*, 'and while it is admitted that some have made good husbands the intermarriage of black and white women, not to mention other relationships, has created much feeling.' The violence which erupted in early June put the whole black community in danger. 'White men appear determined to draw out the blacks, who have been advised to remain in doors. This counsel many of them disregard.' They ignored this advice at their peril. 'Whenever a Negro was seen he was chased and, if caught, severely beaten.'[11] Over three days, tension and violence escalated. Blacks were chased through the streets by baying mobs of up to 2,000 whites, the trouble having attracted 'the passions of the hooligan class'. Black homes were wrecked and hundreds forced to take shelter in the police headquarters. But when suspects were brought to court Negroes greatly outnumbered whites, a syndrome of arrest and prosecution which is the cause of much of the present-day black complaints against police. All neutral observers agreed that the black community was on the defensive and yet its members, in trying to defend themselves were arrested and prosecuted for their attempts at self-defence, while all but a handful of the white aggressors went unchallenged.[12]

A similar pattern of events unfolded in Cardiff where the violence was worse, resulting in at least three deaths and dozens of injuries. The Cardiff *lumpen*, led by men in uniform, went on a four day rampage against local Negroes. Again, unemployment seems to have been the basic cause behind the clash, despite the ironical fact that some 1,000 local Negroes were also unemployed. White mobs chased their black victims into 'an area known to the Cardiff people as "Nigger Town". Here there is a large colony of negroes many of whom have married white wives.' Black property was destroyed, guns were used and white girl-friends of local Negroes roundly insulted. As in its coverage of the Liverpool riots, *The Times* tried to understand the motives of the rioters. 'Some of the more soberminded citizens of Cardiff consider that the coloured-men are not alone to blame for the disturbances, although at the same time, they deplore the familiar association between white women and negroes, which is a provocative cause.' After noting the basic loyalty of the Negro, particularly during the war, *The Times* added disparagingly, 'His chief failing is his fondness for white women'. In expressing the feelings of the Cardiff whites *The Times* came perilously close to sharing their views. It even went so far as to report the comments of an American visitor on the 'laxity of the British law' governing relations between black and white. As the violence continued, three people were shot as white mobs continued to storm black homes, and yet, despite the effort of black leaders to keep their community within the bounds of the law, more Negroes were arrested than whites. Following terrifying incidents where mobs, led by soldiers, had pillaged Negro homes in the course of which 'The relations of coloured men with white women were referred to angrily', a mere four whites were arrested compared with fifteen Negroes. In Newport, where similar events took place, the figures were even more disparate: twenty-seven Negroes arrested and only three whites.[13]

Both in arrest and detention the Negroes, who were the victims of the violence, were subjected to scandalously biased treatment. Those arrested in Liverpool were removed from the gaols and 'placed in an internment camp pending repatriation', despite the fact that their actions had been simply to defend themselves against youths who had climbed onto their houses, 'broke up the slates and threw them on the negroes.' [14] Gross injustices inflicted on the various black communities in 1919 came, not solely from the mobs, but also at the hands of the police and the courts, although in London legal discrimination seems to have been absent. Though not as crudely or blatantly administered as in the eighteenth century, English law once again proved itself unequal to the task of safeguarding the rights of Negroes in a white society.

The riots had profoundly divisive effects on the black community. Memories of that harrowing June lingered on among those Negroes who remained in the country, but others took the hint from the mobs and returned home to the colonies. Even the government took the opportunity afforded by the unhappiness induced by the riots to encourage repatriation. Shipping lines were given governmental encouragement to offer berths to Negroes seeking a passage home, and by August 1921, 627 had returned under this scheme. Repatriation had of course been behind the Sierra Leone scheme of 1787; it was used after the troubles of 1919 and was to receive even more powerful support in the 1960s. Whenever British society ran into social trouble with the black minorities it had created and exploited, repatriation was its first political response.

Throughout the 1919 riots sexual jealousy had been an open element in the response of white mobs to the Negroes. Fears, alarmingly similar to those whipped up by the eighteenth century planters, reappeared. Evidence of a new wave of feeling against the Negro because of his attraction to white women was noticeable in comments about late nineteenth-century travelling Negro shows.[15] By 1919 this by now traditional resentment was directed against the new black community. Since a majority of it was male, it was inevitable that some would turn to local women for companionship. In this respect the mating patterns of the Negroes in the early twentieth century were similar to those of the eighteenth; so too was the animosity shown towards black-white relations by white males. Although difficult to prove, it would seem that interracial sexual relations and the hostile response towards them constitute

Into the Twentieth Century: 1900–1945

one of the most important ingredients in the slow germination of English racialism, from the sixteenth century to the twentieth. For long periods this sexual resentment remained inert and only came to the fore when economic and social distress projected the black community into the forefront of political controversy. This was particularly the case in the late eighteenth century. In 1919 on the other hand it was unemployment and postwar dislocation which brought about the revival of such resentment. Upon local Negroes a confused alliance of the unemployed, remnants from the armed forces and the fringe of urban criminal groups heaped their collective frustrations and tensions. Oddly enough, the most commonly heard complaint – black relations with white women – had nothing to do with the economic situation of the rioters. This resentment was in fact not an articulated complaint but an inbred response.

Repatriation of Negroes after 1919 failed to compensate for the number of new arrivals in the major towns and ports. On the contrary, black immigration strengthened the black communities in the interwar years. In London the bulk of new arrivals were added to the groups of stranded seamen in search of work.[16] In Cardiff the situation was even worse, for the contraction of the shipping industry threw local Negroes into stiff competition with white sailors for limited employment.[17] Some indication of their plight in Cardiff can be gauged from the fact that in June 1936 of 690 registered unemployed firemen on the Cardiff Docks Register 599 were black (or 'coloured').[18] Their plight was worsened by the refusal of the trade unions to accept them for what they really were: 'a sector of the same labouring class striving for livelihood on exactly the same basis as any other union member.'[19] Furthermore the Labour Party in opposition spoke up in defence of the unions' complaints against 'coloured labour'. Not for the last time the Labour Party openly sided with racial discrimination, guided in that direction by the amazing belief that the working class was, necessarily, white.

In Cardiff the black community fared worse than most others at the hands of the police. The Cardiff police enforced the Aliens Order of 1925 in a unique way, obliging all 'coloured' seamen, and not just aliens as the Act intended, to register with them. In registering with the police those black citizens who were British were obliged to prove their citizenship. Many, naturally, were unable to do so (as would many poor whites if placed in a similar position) and were automatically relegated to the category of alien. As such they were liable to arbitrary deportation.[20] The process of registering local Negroes also gave the Cardiff police a convenient tool for harassment. In 1935 the League of Coloured People discovered to its horror that the zealous Cardiff force had registered *all* local 'coloureds' as aliens.[21] This fact ought to be a sobering injunction against placing similar powers in police hands.

In the 1920s and 30s the black community began to experience new problems, problems which bring this study into the realms of contemporary sociological analysis. A new generation of children were growing up whose fathers were black unemployed workingmen. It was a generation which was British in every respect – but it was black and began to experience, for the first time in the twentieth century, that unique disqualification of being both working-class and black. In London, Liverpool, Swansea, Cardiff and Manchester this new generation of black children was nurtured on Public Assistance. To add to their problems, on leaving school they had even greater difficulty than their contemporaries in finding work, more particularly in the case of girls.[22] 'Is it generally known,' asked a black spokesman, 'that at present no coloured boy or girl can procure a job in an office no matter how qualified he or she may be?'[23] British society was putting into operation the hidden controls on complete integration and equality which have become so pronounced since 1945. Since most of these obstacles to black equality were hidden from white society, it was widely believed, as indeed it still is, that such discrimination did not exist.

Manchester and London were similarly affected by social tensions attendant on the rise of a black community which was unwelcome to the locals. But, once again, Cardiff excelled in its reaction to the 'problem'; 'in connection with the association of coloured seamen with white women and the consequent growth of a half-caste population, alien in sentiment and habits to the native white inhabitants, the Chief Constable of Cardiff has reported to the Watch Committee and suggested the desirability of bringing into existence legislation similar to that found necessary in South Africa to check this demoralizing development.'[24]

In the interwar years the black community offers an extreme example of the problems facing certain regional sections of the working-class in that period. Unemployment, with all its ancillary

Into the Twentieth Century: 1900–1945

troubles, was clearly not the unique experience of Negroes, but it was proportionately more widespread among them, and all the more appalling, because it was aggravated and in some cases caused by discrimination on the part of management, unions, local authorities and even the government and opposition. When in the mid 1930s Mosley's Fascists stirred up racial hatred in the East End, their target was not simply the Jews. In King's Cross, Canning Town and Shoreditch there lived black working men who remembered the painful events of only seventeen years before when white violence had erupted against them. Working-class Negroes had experienced the venom of white society long before the fascists gave it a creed and organization. Their children and grandchildren were to taste similar bitterness in succeeding years.

Not all Negroes in Britain in the 1930s belonged to the depressed working-class, for in that decade there developed a black intellectual group which was to exercise a political influence out of all proportion to its numbers in the years after 1945. London in particular provided a base for some of the most important black activists of the twentieth century. Black nationalists from Africa, the West Indies and the United States found in London a focus for their actions and a source of black cooperation. Jomo Kenyatta arrived in 1931. C. L. R. James in 1932, Marcus Garvey in 1934 and George Padmore in 1935.[25] Paul Robeson, perhaps the most famous Negro living in London at the time, used the city as his base in his unique private struggle for the black cause. But all entered a black society whose political and economic organizations were varied, confusing and sometimes contradictory. There were rivalries among Africans, among West Indians, among black students, black workers and frequently among all groups together. On the eve of World War II there were at least sixteen black organizations claiming to speak for various sectional interests. But they had certain bonds of unity. The Italian invasion of Abyssinia, for example, had drawn together diverse black political groups. 'With the realization of their utter defencelessness against the new aggression from Europeans in Africa, the blacks felt it necessary to look to themselves.'[26]

Led by C. L. R. James, black agitators set out to win to their side all shades of black opinion on both sides of the Atlantic, as well as influential friends on the British left.[27] Eventually in March 1937 the International Friends of Abyssinia was absorbed by the International

African Service Bureau, which in its turn became the enormously influential Pan-African Federation of 1944. From the combined efforts of British-based Negroes, a wave of black publications rolled off the presses in the late 1930s. In them the British government was harangued on a wide range of issues, from Ethiopia itself to the serious Jamaican riots of 1938. Some of their campaigns were immediately successful. It was pressure from black ginger groups which for instance cracked open the colour bar in the British armed forces. On 19 October 1939 the Colonial Office announced that 'British subjects from the colonies and British protected persons in this country, including those who are not of European descent, are now eligible for emergency commissions in His Majesty's Forces'.[28] Once again the British called upon the empire to fight the mother country's war.

Like the 1914–18 war, World War II witnessed a massive influx of Negroes, both colonial and American, to man the armed forces and industry. By 1945 some 8,000 Negroes had been recruited for service in Britain, about half of them in the R.A.F.[29] Skilled labour from the West Indies was again recruited to work in the ordnance factories. In 1941 a group of fifty black technicians from Jamaica landed in Scotland, to be greeted by a telegram from Lord Moyne, the Secretary of State for the Colonies, welcoming them to Britain.[30] Only twenty years before the British government had actively encouraged the repatriation of an earlier generation of Negroes who had helped to fight the war. A similar pattern was repeating itself. When economic need demanded black labour, Britain was eager to house black workers; once the need had passed Britain was unwilling to contemplate the full consequences of black settlement.

With the exception of men in the armed forces, the largest black occupational group to develop in World War II consisted of sailors. In this, as in so many other respects, the contribution of the black colonies to the task of maintaining Britain's vital sea-links in times of war has been virtually ignored. There was of course nothing new in this. Since the eighteenth century, large numbers of British ships had used black sailors, but in the years 1914–18 and 1939–45, this labour was all the more vital because of the importance of maritime links.

On the conclusion of peace most of the black servicemen returned home but, following the pattern of 1918, large numbers of

Into the Twentieth Century: 1900–1945

black sailors stayed. Figures are hard to come by, but it was calculated that the total black population of Britain in 1945 was in the region of 10,000.[31] The great majority of them were working-class, although there was a sprinkling of professional people – doctors, professional artists, students and nurses. Ironically, during and immediately after the war, black nurses frequently had great trouble in securing hospital posts, despite efforts on their behalf by the League of Coloured Peoples.[32] They were openly discriminated against and yet, in the years since 1945, black nurses have become vital to the British medical services, another illustration of the way British tolerance of Blacks has been closely related to economic need.

The condition of any individual Negro in the war would clearly depend on his social class. Professionals were fully accepted into their natural class by the British. But the overwhelming majority of Negroes were working-class, facing much more serious problems than even the traditional working-class community.[33] The stage was thus set, even before the waves of new immigration in the 1950s and 1960s, for a pattern of discrimination and social deprivation similar to that which had haunted black settlers after 1918.

Violence on a small scale did break out between black and white,[34] but more significant was the creeping racial discrimination which became ever more noticeable in the war years. One basic cause and object of this discrimination was the large number of black American troops stationed in Britain. Discrimination was so widespread by the autumn of 1942 that the Labour M.P. Tom Driberg questioned the Prime Minister about 'the introduction in some parts of Britain of discrimination against negro troops'. Churchill refused to be drawn on the issue, pointing out that the Minister of Information had already put on record the government's opposition to any form of discrimination.[35] At its most blatant, discrimination consisted of open refusal to serve Negroes in public places. Such refusals became commonplace, so much so that one American Commanding Officer took to issuing his black troops with a covering letter: 'Pte—— is a soldier in the United States army and it is necessary that he sometimes has a meal, which he has on occasions, found difficult to obtain. I would be grateful if you would look after him.'[36] Nor were such rebuffs the preserve of American Negroes. In Liverpool, a West Indian electrician was refused entry to a dance, only to return dressed in his Home Guard uniform. Refused entry again, the despairing man subsequently refused to parade with the Home Guard and was promptly fined.[37] Cases which caught the public eye were exceptional but the discrimination which became public knowledge was merely the tip of the iceberg, for the black community was increasingly subject to all forms of racial discrimination.[38]

Of all such incidents during World War II few brought home to the public the full implication of the spread of racial discrimination better than that involving Learie Constantine. This well-known and respected West Indian cricketer was employed as a welfare officer for black workers in the North West. In the summer of 1943, while in London to captain a West Indian cricket team, Constantine was refused entry to a London hotel, despite having a prior booking. The reason for his exclusion was simple. 'We are not going to have these niggers in our hotel.'[39] Constantine brought the issue to court in a case which received wide publicity and which he succeeded in winning (securing damages of a mere £5).[40] In the eighteenth century there had been a permanent gap between legal decisions and the actual course of events which were supposed to be shaped by legal decisions. The same pattern prevailed into the twentieth century. Constantine's case had established the technical illegality of discrimination in public places. Nonetheless it continued. It had become so pronounced by the end of the war that strong pressure built up to stem it by refusing licences to any establishment which refused to serve a person because of his colour. The postwar Labour government however refused to take any such positive steps.[41]

In many of the racial incidents examined here, a great deal of tension had been generated by the sexual relations which flourished between white girls and Negroes. World War II saw an exaggeration of this tension, particularly in relation to black Americans. In one incident the mutual attraction caused a virtual riot.[42] The impending embarkation of black American troops for the U.S.A. in September 1945 triggered off an amazing sequence of events in a camp near Bristol. Local police were called in to protect black troops from a mob of local girls, distressed to hear of their impending departure. Lining the camp, singing 'Don't Fence me in', the girls proved irresistibly tempting to the troops who broke out of camp. They were only separated from the waiting girls by the arrival of reinforcements of Military Police. Similar scenes were repeated on the following day at the railway station. Although unusual in its scope

Into the Twentieth Century: 1900-1945

and frankness, this display of affection for Negroes was repeated on a minor scale in many parts of the country. It could have done little to ease the traditional phobias of English males in their attitude towards interracial sexual contacts.

By the time this incident took place Europe had settled into an uneasy peace. The years which followed, bringing fundamental changes throughout the British empire, saw the dramatic acceleration of immigration into Britain. After 1945 the subject of immigration and race relations enters the more modern realm of social investigation. The full story of modern immigration is a new chapter in a story which stretches back to the sixteenth century, but it is a chapter which the present author is not equipped to handle. Suffice it to say that the events of the postwar years, while different in scale and impact, form a continuation of the well established history of black people in this country, rather than being a new story. In retrospect it feels as though history had begun to repeat itself.

Notes

CHAPTER THIRTEEN: *Into the Twentieth Century: 1900-1945*

1. *Report of the Committee on Distressed Colonial and Indian Subjects*, 1910, P.P., 1910, xxii, from which the following details are taken.
2. Little, 34–5; Dilip Hiro 'Three Generations of Tiger Bay', *New Society*, 21 September 1967.
3. Little, 34–5.
4. Sidney Collins, *Coloured Minorities in Britain*, London, Lutterworth Press, 1957, 11–12.
5. Banton, *The Coloured Quarter*, 33; Little, 56.
6. C. L. Joseph, 'The British West Indies Regiment, 1914–18', *Journal of Caribbean History*, ii, May 1971.
7. Collins, 36.
8. Little, 56.
9. Banton, *The Coloured Quarter*, 33.

10. *The Times*, 13 May 1919, 7.
11. *The Times*, 10 June 1919, 9.
12. *The Times*, 11 June 1919, 9.
13. *The Times*, 13 June 1919, 9.
14. ibid.
15. Chapter Twelve above.
16. Banton, *The Coloured Quarter*, 34–5.
17. Little, 60.
18. ibid., 74.
19. ibid., 61.
20. ibid., 63–4.
21. D. A. Vaughan, *Negro Victory*, London, Independent Press, 1950, 77.
22. Little, 69–70.
23. Vaughan, 80.
24. Quoted in Banton, *The Coloured Quarter*, 35.
25. For this information I rely upon R. Macdonald's unpublished paper, *London as a Focus for Black Anti-Imperial Agitation, 1934–1939*, Syracuse University, 1970.
26. ibid., 4.
27. ibid., 5–6.
28. Quoted in ibid., 13.
29. 'The Negro in Britain', *The Negro Year Book*, Alabama, 1947, 584.
30. ibid., 592; F. J. Klinberg, 'As to the State of Jamaica in 1707', *Journal of Negro History*, 27, 1942, 288.
31. 'The Negro in Britain', *The Negro Year Book*, 583.
32. ibid., 593.
33. ibid., 584.
34. ibid., 584–5.
35. *The Times*, 30 September 1942, 8.
36. Letter to *The Times*, 2 October 1942, 5.
37. *The Times*, 2 August 1944, 2.
38. Letter from Dr H. A. Moody to *The Times*, 10 August 1944, 8.
39. 'Constantine v. Imperial Hotels', Law Reports, *The Times*, 20 June 1944, 2.
40. *The Times*, 29 June 1944, 2; H. Montgomery Hyde, *Norman Birkett*, London, 1964, 487–90.
41. *The Times*, 21 December 1945, 8.
42. George Padmore, *Pittsburgh Courier*, 1 September 1945; *Sunday Pictorial*, 25 August 1945.

Conclusion

This book ends with a reaffirmation of the point made at the beginning. Negroes have lived in England since the mid-sixteenth century. In various roles and relationships, their individual and collective experiences have been inextricably woven into the structure of English society.

The elements of continuity in black history in England are more striking than the historical breaks, and more significant than the distinctions marking off one generation from another. Equally, white English responses to black minorities have proved similar, if not precisely the same, in a number of greatly differing historical and social contexts. Between the late seventeenth and mid-twentieth century black society evolved out of the experience and life style of the black pre-industrial poor (and more recently from daily life in the lower reaches of the urban working class). But the Negro's economic role in English society has been traditionally determined, or justified, by considerations of colour, a fact which, when coupled with the African and West Indian cultural inheritance, has cut him off from Englishmen of a similar socio-economic level. In response to the English evaluation and treatment of Negroes on colour lines, Negroes have been forced to look to themselves – to their own numerical strength and sense of ethnic identity – in their search for a solution to their peculiar problems.

In the eighteenth century, as in the twentieth, Negroes lived in black enclaves which were, at once, a haven from a hostile host society and a source of friction with those elements in white society which resented their presence. From the depths of the black community spokesmen were occasionally thrown up who spoke with a concern, flowing from a realisation of their ethnic isolation, for their brothers on both sides of the Atlantic. The tone of international sympathy so vital to contemporary black radicalism is in keeping with, though quite different from, this historical precedent of black brotherhood.

White reactions to Negroes are often difficult to distinguish from white reactions to other non-whites, but in both cases the evolution of racial attitudes – friendly or hostile – is a historical phenomenon, only to be fully comprehended in a historical setting. Often the English have learned about Negroes at first hand; more often however their views have been moulded by second-hand garbled mythology. Consequently the roots of racial prejudice against the Negro lie buried in different layers of historical experience. As the social and economic setting changed, so too did the contours of relations. That said, there has nonetheless been a law of historical inheritance which has bestowed the racial attitudes of one generation upon their children.

Black chattel slavery existed in England for two and a half centuries. But it was not the same as West Indian slavery, nor a development of medieval villeinage. It was fundamentally a colonial institution transplanted into England, where it was kept uneasily afloat by certain English traditions about property which were ill-designed to cope with the concept of property in human beings. In all this, English law played a crucial role both in reflecting, and helping to mould, social reality.

Black society as a historical force in England has been almost totally ignored, and this attempt to survey its relationship with white society has produced a story which will affect readers differently. To the author the story which has unfolded has been largely depressing; the excitement of historical discovery has been dulled by both the long-term and the immediate implications of the facts uncovered. In some respects English responses to the black presence have been more revealing about white society than they are about black experience. But it seems clear that these responses, with the odd exception, have been bounded on the one side by open and legally approved cruelty and on the other by indifference and moral insensibility.

All this is not to claim that the history of the black community in England will explain the nature of present-day black society and race relations. But it seems reasonable to the author to assert that without at least an acknowledgment of the historical dimension, any analysis of relations between black and white will be incomplete. In this I take as a fundamental principle the powerful words of C. Wright Mills: 'The problems of our time ... cannot be stated adequately without consistent practice of the view that history is

Conclusion

the shank of social study, and recognition of the need to develop further a psychology of man that is sociologically grounded and historically relevant.'[1] The history of Negroes in England is a history which both black and white need to learn if they are to know each other and themselves more thoroughly.

CONCLUSION

1. C. Wright Mills, 'Uses of history', in *The Sociological Imagination*, Penguin Books, 1970, 159.

Bibliography

MANUSCRIPT SOURCES

Granville Sharp Papers, Hardwicke Court, Gloucester
Granville Sharp, Letter Book, Minster Library, York
Minutes for the Relief of the Black Poor, Public Record Office:

T. 630.1000	T. 634.2012
631.1000	634.1903
631.1304	634.1946
631.1333	636.2430
631.1359	638.2744
632.1513	638.2864
632.1623	641.140
633.1673	643.487
633.1707	644.777
633.1815	645.968
	647.1572

PRINTED PRIMARY SOURCES

Acts of the Privy Council
Calendar of State Papers, Domestic. (Cal. S.P. Dom.)
Calendar of State Papers, Colonial America and West Indies (Cal. S.P. Am. W.I.)
Howell's State Trials, XX
Parliamentary Papers, 1814–15, III, 1816, V, 1842, XXXVIII, 1866, XXXI, 1910, XXXII
Proclamation by the Lord Mayor of London, September 1731, City of London Record Office
Public General Statutes
Records of the Africa Association, 1788–1831, ed. R. Hallett, London, 1964
Returns of Aliens in the City and Suburbs of London, Huguenot Society, 3 vols, Aberdeen, 1900–7
Reports of the African Institution, London, 1807–26

Reports of the House of Commons, 1785–1807, X
Statutes at Large

PAMPHLETS

The African Company's Property to the Ports and Settlements in Guinea considered, London, 1709
JAMES ANDERSON, Observations on Slavery, Manchester, 1789
An Appeal to the Candour and Justice of the People of England . . ., London, 1792
WILLIAM BECKFORD, Remarks upon the Situation of Negroes in Jamaica, London, 1788
The Black Prince, London, 1810
Britannia Liberia, or a Defence of the Free State of Man in England, London, 1772
A BRITISH PLANTER, Negro Emancipation made Easy, London, 1816
A BRITON, Considerations on certain Remarks on the Negro Slavery and Abolition Question, London, 1827
Christian Directions and Instructions for Negroes, London, 1807
THOMAS CLARKSON, On the Slavery and Commerce of the Human Species, London, 1786
The Common Sense Book, I, London, 1824
Common Sense to John Bull, Leicester, 1829
Considerations on the Emancipation of Negroes, London, 1788
Considerations on the Negro Cause, by a West Indian, London, 1772
THOMAS COOPER, Facts Illustrative of the Condition of Negro slaves in England, London, 1824.
Cursory Remarks upon the Rev. Ramsay's Essays . . ., London, 1785
WILLIAM DICKSON, Letters on Slavery, London, 1789
Discourse on the Advantage of the African Trade to the Nation, n.d.
An Essay upon the Trade to Africa, London, 1711
Free Trade in Negroes, London, 1849
G. FRANCKLYN, Observations on the Slave Trade, London, 1789
JESSE FOOT, Observations, 1805
MORGAN GODWYN, A Supplement to the Negro's and Indian's Advocate, London, 1681
A Guide to Prayer for the Young, London, 1830
R. HARRIS, Scriptural Researches on the Treatment and Conversion of Slaves, Liverpool, 1788

Black and White

ANTHONY HILL, *After Baptzatus* . . ., London, 1701–2
The History of Mary Prince, London, 1831
JAMES HOUSTON, *Some New and Accurate Observations* . . ., London, 1725
Inquiries relating to Negro Emancipation, London, 1829
Instructions for the Treatment of Negroes, London, 1797
An Important Appeal to the Reason, Justice and Patriotism of the People of Illinois, 1824
J. JEREMIE, *Four Essays on Colonial Slavery*, London, 1831
HANNAH KILHAM, *Report on a Recent Visit to the Colony of Sierra Leone*, London, 1828
The Claims of West Africa to Christian Instruction Through The Native Languages, London, 1830
W. KNOX, *Three Tracts* . . ., London, 1768
A Letter from a Merchant in Bristol . . ., 1709
A Letter from Capt. J. S. Smith . . ., London, 1786
A Letter To Philo-Africanus . . ., London, 1787
EDWARD LONG, *Candid Reflections* . . ., London, 1772
J. MARRYAT, *More Thoughts* . . ., London, 1815
J. MATTHEWS, *A Voyage to the River Sierra Leone*, London, 1788
H. M'NEIL, *Observations on the Treatment of Negroes* . . ., London, n.d.
Negro Emancipation Morally and Politically Considered, London, 1824
The Negro's Friend or, the Sheffield Anti-Slavery Album, Sheffield, 1826
The Negro's Memorial, by an Abolitionist, London, 1825
The Negro Servant, London, 1810
Negro Slavery . . ., London, 1823
Negro Slavery described by a Negro, ed. S. Strickland, 1831
R. B. NICKOLLS, *Letter*, London, 1788
R. NORRIS, *Memoirs of the Reign of Bossa Ahadee*, London, 1789
No Rum!, No Sugar!, London, 1792
Observations on the Bill . . ., London, 1816
Observations on the Evidence given before the Committees of the Privy Council and the House of Commons, London, 1791
Observations on Some of the African Company's late Printed Papers, 1709
An Oration Pronounced on the 29th of July, 1829, London, n.d.

A. PLANTER, *Commercial Reasons for the Non-Abolition of the Slave Trade*, London, 1789
M. POSTLEWAYT, *The National and Private Advantage of the African Trade*, London, 1746
The Principles, Plans and Objects of the 'Hibernian Negro's Friend Society' . . ., Dublin, 1831
J. PUGH, *Remarkable Occurrences* . . ., 1788
J. RAMSAY, *On the Treatment and Conversion of Slaves*, London, 1784
H. SMEATHMAN, *Substance of a Plan of Settlement*, London, 1786
G. SHARP, *A Representation of the Injustice* . . ., London, 1769
T. THOMPSON, *An Account of Two Missionary Voyages* . . ., 1758 (?)
R. THORPE, *A Letter to William Wilberforce*, London, 1815
J. TOBIN, *A Short Rejoinder* . . ., London, 1787
J. WESLEY, *Thoughts on Slavery*, 1774
A WEST INDIAN PLANTER, *A Letter to the Members of Parliament* . . ., London, 1792
A WEST INDIAN PLANTER, *Letter to the Most Hon. The Marquis of Chandos*, London, 1830
A Word from the Bible . . ., London, 1829
A Very New Pamphlet Indeed! . . ., London, 1792

PAMPHLET AND DOCUMENTARY COLLECTIONS

Goldsmith's Library London, 50 volumes
  Pamphlets on the Slave Trade, 17 vols
  Tracts on West Indian Slavery, 17 vols
  Tracts on the Slave Trade, 11 vols
  Tracts of the Anti-Slavery Society, 2 vols
  Abolition of the Slave Trade, 2 vols
  Abridgement, Slave Trade, I vol
  Broadsides, vols I and IV
J. W. BLAKE, *Europeans in West Africa*, London, 1942, 2 vols
H. T. CATTERALL, *Judicial Cases Concerning American Slavery and the Negro*, 5 vols, Washington, 1926–36
ELIZABETH DONNAN, *Documents Illustrative of the Slave Trade to America*, 4 vols, Washington, 1930–35
C. FYFE, *Sierra Leone Inheritance*, London, Oxford University Press (West African History Series) 1964
RICHARD HAKLUYT, *The Principal Navigations, Voiages, Traffiques*

Black and White

    and Discoveries of the English Nation, 12 vols, Glasgow, 1904
Historical Manuscripts Commission
SAMUEL PURCHAS, *Purchas His Pilgrimes*, 20 vols, Glasgow, 1905-7
Tudor Royal Proclamations, 1588-1603, ed. P. L. Hughes and J. F. Larkin, Yale University Press, 1969
ERIC WILLIAMS, *Documents of West Indian History*, Port-of-Spain, 1963

CONTEMPORARY PRINTED SOURCES

The African Widow, being the History of a Poor Black Woman, London, n.d.
LEO AFRICANUS, *The History and Description of Africa*, ed. Robert Brown, Hakluyt Society, London, 1896
Reminiscences of Henry Angelo, 2 vols, London, 1828
E. ARBER, *The First Three English Books on America*, London, 1895
A. BENEZET, *Some Historical Account of Guinea*, London, 1788
W. BLACKSTONE, *Commentaries on the Laws of England*, Oxford, 3rd edn, 1773
SIR THOMAS BROWNE, *The Works of Sir Thomas Browne*, 4 vols, ed G. Keynes, 2nd edn, London, Faber, 1964
THOMAS CARLYLE, Discourse on the Nigger Question, in *Critical and Miscellaneous Essays*, London, 1872, vii.
THOMAS CLARKSON, *The History of the Rise, Progress, and Accomplishment of the Abolition of the Slave Trade*, 2 vols, London, 1808
GEORGE CRUIKSHANK, *Comic Almanack*, 1835-43, London
Four Hundred Humerous Illustrations, London, n.d.
OTTOBAH CUGOANO, *Thoughts and Sentiments on the Evil of Slavery*, London, 1787; ed. P. Edwards, London, Dawsons Pall Mall, 1969
THOMAS DAY, *The Dying Negro*, 1773
BRYAN EDWARDS, *The History, Civil and Commercial of the British Colonies in the West Indies*, 2 vols, London, 1793
OLAUDAH EQUIANO, *Interesting Narrative of the Life of Olaudah Equiano, or Gustavus Vassa, the African, written by himself*, 2 vols, London, 1789 [cited in references as Equiano]
Equiano's Travels, ed. P. Edwards, London, Dawsons Pall Mall, 1967
SIR JOHN FIELDING, *Penal Laws*, London, 1768
The Original Writings of the two Richards Hakluyt ed. E. G. R. Taylor, Hakluyt Society, London, 1935

Bibliography

Hogarth's Graphic Works, ed. R. Paulson, Yale University Press, 1965
P. HOARE, *Memoirs of Granville Sharp*, London, 1820
EDWARD LONG, *History of Jamaica*, 3 vols, London, 1774
Mandeville's Travels, ed. M. Letts, 2 vols, Cambridge University Press for Hakluyt Society, 1953
J. S. MILL, On the Negro Question, *Fraser's Magazine*, January 1850
Missionary Stories, London, 1842
J. MONTGOMERY, *The Abolition of the Slave Trade*, London, 1814
H. MAYHEW, *London Labour and the London Poor*, 4 vols, Dover Publications, 1968
IGNATIUS SANCHO, *The Letters of the late Ignatius Sancho*, ed. J. Jeckyll, London, 1782; ed. P. Edwards, London, Dawsons Pall Mall, 1968
W. G. SEWELL, *The Ordeal of Free Labour In the British West Indies*, New York, 1861
B. SILLIMAN, *A Journal of Travels in England, Holland and Scotland in the Years 1805 and 1806*, New Haven Conn., 1820
H. TAINE, *Notes on England*, London, 1872
J. THELWALL, *The Vestibule of Eloquence*, London, 1810
ANTHONY TROLLOPE, *The West Indies and the Spanish Main*, London, 1859
H. G. TUKE, *The Fugitive Slave Circulars*, London, 1826
Narrative of the Life of James Watkins, Bolton, 1852
Narrative of the Life of John Williams, London, 1855

SECONDARY SOURCES

J. ASHLEY, *Social Life in the Reign of Queen Anne*, 2 vols, London, 1882
J. V. ASIEGBU, *Slavery and the Politics of Liberation, 1787–1861*, London, Longman, 1970
M. P. BANTON, *The Coloured Quarter*, London, Cape, 1955
Race Relations, London, Tavistock, 1967
C. R. BEAZLEY, *The Dawn of Modern Geography*, 3 vols, New York, P. Smith, 1949
C. F. BECKINGHAM and G. W. B. HUNTINGFORD, *The Prester John of the Indies*, 2 vols, Cambridge University Press for Hakluyt Society, 1961
J. W. BLAKE, *European Beginnings in West Africa*, London, Longmans, 1937

C. R. BOXER, *The Portuguese Seaborne Empire, 1415–1825*, London, Hutchinson, 1969
CHRISTINE BOLT, *Victorian Attitudes to Race*, London, Routledge, 1971
A. T. CAREY, *Colonial Students in London*, London, Secker & Warburg, 1956
R. R. CAWLEY, *The Voyagers in Elizabethan Drama*, Boston, Modern Language Association, 1938
LORD CAMPBELL, *Lives of the Lord Chancellors*, London, 1874
S. COLLINS, *Coloured Minorities in Britain*, London, Lutterworth Press, 1957
M. J. CRATON, and J. WALVIN, *A Jamaican Plantation*, London, W. H. Allen, 1970
P. D. CURTIN, *Two Jamaicas*, Harvard University Press, 1955
The Image of Africa, University of Wisconsin Press, 1964
Africa Remembered, University of Wisconsin Press, 1967
The Slave Trade: a census, University of Wisconsin Press, 1969
BASIL DAVIDSON, *Black Mother*, London, Longman, 1970
K. G. DAVIES, *The Royal African Company*, London, Longmans, 1957
D. B. DAVIS, *The Problem of Slavery In Western Culture*, Cornell University Press, 1968.
H. G. FARMER, *Military Music*, New York, Chanticleer, 1950
C. FYFE, *A History of Sierra Leone*, London, Oxford University Press, 1962
M. D. GEORGE, *London Life in the Eighteenth Century*, rev. edn, London, Penguin (Peregrine), 1966
From Hogarth to Cruickshank, London, Allen Lane, The Penguin Press, 1967
ELSA GOVEIA, *West India Slave Laws of the 18th Century*, Caribbean Universities Press (London, Ginn), 1970
D. GRANT, *The Fortunate Slave*, London, Oxford University Press, 1968.
R. HALLETT, *The Penetration of Africa to 1815*, London, Routledge, 1965
J. J. HECHT, *Continental and Colonial Servants in 18th century England*, Northampton, Mass., Smith College, 1954
BOB HEPPLE, *Race, jobs and the law in Britain*, Penguin Books, 1970
D. HIRO, *Black British, White British*, London, Eyre and Spottiswoode, 1971
W. S. HOLDSWORTH, *A History of English Law*, London, 1903

C. HOLE, *History of the CMS*, London, 1896.

D. HUMPHREY and G. JOHN, *Because They're Black*, Penguin Books, 1971

E. JONES, *Othello's Countrymen: the African in English Renaissance Drama*, London, Oxford University Press, 1965

WINTHROP JORDAN, *White Over Black*, Baltimore, Penguin Books, 1969

Introduction to Scottish Legal History, Edinburgh, The Stair Society, 1958

F. J. KLINGBERG, *The Anti-Slavery Movement in England*, New Haven, Conn., 1926

J. LATIMER, *The Annals of Bristol in the Eighteenth Century*, Frome, 1893

The Annals of Bristol in the Seventeenth Century, Bristol, 1900

M. LETTS, *Sir John Mandeville, The Man and His Book*, London, Batchworth, 1949

K. L. LITTLE, *Negroes in Britain*, London, Kegan Paul, 1948

V. S. NAIPAUL, *The Loss of El Dorado*, London, Deutsch, 1969

J. E. NEALE, *Elizabeth I*, London, Cape, 1934, Penguin Books, 1961

A.P. NEWTON, *The European Nations in the West Indies*, London, A. and C. Black, 1933

Travel and Travellers in the Middle Ages, London, Kegan Paul, 1934

G. W. T. ORMOND, *The Lord Advocates of Scotland*, Edinburgh, 1883

S. OLIVIER, *The Myth of Governor Eyre*, London, Hogarth Press, 1933

R. PARES, *War and Trade in the West Indies*, Oxford, Clarendon Press, 1936

J. H. PARRY, *The European Reconnaissance*, London, Macmillan, 1968

The Spanish Seaborne Empire, London, Hutchinson, 1966

and P. SHERLOCK, *A Short History of the West Indies*, 3rd edn, London, Macmillan, 1968

C. F. PASCOE, *Two Hundred Years of the SPCK*, London, 1967

C. PASTON, *Social Caricature in the Eighteenth Century*, London, 1905

O. PATTERSON, *The Sociology of Slavery*, London, MacGibbon & Kee, 1967

H. W. PEDICORD, *The Theatrical Public in the Time of Garrick*, New York, Kings Crown Press; Oxford University Press, 1954

B. PENROSE, *Travel and Discovery in the Rennaissance*, Harvard University Press, 1960
F. W. PITMAN, *The Development of the West Indies*, New Haven Conn., 1911
L. RADZINOWICZ, *History of English Criminal Law*, 4 vols, London, Stevens & Sons, 1948–68
L. J. RAGATZ, *The Fall of the Planter Class in the British Carribbean*, London, Appleton-Century, 1928
A. H. RICHMOND, *Colour Prejudice in Britain*, London, Routledge, 1954
CAROLINE ROBBINS, *The Eighteenth-Century Commonwealth Man*, Harvard University Press, 1959
R. ROBINSON and J. GALLAGHER, *Africa and the Victorians*, London, Macmillan, 1961
J. A. ROGERS, *Nature Knows No Color-Line*, New York, printed privately, 1952
Sex and Race, 2 vols, New York, 1952
W. RODNEY, *History of the Upper Guinea Coast*, Oxford University Press, 1970
E. J. B. ROSE and associates, *Colour and Citizenship*, London, Oxford University Press, 1969
A. L. ROWSE, *The Expansion of Elizabethan England*, London, Macmillan, 1955
GEORGE RUDE, *Hanoverian London*, London, Secker & Warburg, 1971
R. SHERIDAN, *The Development of the Plantations to 1750*, Caribbean Universities Press; London, Ginn, 1970
M J SMITH, *Plural Society In the West Indies*, University of California Press, 1965
F. SNOWDEN, *Blacks in Antiquity*, Harvard University Press, 1971
W. SYPHER, *Guinea's Captive Kings*, Chapel Hill, North Carolina, 1942
E. P. THOMPSON, *Making of the English Working Class*, London, Gollancz, 1963
D. R. VAUGHAN, *Negro Victory*, London, Independent Press, 1950
G. S. VEITCH, *The Genesis of Parliamentary Reform*, London, 1913
R. WEST, *Back to Africa: a history of Sierra Leone and Liberia*, London, Cape, 1970
R. WINKS, *The Blacks in Canada*, Yale University Press, 1971
ERIC WILLIAMS, *Capitalism and Slavery*, University of North Carolina Press, 1944; London, Deutsch, 1964

History of the People of Trinidad and Tobago, London, Deutsch, 1964
From Columbus to Castro: The History of the Caribbean, London, Deutsch, 1970
J. A. WILLIAMSON, *Hawkins of Plymouth*, London, A. and C. Black, 1949
P. C. YORKE, *The Life and Correspondence of Phillip Yorke*, 2 vols, Cambridge, 1913

ARTICLES

H. APETEKER, 'The Quakers and Negro history', *Journal of Negro History*, xxv, 1940
W. BAKER, 'William Wilberforce and the Idea of Negro Inferiority', *Journal of the History of Ideas*, xxxi, no. 3, 1970
M. COOK, 'J. J. Rousseau and the Negro', *Journal of Negro History*, xxi, 1936
E. FIDDES, 'Lord Mansfield and the Sommersett Case', *Law Quarterly Review*, l, 1934
F. T. H. FLETCHER, 'Montesquieu's influence on anti-slavery opinion in England', *Journal of Negro History*, xviii, 1933
R. A. FISHER, 'Manuscript material bearing on the Negroes in British archives', *Journal of Negro History*, xxvii, 1942
'Granville Sharp and Lord Mansfield,' *Journal of Negro History*, xxviii, 1943
D. HIRO, 'Three generations of Tiger Bay', *New Society*, 21 September, 1967
C. L. JOSEPH, 'The British West India Regiment, 1914', *Journal of Caribbean History*, ii, May 1971
F. J. KLINGBERG, 'As to the State of Jamaica in 1707', *Journal of Negro History*, xxvii, 1942
M. LETTS, 'Prester John', *Transactions of the Royal Historical Society*, 4th Series, xxix, 1947
J. NADELHAFT, 'The Somerset Case and Slavery', *Journal of Negro History*, li, 1966
I. ORIGO, 'The domestic enemy; The eastern slaves in Tuscany in the 14th and 15th Centuries', *Speculum*, July 1955, xxx, no. 3

Black and White

PERIODICALS AND NEWSPAPERS

Annual Register
Bristol Gazette and Public Advertiser
Edinburgh Review
Felix Farley's Bristol Newspaper
Felix Farley's Bristol Journal
Gentleman's Magazine
Notes and Queries
Quarterly Review
The Scot's Magazine
The Times

Index

Abolition (1807), 191
Abolitionists, 68; see Humanitarians
Abolition Society, 183
'Abolition of the slave trade' (poem), 185
Alfred v Marquis of Fitzjames (1799), 135
Alleyne, Mr, 123
Allan, Mrs, 137
Admiralty, 93, 151
Ahadee, Bossa, 169
Andalusia, 1
Anne of Denmark, 9
Annual Register, The, 127
Antigua, 36, 137, 138, 191
American Civil War, 193
American Revolution, 48, 86
Americas, 47
Amerindians, 33
Arabs, 5, 6, 19
Army Council, 205
Armstrong, Thomas, 50
Asa-Asa, Louis, 193
'Atlantic', 149
Africa, 1, 2, 3, 47, 80, 84, 100–1
  animals, 17–18
  commodities, 16, 39, 40
  heat, 3, 6, 17, 19–20
  religions, 170
  trade, 41–2
  weather, 17

Bacon, Roger, 3
Bahamas, 148
Banks, Sir Joseph, 89

Baptist Church of Christ, Bristol, 64
Barbados, 36, 37, 118
Barber, Francis, 53
Barry, 206
Baskerville, Sir Thomas, 8
Beckford, William, 57
Bedford, 58, 198
Belfast, 93
'Belisarius', 149
Benezet, Anthony, 126
Berbers, 5, 19
Bermuda, 36, 136
Best, George, 20, 21
Best, Mr Justice, 137
Beswick (slave), 65
Biblical sources, 21
Biafra, 89
Birmingham, 93
Blacks, American troops, 213–14
  in Canada, 153–4
  and Chain of Being, 182
  labour; English dependence on, 73
  and literary caricature, 159
  myth of indolence, 160, 164–7
  myth of musicality, 70–71, 160, 170
  myth of relation to apes, 168–9
  myth of sexuality, 22, 26, 53, 160, 162, 163, 164
  myth of stupidity, 160, 167–8
Blacks, as Noble Savage, 183–4, 186
Blacks in England, 1, 2, 6, 7, 8, 9, 11, 21, 23, 27, 105, 150, 165, 178, 180, 189, 190 (Chapter 4)
  in armed forces, 205, 212

Index

Blacks in England (contd)
  acculturation of, 63, 66–7, 68–70
  Americans, 58, 189–90, 193
  baptisms, 51, 64, 65, 66; white attitudes towards, 64–5
  beggars, 48, 189, 190
  brutalization of, 59–60, 192
  as commodity, 11, 50, 60, 107, 109–10, 112, 119–20, 177–8
  community, 12, 49, 95, 111, 128, 135, 139, 154, 190, 196, 197, 203, 209, 213, 217 (Chapter 4); relations with poor whites, 57
  crime among, 57–8
  education of, 63
  first impressions of whites, 90
  free, 9, 10, 49, 56, 64
  language of, 62, 63, 99
  and the law, 140
  literacy, 62–3
  loyalty among, 50
  marriage patterns, 99
  metal collars for, 60
  musicians, 70–71, 189
  names of, 66–7, 90, 95
  Nationalists, 211
  population, 46–7; sexual imbalance in, 52, 150, 197, 204–5; dispersal of, 72
  poor, 58–9, 92, 94, 135, 144–6, 151, 189, 190
  professional class, 213
  refugees, 48, 49
  religion of, 64–70, 90–92, 96, 110, 112; fear of, 67; impact of, 67–8; ideology of, 69–70
  repatriation of, 208–9, (Chapter 9)
  runaways, 49, 51, 56
  sailors, 7, 48, 202, 203, 212
  school for, 96–7
  servants, 9, 10, 52, 55, 191, 202; livery of, 10, 27, 62, 77 n.
  skilled artisans, 56, 57
  social life, 61
  social mobility of, 63
  students, 51, 194–6
  threat to white employment alleged, 59, 209
  unemployment, 203, 206, 209, 210–11
  unity among, 49, 61, 87
  workers in heavy industry, 205
'Black Ivory', 17, 40
Blackamoor (blackamore, blakimore), 8, 11, 25
Blackness, cultural value of, 24, 27
  imagery of, 24–5
  and ethnic unity, 61
Blackstone, William, 115, 118, 179
Blake, William, 185
Bluett, Thomas, 82
Blundell, Sir George, 11
Bolt, Christine, 172
Boswell, James, 133
Boxing, 72
Brabantio, 26
Brazil, 31, 33, 166, 192
Bristol, 47, 51, 56, 60, 62, 63, 64, 203, 204, 214
Browne, Sir Thomas, 21
Burke, Edmund, 96, 179
Butts v. Penny (1677), 109
Byron, Lord, 72

Canada, 148
Canaries, 31
Canning Town, 198
Cardiff, 203, 204, 206, 209–10; race-riots in, 207; police, 209–10
Cardington, Bedfordshire, 11
Caricaturists, 54, 159
Carlyle, Thomas, 43, 160, 161, 164, 165, 166, 167, 171, 172, 173, 186

Index

Cartwrights Case (1569), 109
Ceuta, 5
Chamberline v. Harvey (1696/7), 109
Charitable relief (for Blacks), 146
Charles I, 36
Charles II, 10, 12
Chaucer, 3
Cheshire, 58
Cheshunt, 82
Chinese servants, 55
Christianisation (of Africans), 170
Church of England, 67
Churchill, Awnsham and John, 28
Churchill, Winston, 213
Chus, 20, 21
Civil War, English, 36
Clarkson, John, 154
Clarkson, Thomas, 146, 182
Classical sources, 2
Claudio, 24
Colonial legislatures, 106, 108, 110, 114
Colonial Office, 203
Columbus, 32
Committee for the Relief of the Black Poor, 146, 147, 148, 150
Common Law, 39, 40
Condorcet, 179
Constantine, Learie, 214
Convention, American, 149
Coptic Monks, 4
Corresponding Societies, 180
Court of Chancery, 138
Creole Society, growth of, 63
Cribb, Tom, 72
Cruikshank, George, 38, 159
Cuba, 33
Cugoano, Ottobah, 68, 69, 89, 95–100, 151, 152 (Chapter 5)
Cullen, Miss, 95
Cumberland, 58
Customs Acts (1832), 194

Dahomey, 169
D'Alembert, 179
Danes, 35
Davy, Serjeant, 122
Day, Thomas, 179, 184
Denning, Lord, 141
Deptford, 149
Dickens, Charles, 172
Dickson, William, 183
Diderot, Denis, 179
Diego, William, 65
Discrimination, 203
Domestics, white, 59
Dorset, Duke of, 55
Driberg, Tom, 213
Dundas, Henry, 133
Dunning, Mr, 123, 125
Durham, 93
Dutch, 35, 36
'Dying Negro', The, 179, 184

Earls Colne, 65
Earls Court, 199
East End of London, 198, 211
Eden, Richard, 6, 17, 19
Edinburgh, University of, 195
Edinburgh Courant, 132
Edwards, Bryan, 162, 170
Edwards, Paul, 96
Egypt, 3, 5, 161
Elephant, 17
Elizabeth I, 7, 8, 9, 23–4, 34, 35, 36
Emancipation, 140, 196, 197
Enlightenment, 149
Encyclopaedia Britannica, 173
English impressions of the African, 28
English knowledge about Africa, 16
English law, alleged colour-blindness of, 141
English law, and human rights, 108
English law, and property rights, 108

233

Index

English trade to Africa, 1, 2, 7
English views of Africa, 19
Equiano, Olaudah, 52, 62, 63, 65, 66, 68, 69, 89–95, 97, 98–100, 150, 171 (Chapter 5)
Esprit des Lois, 178–9
Ethiopia, 212
Ethiopian, 3, 19, 20, 25, 27
Ethiopian church, 4
'Ethiopian Seranaders', 171
Evangelicals, 68
Explorers, 3, 54
Eyre, Governor Edward, 118, 161, 166, 172

Fascists, 211
Faversham, 58
Forbes v. Cochrane (1824), 136–7
Fothergill, Dr, 126
Fox, George, 160
Franklin, Benjamin, 127
French, 35
French Enlightenment, 178–80
French Revolution, 149
Friston, 11

Gainsborough, Thomas, 84
Gambia, 81, 148
Garrick, David, 71, 84
Garrignano, Giovanni da, 4
Garvey, Marcus, 211
Gentleman's Magazine, 46, 84, 160, 186
Ghana, 95
Glasgow, 203
Gold, 17
Gordon Riots, 87, 134
Grace, The Slave, 191
Grattox, George Alexander, 55, 71
Greco-Roman remains, 3
Greeks, 2, 5
Grenada, 84

Guinea, 1, 6, 11, 22
Guinea Company, 10

Habeas Corpus, 108, 109, 114, 117, 120, 121, 122, 140; Act, 108
Haiti, 174
Hakluyt, Richard, 6, 17, 22, 23, 25, 26
Hamilton, Mary, 113
Hanson, John, 56
Hanway, Jonas, 146
Hardwicke, Lord, 40, 43
Harlequin, 71
Hargrave, Francis, 122, 123, 125, 127
Harriet, 72
Harvey, Joseph, 113
Hawkins, John, 7, 31, 33, 34, 38
Hawkins, William, 2, 31
Henley, Lord Chancellor, 114
Herodotus, 2, 3
Hispaniola, 31, 32, 33, 37
Historians, 124
History of Jamaica (1774), 163
Hogarth, William, 159
Holdsworth, W S., 111
Holt, Lord Chief Justice, 110, 112
Homer, 2
Hospital, for poor Blacks, 146
Houston, James, 168
Howell's State Trials, 127
Hull, 93, 203, 206
Hull, Warren, 65
Humanitarians, 41, 88–9, 140, 145–6, 161, 179–80
Hume, David, 167, 173
Hylas, Mary, 119
Hylas, Thomas, 119

Iago, 26
Immigration, black, 47, 99, 204, 209, 212, 214; fear of, 48–9, 190–91
Indenture, 135, 192

Index

India, 88
Indian Mutiny, 173
Irish, in London, 58
Isidore, 3
Islam, 4, 82
Italy, 2
Ivory, 17

Jamaica, 33, 36, 37, 107, 112, 120, 121, 133, 166–7, 192, 195 212
Jamaican revolt (Morant Bay), 161, 166, 171–2, 173, 174, 187
James I, 9, 36
James, C. L. R., 211
Jeckyll, Dr Joseph, 84
Jennings, Thomas, 58
Jerusalem, 4
Jews, 5
Jobson, Richard, 162
Johnson, Dr, 53, 133
Jones v. Schmoll (1785), 134
Jonson, Ben, 9
John II, 1
Judges, English, 139, 141

Kenyatta, Jomo, 211
Kidnappings, 128
King v. Inhabitants of Thames Ditton (1785), 134
Knight, Joseph, 132–3
Knight v. Wedderburn (1778), 132
Knowles, Capt., 121
Kru, tribe, 198

Labour Government, 214
Labour Party, 209
Lancaster, 51, 66
Las Casas, 33–4
Law, English, role of, 41
Law, and slavery, Chapters 6, 7, 8
League, of Coloured People, 210–13
Legal systems of slavery, 62
Lewis, Thomas, 119–20, 126
Lisle, David, 118

Liverpool, 47, 51, 169, 193, 195, 203, 204, 206–7, 208, 213; race-riots in, 206–8
Limehouse, 82
Lincolnshire, Blacks in, 11
Lisbon, 32
Lofft, Capel, 121
London, 2, 7, 9, 10, 47, 48, 49, 57, 72, 81, 98, 144, 184, 197, 203, 204, 206, 208, 210; Corporation of, 59
London, Jack, 65
Long, Edward, 47, 52, 55, 58, 162, 165, 168, 169, 170, 174
Lok, John, 1, 6, 7, 17, 19

Macomo, 72
Manchester, 93, 206, 210
Mandeville's Travels, 4, 6
Mandingoes, 81, 162
Manumission, 50, 51
Mansfield, Lord; Lord Chief Justice, 42, 46, 49–50, 93, 111, 117, 118, 119, 120, 121, 122, 123, 124, 125, 126, 127, 128, 132, 133, 134, 135, 138, Chapter 7
Mansfield, Mr, 122
Maori Wars, 173
Maritime Trade, 204
Marriage, 52
Maryland, 81
Mason, Charles, 11
Mayhew, Henry, 171, 189, 191
Mayo, Dr, 51
Medieval society, 3
Melbourne, Derbyshire, 180
Mercantilism, 39
Merchant Adventurers, 1, 6, 7
Methodism, 91–2, 181
Midgham, 54
Midsummer Nights Dream, 25
Mile End, 48, 146

235

Index

Mill, John Stuart, 165–6, 186–7
Mills, C. Wright, 218
Mina, 6, 17
Miscegenation, 54, 55, 197
Molineux, 72
Montagu, Duchess of, 84–5, 88
Montagu, Duke, of, 83, 84
Montesquieu, 178–9
Montgomery, James, 185
Montserrat, 36
Moors, (Mooren, Moores), 6, 19, 20, 48
Morant Bay; See Jamaican revolt
More, Hannah, 60
Morrett, Charles, 52
Moyne, Lord, 212
Much ado about nothing, 25
Mythology, about Africa, 6, 28; See also Blacks

Navigation Acts, 39, 107
Negroes, see Blacks
   Bozal, 32
New Brunswick, 97, 148, 153
Newspapers, 123, 126–7
   slave advertisements, 10, 62, 63, 115, 192
New World, 32, 34, 105, 106
New York, 58, 72, 190, 193
Nevis, 36
Nile, 3
Noah's Curse, 20
Nobility (English), 55
Noel v. Robertson (1687), 109
Norris, John, 169
North, Lord, 126
North Ashton, 52
North and South Shields, 204
Nottingham, 93
Nottinghamshire, 11
Nouvelle Héloïse, La, 179
Nova Scotia, 148, 153
Nubia, 5

Odysseus, 2
Oglethorpe, James, 81
'Oran-Outang', 168
Othello, 25–6
Oxford, 81

Paddington, 48, 146
Padmore, George, 211
Paine, Tom, 180
Pall Mall Gazette, 172
Pan African Federation, 212
Papal Bulls, 1
Papillon, Thomas, 50
Parliament, 106, 124, 190, 202
   legislation, 39, 40
Pearce v. Lisle (1749), 112
Penis, 162
Pepys, Samuel, 10
Perthshire, 133
Philadelphia, 149
Philanthropists, 46, 50
Philips, Dr John Baptista, 195
Pitt, William, the younger, 48, 152
Plantations, 34, 36, 38, 39, 106, 162
Planters, 38, 47, 54, 107, 124, 162, 190, 196
Pliny, 3
Plymouth, 94, 160, 193
Popular radicals, 94
Portraits, 62
Portugal, 34
Portuguese, 1, 2, 4, 5, 17, 32, 36, 106
Prester John, 4
Prevost, Abbé, 178
Prince Henry, the Navigator, 5, 6
Prince, Mary, 138
Principal Navigations, 6, 17
Privy Council, 38, 40, 107, 138
Puerto Rico, 33
Purchas, Samuel, 28

Queen Mary, 1
Queensbury, Duchess of, 53

Index

Race riots (1919), 206–8
Racial attitudes, 189;
  hatred, 60–61, 73, 86, 97
Racialism, 73, Chapter 10
Ramsay, James, 146, 182
Raynal, Abbé, 179
Re-enslavement (in England), 59, 60
Repatriation, 208, 209
Restoration, The, 36, 37
Richmond, Bill, 72
Rights of Man, 180
Robeson, Paul, 211
Rodney, Lord, 47
Romans, 2, 5
Romanticism, early, 183–5
Rousseau, Jean Jacques, 179, 184
Royal African Company, 36, 38,
  41–2, 83, 107–8, 168
Royal Air Force, 212
Royal Navy, 58, 136, 148, 149
Royal Proclamation (1601), 8
Royalty (English), 55
Rudd, William, 50
Runaways, 135–6
Rural England (Blacks in), 48
Ruskin, John, 172

Sabina, 50
St Giles, 71
St Ives, 193
St Kitts, 36
St Lucia, 195
St Preux, 179
St Vincent, 202
Sailors, black, 51, 59, 198;
  English, 48;
  see Blacks
Sallust, 3
Sancho, Ignatius, 61, 62, 63, 68, 69,
  71, 85–9, 94, 96, 97, 98–100,
  Chapter 5
Sancho, William, 89
Sambo, Maria, 65

Scotland, slavery in, 132–3
Scot's Magazine, 126
Scriptures, 3
Senden, Casper van, 8
Servants, black, 5, 7, *see* Blacks
Sewell, William, 166
Sexual relations, black and white,
  52, 53, 54, 100, 164, 208–209,
  214; *see* Blacks
Shadwell, 71, 197
Shakespeare, William, 23, 27, 162
Shanley, Edward, 113
Shanley v. Harvey (1762), 113
Sheffield, 93
Shrewsbury, 58
Sharp, Granville, 21, 47, 60, 92, 93,
  95, 96, 109, 114, 117, 118, 120,
  120, 121, 122, 124, 125, 126,
  146, 147, 149, 150, 151, 154,
  177, 178, 180, 181, 183, 186,
  187, Chapter 7
Sharp, Dr William, 117
Sierra Leone, 31, 48, 51, 54, 94, 95, 97,
  147, 148, 149, 164, Chapter 9
  Canadian Blacks in, 153–4
  Cost of mission to, 150, 153
  deaths in 150–51
  Sharp's views on, 145, 155, 186,
    193
  Company, 153, 196
Slave, Grace (1827), 137–8
Slaves, 32, 33, 36, 37
  importance to British economy,
    12
  in England, 7, 8, 9, 10, 47, 48, 49,
    50, 138–9
  in England, sales of 49–50, 55–6
  in England, freed, 193
Slave Cases, 48
Slave Lobby, 46, 50, 73, 110, 141,
  161, 174, 186
Slavery, in England, 105, 111, 112,
  120, 124, 128–9, 133, 218

237

Index

Slavery in England, illegal, 109, 111, 113
Slave Trade, 9, 10, 12, 31, 32, 35, 36–7, 39
Sloane, Sir Hans, 83
Smeathman, Henry, 146–7, 148
Smith v. Gould (1706), 110
Social Darwinism, 161
SPCK, 66, 82, 83
Solicitor General, 39, 108
Solomon, Job ben, 80–3, 84, 90, 91, 98–100, Chapter 5
Somerset Case (1772), 46, 111, 115, 116, 121–9, 132, 137, 139, Chapter 7
Somerset, James, 49, 121, 124, 125, 126, 128, 129
Soubise, 53, 71–2, 88
South Sea Company, 40
Spalding, Gentleman's Society of, 83
Spain, 34
Spaniards, 17, 32, 33, 106
in New World, 7, 31
Spectator, 88
Stapylton, Mr, 119–120
State Papers, 107
Stepney, 51, 198
Sterne, Laurence, 84, 86
Stewart, Charles, 121, 123
Stowell, Lord, 137–8, 191
Strabo, 3
Strong, Jonathan, 60, 117, 118, 119, 179
Sugar, 12
duties, 196
empires, 165–6
Swansea, 210

Taine, H, 71, 198
Talbot, Charles, 111
Tennyson, A, 172
Theatre, 71

Thelwall, John, 184
Tilbury Docks, 203
The Times, 172, 173, 187, 192, 206, 207
Towerson, William, 22
Trade Unions, 206
Treasury, 146, 148
Travel, accounts of Africa, 2, 3, 22
Triangular Trade, 38
Trinidad, 33, 195
Trollope, Anthony, 160, 161, 166, 171, 173
Tsarina of Russia, 48
Tuscany, 5
Tyneside, 204, 205

Uganda, 198
Urban Poor, 57–8
Utrecht, Treaty of, 40

Vassa, Gustavus; *see* Equiano
Vauxhall, 86
'Vernon', 149, 150
Vice-Admiralty Courts, 137
Villeinage, 106, 107
Virginia, 110, 132
Voltaire, 179

Wallace, Mr, 123
Walpole, Horace, 60
Warfield, 65
War Office, 205
Waterman, Walter, 26
Waters, Billy, 71
Watkins, James, 193
Wedderburn, John, 132–3
Wedgwood, Josiah, 146
Wesley, John, 66, 70, 170, 181–2
West Africa, 1, 2, 5, 6, 7, 12, 31, 36, 51, 164, 167, 168
West Country, 93
West Hartlepool, 203

West Indies, 10, 11, 12, 31, 37, 39, 47, 51, 136, 137, 155, 161, 164, 165, 167, 191, 192, 195, 196, 202; education in, 195
West Indians, 202–205
'White Raven', 146
Wilberforce, William, 53, 146, 190
Wilkes, John, 128
Williams, Eric, 180–81
Williams, Francis, 84
Williams, John, 193
Windham, John, 6, 17
Woburn, 11

World War I, 202, 205
World War II, 211

York, 52
  Archbishop of, 120
  Duke of, 36
Yorke, Philip, 111, 112
Yorke-Talbot, Opinion (1729), 111–12, 118, 119, 120
'Yorkshire Stigo', 146

Zeno, Richard, 11
Zong, Case of the Ship (1783), 42, 92–3, 134